THE FOX HUNT

Mohammed Al Samawi, a Zaydi Shia'a Muslim, was born on 30 November 1986 in the old Yemeni city of Sana'a. Brought up to believe that the Jews were responsible for all his people's troubles, his life changed when he read the Old Testament, 'friended' Jews in Israel, and joined social-action groups aimed at promoting dialogue between Muslims and Jews. Soon, he started receiving death threats from his compatriots, and when he fled to the southern city of Aden he found himself caught up in a brutal civil war. Trapped and desperate, he could find no one to help him, until strangers from overseas pitched in and eventually saved his life. He escaped to the United States, where he now lectures widely to promote inter-faith relations.

MOHAMMED AL SAMAWI

THE FOX HUNT

FOUR STRANGERS, THIRTEEN DAYS, AND ONE MAN'S AMAZING JOURNEY TO SAFETY

SCRIBE

Melbourne • London

Scribe Publications
18–20 Edward St, Brunswick, Victoria 3056, Australia
2 John St, Clerkenwell, London, WC1N 2ES, United Kingdom

Published by Scribe 2018

This book is a work of memoir; it is a true story based on my best recollections
and the information I have since received. The names and identifying characteristics
of some of the individuals in this book have been changed to protect their privacy,
and certain events have been adjusted for security purposes or compressed in service
of the narrative.

Unless otherwise noted, interior images are courtesy of the author. Additional photo
credit information: Map of Yemen: United Nations Department of Peacekeeping
Operations. Pages 1, 207, and 213 © Karam Kamal. Pages 19, 33, 45, and 57:
New York Public Library. Page 123: Sallam/Flickr. Page 151: NASA. Page 221:
T3n60. Page 275: Skilla1st.

Printed and bound in the UK by CPI Group (UK) Ltd, Croydon CR0 4YY

Scribe Publications is committed to the sustainable use of natural resources
and the use of paper products made responsibly from those resources.

9781911344988 (UK edition)
9781925322798 (Australian edition)
9781925548693 (e-book)

CiP records for this title are available from the British Library
and the National Library of Australia.

scribepublications.co.uk
scribepublications.com.au

To my country.
To everyone who's different.
To all the people who said "yes."

CONTENTS

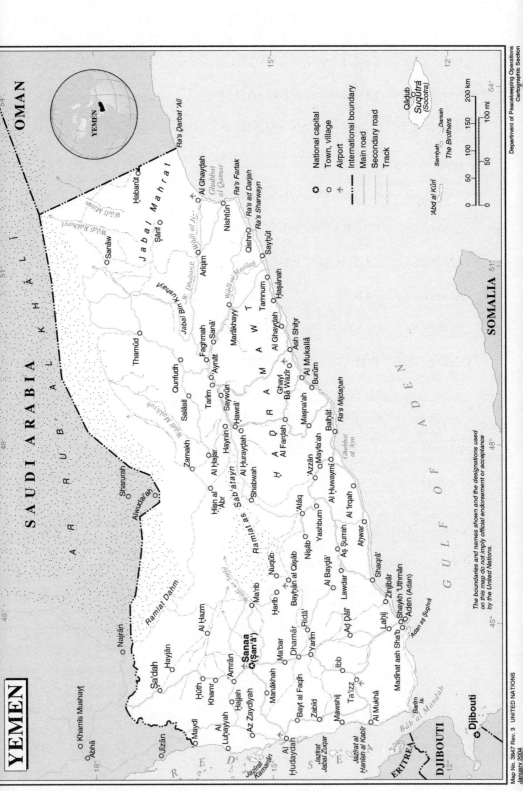

YEMEN

OMAN

SAUDI ARABIA

A L   R U B '   A L   K H Â L Î

Khamis Mushayt

Abhā

Najrān

Jizān

Sharurah

Alwurtal'ah

Sa'dah

Hayjān

Hūth

Khamr

Hajjah

'Amrān

Al Luhayyah

Az Zaydīyah

Al Hudaydah

Zabid

Bayt al Faqīh

Mawshij

Al Mukhā

Jazīrat al Hanīsh al Kabīr

Jazīrat Jabal Zuqar

Kamarān

Ta'izz

Ibb

Madīnat ash Sha'b

'Adan (Aden)

Shaykh 'Uthmān

Lahij

Az Zaydīyah

Ad Dāli'

Yarīm

Dhamār

Ma'bar

Ridā'

Al Hazm

Manākhah

Ma'rib

Harib

Nuqūb

Bayhān al Qisāb

Nisāb

Al Baydā'

Lawdar

As Surrah

Yashbum

Atāq

'Azzān

Al Irqah

Afyar

Shaqrā'

Zinjibār

Ramlat Dahm

Ramlas Sabatayn

Hisn al 'Abr

Shabwah

Al Hajar

Haynīn

Zamakh

Wādī al Masilah

Wādī Hadramawt

Qurfudh

Salāsil

Tarīm

'Aynat

Saywūn

Al Hawra'

Al Furdah

Al Huraydah

Mayfa'ah

Al Huwaymī

Masna'ah

Ra's Mijdahah

Ghubbat al 'Ayn

Balhāf

Burūm

Ghayl Bā Wazīr

Al Mukallā

Ash Shihr

Al Ghaydah

Marākhayy

Sana'

Faghmah

Thamūd

Jabal Bin W. Dhuhays

Wādī al Jīz

'Irqim

Sanāw

Wādī Rabhārt

Wādī Mitan

Jabal Mahrat

Habarūt

Sharif

Al Ghaydah

Ghubbat al Qamar

Ra's Fartak

Ra's ad Darjah

Ra's Sharwayn

Nishtūn

Qishn

Sayhūt

Hasānah

Tamnum

H A D R A M A W T

M A H R A T

G U L F   O F   A D E N

SOMALIA

ERITREA

DJIBOUTI

Djibouti

Barīm Is.

Bāb al Mandab

'Adan as Sughra

R   E   D   S   E   A

Ra's Darbat 'Ali

Qādub

Suqutrā
(Socotra)

'Abd al Kūrī

Samhah — Darsah
The Brothers

⊛	National capital
○	Town, village
✈	Airport
·—·—·	International boundary
——	Main road
——	Secondary road
——	Track

The boundaries and names shown and the designations used
on this map do not imply official endorsement or acceptance
by the United Nations.

```
0    50   100  150  200 km
0       50      100 mi
```

Map No. 3847 Rev. 3   UNITED NATIONS
January 2004

Department of Peacekeeping Operations
Cartographic Section

CHAPTER I

◇◇◇

WEAK TIES,
STRONG BONDS

Aden, March 2015

I counted my steps. Three to get from the door to the wall; two between the toilet and the mirror. My new apartment in Aden was big for one person, but I hadn't planned on taking refuge in its bathroom. The gray-green light from the single fluorescent bulb scattered off the mirror, blanching the walls, the ceiling, the floor. It had nowhere to go.

Trapped.

My eyes, red-rimmed and shot through with blood, had been hollowed by sleeplessness and stress. They'd retreated, withdrawn from the front lines, as if unwilling to watch Yemen tear itself apart. Rubble-strewn streets; soldiers and citizens shouting and firing weapons; social media emblazoned with the slogans "God is great! Death to America! Death to Israel! Damn the Jews! Victory to Islam!"

The power shut off. I glanced at my phone and tried to calm myself by taking inventory.

It was March 22, 2015. Seven days earlier I'd fled my home in Sana'a, Yemen's official capital city, to escape the threats on my life and the violence of the earliest days of what was now a full-on civil war. On one side was President Abdrabbuh Mansour Hadi and the loyalist forces; on the other were the opposition forces, the Houthis and their Supreme Revolutionary Committee, backed by the former president Ali Abdullah Saleh.

I thought I was running toward safety, but the violence followed me.

First went the airport from which I'd departed, seized by the Houthis. Then came fighting between the Hadi loyalists and the Houthi rebels at the airport here in Aden. Would the bombing spread from there? Everyone prayed that the conflict would die down, but the fight was only just beginning. Was Yemen, the poorest nation in the region, about to become the battleground of a well-funded proxy war between Iran and Saudi Arabia?

Whispers flew from door to door. Iran, a Shia nation, was said to be funneling weapons to its fellow Shias, the rebels from the north—the Houthis. Meanwhile, Saudi Arabia, a Sunni nation, was supposedly backing President Hadi, a fellow Sunni. To make matters worse, the Sunni network extended to Al Qaeda in the Arabian Peninsula (AQAP) and the Islamic State of Iraq and the Levant (ISIL), both of which had started to claim control of various parts of Yemen. The Sunni-Shia balance of power in Yemen could help tip the Middle East in one direction or another; all these different groups with only the loosest affiliations seemed willing to unite in order to move that needle.

From my window, I watched as fighters patrolled the streets. There were only two roads out of the city, and both went around the airport, which was one of the centers of the battle; it didn't look like I could escape using either of them. The situation was delicate for everyone, and downright deadly for anyone with ties to Israel, Jews, or interfaith activism. I had all three.

As a peace activist who promoted understanding between Jews, Christians, and Muslims, I'd been targeted before. But this was different. This was worse.

If anyone were to find out who I was, where I was from, or what I'd been doing for the last several years . . .

Capture.

Torture.

Execution.

How much longer could I survive on little more than adrenaline and intermittent Internet and cellular connectivity?

I shut my eyes and rested both hands on the sink. My forehead touched the mirror and slipped down the glass in its own sweat. I ran my tongue across my cracked lips, resisting the urge to tear at the loose flesh with my teeth. My stomach roiled from hunger and worry.

A faint pop of gunfire pulled me back up.

I planted my bare feet on the tile floor and wondered if the impact of a shell could work its way up from the street to my fourth-floor apartment.

I hurried out of the bathroom back to the window, pressed my body against the wall, and peered around a small gap between the drawn curtains. The power lines formed a messy web. Just down the block, two men stood watch at what looked like an AQAP checkpoint. Their black *shemaghs* hid their faces. The wind wrapped their white robes around the bandoliers crossing their chests; dust devils danced at their feet. Their rifle barrels pointed skyward.

Why did I put myself in this situation? I thought to myself. *Why did I leave my home in Sana'a?*

Ana hemar. I am a donkey.

I wished that I was with my sisters, safe in my room, watching an old Hollywood movie. The good guys would win. The problem was that here, under so many layers of dirt and blood, the good and the bad were sometimes indistinguishable. Publicly, each group made righteous claims, but behind the scenes they were united by violence. The Houthis, the so-called rebels from the north, were heroes to some, terrorists to others. The Al Qaeda fighters, the foot soldiers from the south, had their own supporters, their own enemies. Good, bad. Right, left. Nothing was as it seemed.

What would happen when the two armies met? The Houthis had just taken Taiz, the third-largest city in the country, a strategic stronghold between the north and the south. They were only about 100 miles away now, readying for a military offensive, marching straight toward Aden. Right toward me.

With my eyes shut and my jaw clenched, I heard rather than saw the flicker of lights coming back on. Was this a sign from God? I couldn't waste much time considering. Electricity was a scarce and valuable commodity.

In the living area, I crouched in front of my now charging laptop. My cell phone sat in the kitchen plugged in.

I checked Facebook. I refreshed Twitter. I scanned Al-Masdar News. Everyone knew it was a mouthpiece for the al-Islah party, the Islamists, but they were the only ones directly reporting from the ground. Them and a freelance American journalist named Adam Baron. The state-controlled channels were useless. As far as they were concerned, there was no war, and no one was dying.

Overwhelmed by fear and facts, I shut my laptop. Scanning the apartment, I spotted my remaining foodstuffs. The few bottles of water, juice, bars of chocolate, cans of tuna, and packets of cookies and chips were all that remained.

My stomach groaned against my ribs. Hunger and thirst. The water that spurted from the faucets wasn't potable. With nothing else to do, I reopened my computer, the safest window to the outside world.

I checked my messages. Nothing. I'd spent the day in front of my laptop, curled like a shrimp over its screen. I'd scrolled through my recent calls, my emails, my Facebook friends, and sent messages to everyone I could think of. *Help me. Please.* But no one knew what to do. People needed to save themselves, their families. No one was willing to drive a car through a war zone to save a stranger—or a friend. People sent their regrets, their prayers. I appreciated the sentiment, but I couldn't fly away on a prayer.

I needed to get out.

Right before midnight, I sent one more message.

◇◇◇◇◇◇

Packets of data flew through a network of networks. They bounced from one router to another until they reached their destination. Within a matter of seconds they reassembled halfway around the world.

MOHAMMED AL SAMAWI: Daniel, I hope everything is great in your side!

I hope you still remember me . . . I thought it will be a good idea if I ask you if you can help me out . . . If you watch the news lately, you may have heard about what's happening in Yemen. For that I am writing the following request. If you know someone who could help please let me know.

Daniel Pincus was standing by himself at the cocktail hour of a Jewish wedding in Brooklyn. Tall and energetic, with a knack for finding himself in impossible situations, he ran a hand through his hair. He was flying solo in a crowd he didn't know, and between the cheese and the canapés, he checked Facebook. There he saw a short, desperate letter from a guy he barely remembered. Grateful for an excuse to leave the party, he tapped out a response and stepped into the hallway to place a Skype call to Yemen.

Meanwhile, Megan Hallahan, an American woman with big eyes and a crown of curly brown hair, was sitting in front of her laptop in her apartment in Tel Aviv. A young man she'd met on Facebook three years earlier was stuck in Yemen, trapped in a war zone. For two weeks, she'd been trying to find a way to get him out of the country, but she'd come up short and was nearly out of hope. She typed a fresh email and blasted it to yet another circle in her social network. Then she fell asleep.

Natasha Westheimer, an Australian American in Israel, was still awake, answering emails for EcoPeace Middle East, when she saw a message from Megan, a girl she'd met three weeks prior at a social action conference in Jordan. The subject read: "Urgent—My Friend in Yemen." She adjusted her glasses and pushed her thick red hair behind her ears. Natasha would be attending Oxford University in the fall to pursue a master's degree in water science. She knew about filtration, not exfiltration. But after only the briefest pause, she hit reply.

Justin Hefter, a recent Stanford graduate, was in Utah skiing. Exhausted from a weekend with the guys, and with an ungodly flight the following morning, he turned in early. At 4:00 A.M., he crawled into his Uber to the airport and checked his email.

Dear friends,

I'm sorry to bother, but my friend's life is really in danger and he just needs an excuse, any excuse to get out of Yemen—he will go anywhere and do anything as long as he is able to meet his basic survival needs. Any idea or contact will help, please pass the word along as far as possible and let me know of any thought you may have. Thank you in advance, Megan

Justin dug around in his wallet until he found the business card of a twenty-something Yemeni he'd met briefly at the same conference in Jordan three weeks earlier. He sent a quick email:

Hey Megan, Mohammed Al Samawi lives in Yemen and was at the GATHER conference. He may have some ideas . . . you can reach him on Facebook at: (link).

Within hours, Megan snapped off a reply:

Hi Justin, It's Mohammed that I'm talking about . . .

◇◇◇◇◇◇

They were talking about me. I am that Mohammed.
　This is my story.
　It begins and ends with a book.

CHAPTER 2

◇◇◇

CONTRADICTIONS

At school with my classmates

For as long as I can remember, I was set apart from others. My parents told me I was blessed by God; they told me I was cursed by evil. I was special; I was odd. I was loved; I was resented. I was pitied; I was despised. All because of an event over which I had no control, of which my family rarely spoke, and when they did, only in the vaguest of terms.

I grew up without any recollection of the time before, the time when things were normal. When most kids were learning to walk, I was stuck on my stomach. It wasn't until I was four that I was able to propel myself around in a walker, lurching and staggering, regarding my right leg with curiosity and anger when it refused to behave. Why was one side of me so compliant, so willing? Why was the other so stubborn, so unyielding? Why did it seem as though I couldn't move in any unified manner?

When I was old enough to speak, I asked my mother why my body was different, why my right hand looked like the beak of the Arabian partridge.

"What's wrong with me?"

"There's nothing wrong with you. You had an accident. You will get better."

"When?"

"Soon."

"How soon?"

"Mohammed, you are fortunate to be as you are. It makes you unique."

It didn't make sense. I was less capable than others, and that made me fortunate? If I got better, would I lose what made me unique? Too young to pick apart the philosophical threads, I made do as best as I could, believing things would one day change. It was 1990. Both my parents were doctors. Medical advancements were coming at a rapid pace, and we were taking full advantage of them.

If I hadn't been born into a prominent family, I wouldn't have been so fortunate. Yemen was the poorest country in the Middle East, but we were fairly well off. My paternal grandfather was a respected elder in the community, a kind of judge who settled disputes. He earned enough money from his work and landholdings that he was able to send his sons to university. There, they studied law. My father, exercising his independent streak, became a doctor instead. With his income, we could have lived in the most exclusive neighborhood in Sana'a, but my father didn't want that. Instead, we resided in a more mixed-income area near the Old City.

The Old City, situated in a high mountain valley, with distinctive rammed-earth buildings and towers, was settled more than twenty-five hundred years ago. Through the seventh and eighth centuries, it was a regional center of Muslim culture, and historically significant areas from the eleventh century were named part of a UNESCO World Heritage Site in 1986—the same year I was born.

When I was a child, my thoughts wended through the narrow streets and the market stalls, between the mountains of coffee beans and exotic spices, while I spent nearly every moment at home.

I'd barely reached my mother's knees when she bundled me into an airplane and we traveled to India, Egypt, and Jordan to see specialists and undergo surgeries. Time after time, I returned to my bed to recover, hopeful that this time I would join the children I heard running through our neighborhood. Their shouts reached my room on the ground floor of our five-story home, but as I lay on my mattress, needles projecting from my body and my face, the acupuncturist murmured, "Stay still. Stay still." I was a mounted specimen, pinned and wriggling, anesthetized but keenly aware.

All I wanted to do was move, to run through the alleyways chasing the sun. But after that soft-spoken command, I froze, unwilling to do anything that might interfere with the cure that I prayed every night God would grant me. But God must have been busy somewhere else. Instead of buying me a bicycle to ride up and down the street outside our gate, my mother bought me a book about a boy and a bicycle. "This is just as good," she said. She—Nawal—and my father—Khalid—started working with me in the evenings, teaching me how to recognize, pronounce, and write the twenty-eight main letters of the Modern Standard Arabic *abjad* system. Soon enough, I could read. Words opened up another universe, but still I couldn't reach the world outside my front door.

My mother told me I'd get better.

Soon.

But when was soon?

On my first day of school, I stood in the parking lot hunched under a backpack stuffed with dread. I had no friends and very few interactions with children other than my older brother, Hussain; my older sister, Lial; my younger brother, Saif; and my baby sister, Nuha. I fidgeted in my uniform—a pair of navy cotton pants, a T-shirt, and a white button-down shirt—as my classmates bolted from their cars. As my mother and I approached the building, we walked through a collection of bodyguards lounging on the limousines and Toyota Land Cruisers of the wealthy. I looked up at my mother. She was one of the few parents within sight.

The school, a forty-five-minute drive away, was in the well-to-do section of Sana'a called Al Seteen. Though the public school was much closer to our home, it didn't provide the kinds of opportunities that Azal Alwadi School did. In the public school system, the main emphasis was on the teaching of Islamic principles. That, of course, was part of every school curriculum. But here there would be other subjects, too, such as earth science, geography, history, and mathematics. My parents, both doctors, understood the importance of a rounded education.

Before we entered the classroom, my mother reassured me with a smile, but when she bent down to straighten my clip-on tie, her hand shook. She was on edge; after all, she was going to be attending this new school along with me. She'd decided that for the first day, she would sit in the back of the room to monitor how the other students treated me.

We entered together and I found a desk in the first row while my mother settled into a chair along the wall. I pulled out my books and tried to look important in a pantomime of pencil arrangements. I couldn't have been more grateful than when the teacher clapped his hands and signaled that class was about to begin.

That first day consisted of a basic introduction: the alphabet, counting, rudimentary facts about Yemen and Islam. I could already read and do basic arithmetic. Why couldn't the rest of these children?

The second day, my mother sat just outside the classroom, visible through the windows. My classmates pointed to her and nudged each other, whispering behind their hands.

I didn't understand the issue. My mother took me everywhere with her. True, I was often the only child—and the only male—in a group of women. But even at weddings, when people were explicitly asked not to bring kids, there I was. I got a lot of attention from the adults, and I felt special, loved, and cared for. My brother Hussain, six years my senior, got jealous and picked fights with me, which only seemed to prove that the extra attention from my mother was a good thing. But here, for the first time, it was a clear liability. And after the first couple of weeks, my mother and I agreed that she should stop coming with me; our driver, Taha, would take me instead.

It was too little too late. I was already marked. I was the disabled boy, the mama's boy, the dope. I needed to create a new identity. I thought of all my strengths. I couldn't run, and I couldn't ride a bike, but I could read. At home, I studied as much as I could. I squirreled away Hussain's math books, and took Lial's novels. Academics was a race I knew I could win; I would be the MVP of the classroom. I made it my goal to arrive first. To raise my hand first. To finish my exams first. Every day, when I completed my assignments, I made a quiet show of putting my pencil down, rising from my seat, and looking around to measure everyone else's progress. In no time, I was appointed the class monitor whenever the teacher left the room. When he came back and asked if anyone had acted out, I made a full report, pointing out anyone who had been talking when we'd been instructed to work quietly.

I quickly learned that volunteering to answer *every* question my teacher asked was a ticket to abuse, and I paid for the hit of pride with isolation. I didn't know which was worse—people looking at me, or people looking away. I learned to fade out with the years. When my teacher asked a question, I sat on my good hand and waited for someone else to name the major international airports in each of the countries in the Arab world. In the silent void that followed, I silently mouthed the answers: Dubai International, Hamad International, King Abdulaziz International, Abu Dhabi International. I'd been through many of them on my way to visit this or that doctor.

Those years of my life were dim—literally. The ground floor on which I lived was nearly windowless, which meant that I couldn't even watch Hussain playing football (soccer) with his friends. I could hear the groans and the shrieks, but I couldn't see anything. Whenever the gang of older boys came in for water and cookies, I limped over to whichever part of the house they were in, eager to be a part of the action. Inevitably, Hussain would roll his eyes, gather himself, and then take me by the hand to find my mother. With little variation, the shouts and protestations would echo through the house. I'd stand there listening, feeling even smaller and less significant than usual, as my eldest brother railed at my mother and she was left crying.

Ana hemar, I would berate myself. *I am a donkey.*

By the time I was seven or eight, I'd learned to create another world in my head. Every morning, Taha the driver would wait for me to clamber into the car, and then he'd whisk me away. For a stretch of forty-five minutes, surrounded by the blaring mayhem of Sana'a traffic, I would stare out the window, down the maze of minarets and stone-work houses towering five to nine stories high. The rammed-earth and burnt-brick buildings, trimmed with white, would bake in the sun like gingerbread houses from a fairy tale. As the engine thrummed, I lost myself in fantasies, in visions of another life. I could be a doctor, a lawyer, a Hollywood actor. Or, the best dream of all, I could be a football star.

Football was my white whale. The World Cup was the most antici-pated event of my life, followed closely by the Sana'a International Book Fair. I sat glued in front of the television whenever possible, watching players dribbling the ball, sprinting down the pitch, legs like machine-powered scissors slicing through the grass as they made their way to-ward the goal. Even when I wasn't watching the games, when I was being driven to school, I lost myself in a world in which I was the superstar, weaving across the green, scoring the winning goal. Too soon, Taha would stop short, right outside the evil fortress—my exclusive private school.

On one particularly perfect day, my classmates were wiggling out of their seats. The sun was glowing in the sky like a crystal ball, and every tick of the clock beckoned us one second closer to exercise pe-riod. Finally, our geography lesson ended, and we were dismissed. My classmates bounded onto the sports field, and I took my spot on a hard wooden bench, shifting uncomfortably from one butt-numbing po-sition to another. The black-and-white ball rolled onto the grass, and I watched as my schoolmates flailed, the ball lost between their feet. They made stuttering runs that had them throwing their hands up in despair at the unfairness of the football gods. What did they know of unfair? I sat still as a stone, staring blankly as they wandered over.

"Mohammed the maimed," one said.

"Mohammed the mama's boy," another added.

I looked to our teacher, his back to me, well within earshot. He didn't hold up a red card or yell foul. Instead, he turned around and smiled at some of the more original turns of phrase.

The entire drive home I looked up to the clear, cloudless heavens. *Why me?* I asked God. *Is this some divine test?* I opened the door to my house and greeted my caretaker, a woman from India, and the housekeeper. I avoided my mother and went to my room to read my favorite book, *Majid*. I lost myself in the comics, imagining myself as the young boy after whom the series was named. Unlike me, he enjoyed many different adventures; like me, he almost always wound up getting in trouble.

"Salaam, Mohammed." My mother stood in the doorway. "And how was your day?"

I didn't want to get caught in a series of complaints. I knew that no good could come of my parents running interference. My mother had spoken with my classmates' parents before, and my father had even tried bribing my teachers to be more vigilant—but this only led to more teasing. I didn't have the energy to file a report, or dissemble in half-truths, so instead I asked if I could go to the neighborhood shop to buy some sweets. She shook her head.

"Hussain can go by himself!" I screamed, letting out all the pain of the day.

"But Lial cannot."

"Lial is a *girl*. I am a *man*. It's not fair!"

My mother looked at me as if my pain was her own.

"Hussain?" she called, deliberating. "Take your brother out. He wants some candy."

A minute later, Hussain showed up, eyes rolling, shoulders slumping, looking at me with disgust. "Why do I have to go?" he said, registering his complaint.

My mother, hands on hips, radiated hurt and guilt. "What kind of dog are you? Why do you ask such things?"

"I don't want to go." Hussain bit down on the words.

"Go."

Torn between a sense of duty and injustice, he turned on his heel, waggling his fingers behind his back to indicate that I was to follow.

I tried to copy the rhythm of his feet as we made our way past the gates of our home. When we got into the street, he paused and glanced around. A gang of boys stood at a corner a few streets down, their long shadows exaggerating their height. Hussain exhaled loudly.

"We don't—" I began.

"This way." Hussain clamped his hand on my shoulder. I winced and followed.

We got maybe fifty yards before the footfalls caught up to us. I heard a shrill whistle. Another.

Next, I heard an expulsion of air, a grunt. Hussain had his hand spread across the back of his head. He brought it toward his face, and in the webbed skin between his thumb and index finger, a worm of blood writhed down his wrist and burrowed beneath his shirt cuff. He muttered a string of curses.

The sound of shouting and laughing reverberated off the stone walls surrounding us. A few more rocks whistled past and skittered along the ground harmlessly. A bit of wood clattered and came to rest alongside me, its edges corrugated like shark teeth. I wanted to kick it away, but my right foot was heavy in defiance. I scraped my shoe along the rough surface, watched it judder and spasm, but the wood only moved an inch. I felt my breath scratch my throat as I watched Hussain fold in on himself, his chin tucked to his chest. Shaking, he put his hand back on his skull and raised it, showing our enemy the results of the blow to his head.

Back home, he took the lead in explaining to our mother what had happened. It was the neighborhood kids. Half of them had already dropped out of school, some of them to help their parents make ends meet. It was a problem: only half of all Yemeni males enrolled in elementary school went on to secondary school, and only one-third of females did the same. They had time on their hands, and they filled it with trouble. My mother had spoken to their parents before, but nothing had changed. These children were ignorant, my mother concluded, using the word in the strictest sense. From how she said it, I understood that they were the ones to be pitied, and that I should avoid this state of being at all costs. My main concern wasn't to avoid those people, but to avoid being like them.

Hussain identified the boys involved, but as each name left his lips, I couldn't help but feel that he was saying *Mohammed, Mohammed, Mohammed*. He blamed me. So I did the only thing I could: I blamed my mother.

After dinner, I sat propped up in bed, my mother alongside me. She worked some massage oil between her two hands and then began kneading it into my gnarled, knotted right hand. After a few minutes, she switched to my leg, the familiar routine of it comforting, frustrating. The two of us spent every evening together like this. After my mother finished her evening prayers, she came to my room. These physical therapy sessions were a blessing and a curse. They were helpful, yet painful. They symbolized a special bond between my mother and me, and created a fissure of resentment with my siblings.

Before my mother began the painful process of stretching and manipulating my limbs, I found my opening.

"Why can't you tell me the truth?"

Her eyelids fluttered involuntarily, as if they'd caught a speck of dust, or an insect. She stopped massaging my leg, and then resumed. Her mouth formed an imperfect *O,* and she exhaled through it, her breath whistling between her teeth.

"Things will never change, will they?"

"I'm sorry, Mohammed," she began, her voice even, matter-of-fact. "I thought it was best. I hoped—" Her words were strangled by a sob. She looked to the ceiling and shook her head. Tears wended their way down her face, washed against her hijab.

I was not yet one year old, she said. Both she and my father were at work, treating patients. I was at home with Hussain, who wasn't yet seven, and Lial, who would have been approaching four. My brother noticed that something was wrong with me. I was unusually quiet. But that was a good thing, wasn't it? That I wasn't crying? That I was just lying there, very still? By the time my mother came home from work, the damage was done. A small stroke on the left side of the brain had withered my right side—arm, hand, leg, and foot.

My mother stopped working right after. She blamed herself. If she had been home, if she had been like the other mothers, this never would have happened. She would have noticed I was sick; she would have rushed me to the hospital. But she was taking care of strangers rather than her own son.

I wouldn't be better soon, as my mother once promised. Only a miracle would cure me. So we started chasing miracles.

CHAPTER 3

◇◇◇

REASON AND RELIGION

A sixteenth-century image of the King of Yemen

As I tipped into double digits, I learned a very important lesson: reason and religion don't always go together. When I was nearly ten, my mother decided that if medical science wasn't going to do the trick, we needed to double down on faith. I was happy to oblige. I'd been praying to God my entire life and was still waiting on the returns.

One morning, after I left for school, my mother the doctor went to the imam and purchased incense. When I returned home, she led me by the shirtsleeve through the main hallway and living area to our small alcove. She held her finger to her lips to keep me silent. In the center of the little room stood a stick of incense bisecting a plate. She bent down to light it, and as she rose, so did a spire of smoke. It smelled like our local mosque.

"Mohammed," she whispered, terse and serious, "the evil eye has been cast on you."

This was something I'd heard for years now. Islamic culture has a marked bias toward the right. Religious stricture dictates that the right hand be used for anything that's good and honorable, such as writing and shaking hands, eating and drinking; conversely, it demands that the left hand be used only for excretory functions. These rules might have made sense once upon a time. Don't eat where you . . . and all that. But with modern-day innovations—like soap—what was the logic? Nonetheless, I wanted to be pure. So I twisted my body to shake hands with my right side; I washed the fingers on my left hand until they puckered. But still, it was not good enough. Eating with my left hand, no matter how clean, was considered an abomination, a kind of blasphemous insult to Allah. People questioned my belief in God based on my "refusal" to eat in the manner that God commanded. Strangers came up to me and shouted that I should stop offending God and eat the right—correct—way. I explained my situation—over and over again—but still, pious men and women ignored my physical limitations and told me to honor God properly. *You are cursed by the evil eye,* they'd say, while my mother would herd me along and tell me to ignore the ignorant. At least until now—

"The only way you can be better," she said, "is if you listen to me and do as I say."

The thought that I could be cured was thrilling. "Of course," I said. "I'll do anything."

For the next few minutes I walked in a tight circle around the lit incense stick. While I did this, my mother recited a series of passages from the Quran. I don't know if it was the tight circles, the smell of the incense, or my own clumsiness, but I staggered. Before I could catch myself, I kicked the incense stick and the fringe of the rug flared up. The fire started to run down the length of the hallway, adding the scent of burning wool to the air.

My mother looked at me, horrified. "What have you done?"

She tucked the Quran under her arm and stamped up and down the singed rug. *Ana asif, Ana asif,* I apologized, over and over again. I don't know which of us was more upset. I was still disabled, and she was now going to have to explain to my father how a very beautiful and expensive carpet got damaged. It seemed I was, indeed, marked by the evil eye.

So I decided to exorcise the devil by devoting myself to God. I committed to studying the Quran—the word of Allah as dictated to the Prophet Muhammad by the angel Gabriel—as well as the hadith, an account of the words and deeds of the Prophet. My father encouraged me. He took me (and my brothers) to the local mosque every Friday afternoon, and we discussed the imam's sermons over lunch. I wanted to be like my *abi.* I admired his patient devotion, his complete dedication, particularly since for much of his adult life he hadn't been a religious man. He'd been a completely different person—until I almost died.

Back when I was a child, my father drank alcohol. It was *haram,* forbidden, and even though the sale of alcohol was illegal in Yemen, he used to buy bottles of vodka on the black market and host parties; my mother would hide in the kitchen, hurt, confused, not sure what to do. One weekend when I was five or six, my father took me with him to the Sheba Hotel, one of the many hotels that made alcohol readily available to westerners, to which the police and imams turned a half-blind eye. The men sat together poolside, and the conversation devolved into energetic grunts and gesticulations.

I watched the crystalline water capture the sunlight, and I asked my father if it was okay if I went in. I didn't know how to swim, but I'd seen Hussain and Lial do it, and I figured I could lie on my back or stay in the shallow end and splash around. I would be careful, I promised. I dipped my toes in the water, then my feet, then my ankles and calves. By the time I was fully submerged, I felt all my inhibitions drift away. I felt like I'd found my miracle. I was buoyant and light. I was able to move like I couldn't on land. I imagined that this was how everyone else felt all the time, unburdened, floating.

I held on to the cool tile at the edge of the pool with my good hand, letting the water cover my lips, my nose, my eyes, my head. And then I lost my grip. I drifted from the wall, thrashing with my good arm, which only sent me farther from safety. I shouted and shouted, gasping for air, until the water pressing me down drowned out the sound. In the throbbing silence, I heard my father's voice. "Help him! Help him! My son! He can't swim!" Then I felt myself sinking, slowly, slowly, the muffled sounds of the world lost in an explosion of bubbles.

When I opened my eyes, I was on the deck. Someone's hands were on my chest, and I spit up a mouthful of water. I gasped and sputtered. The back of my head felt itchy from the inside out. My eyes stung and water dripped down my face, but I couldn't tell if it was tears or chlorinated water. I saw my father's image dissolve and re-form, dissolve and re-form.

As far as I know, my father never drank again. Already a serious man, he grew even more somber in his sobriety. After the pool incident, he was more likely to scold than to laugh, more focused on sins than on beauty. He became more observant, more traditional in his views.

In the evenings, when he took out his Quran, he would tell me about my grandfather, Hakim, who served as a judge. In Yemen, the main law was Islamic law, sharia. Literally, this word means "the right path" or "guide." And though fundamentalists interpreted this law as it was written centuries ago, most people I knew understood that the law needed to evolve with the times.

Many Muslims were united in this belief, and for years we lived together in Yemen in peace, despite our different practices concerning ideology and the lines of succession, which can be traced back to the death of the Prophet Muhammad. The question of the Prophet's successor split his followers in two. Some believed that the Prophet selected his cousin and son-in-law, Ali, as his rightful heir. These people were called the *Shiat Ali*, the ones who followed Ali—or the Shia, for short. The Al Samawis belonged to this group and identified as the Shia subset known as the Zaidi, which originated with Zaid, the great-grandson of Ali.

Sunnis, on the other hand, did not accept that the caliphs should be descended from Muhammad. They believed that the religious leaders should be chosen by the people.

Where I lived, in the north of Yemen, Zaidi Shia was the dominant practice, but in many ways, Saudi Arabia, a Sunni majority country, was the spiritual home of Islam. To be good Muslims, we were expected, if we were able, to travel to Mecca on a pilgrimage, or hajj—a religious obligation so profound that it's one of the Five Pillars of Islam. Saudi Arabia was also the site of another of the holiest places in our religion, Medina, where Muhammad led his followers after being ousted from Mecca and where he was buried.

Since Saudi Arabia owned the religious sites and monuments, it exerted a great deal of influence throughout the region, politically and spiritually. In fact, religion and politics were nearly inseparable. Saudi Arabia was viewed as a leading center of Islamist thought, a place where the desire to keep the West and modern influences out of our religion and culture was often felt most strongly. I was taught in school that Saudi Arabia was the *Ashaqiqah Alkoubra*—the Big Sister—of Yemen, who wanted to help her less fortunate siblings.

This "help" spread to our mosques and schools, many of which were built by the Saudis. They influenced much of our curriculum as well. Early on, I was taught that the three flags that flew at our school— Yemen's, Iraq's, and Saudi Arabia's—were to be venerated and never allowed to touch the ground. I learned that Saddam Hussein was a leader who was working to make life better for his people, our brothers and sisters. And of course our Big Sister Saudi Arabia saw that no harm befell us. Yemen was poor but we had others looking out for our best interests. We were one Muslim family.

Country, religion, family, legacy. They were all bundled together, bound and secured by the Quran. I organized my faith into basic principles.

Islam for "divine law."

Iman for "belief."

Ihsan for "ethics and moral character."

But over and over again, I found myself returning to one basic principle: *rahmah*—mercy. As Allah stated in the Quran, "And we did not send you [O Muhammad] except as a mercy for all creation" (21:107). Or as the Prophet said in a hadith, "The Most Merciful shows mercy to those who have mercy on others. Show mercy to those on earth, and the One above the heaven will show mercy to you."

I would sit in class or kneel at the mosque and wonder if my tormentors heard these words. And if they did hear them, then why didn't they understand them? Why didn't they put mercy into practice as our God directed us to do?

In search of an answer, I threw myself into my religious studies. Each term, every day of the week, we had a class specifically devoted to sharia. We were instructed that Islamic law springs from two sources: divine intervention and human reason. Sharia is most aligned with the first, while *fiqh* is mainly the product of the second. *Fiqh* refers to human understanding and knowledge. The two work in concert to help us to determine how to conduct ourselves. We can't simply accept the rules as written; we have to use our independent reason and employ our minds and our intellect as fully as possible. In other words, the kids who tormented me were taught *rahmah* (mercy), but it was up to their human reason to make the right choices to behave properly. I tried not to judge them, to feel no resentment.

But forgiveness and mercy had their limits.

When I was just entering my teenage years, my teacher strode to the front of the classroom to begin a lecture on "How the Jews tried to fight and kill the Prophet Muhammad." The teacher carefully articulated each part of the story: the Jews followed Muhammad through the streets, called him names, and threw rocks to draw blood. As I listened, I could feel the words piercing me like stones. The Jews made Muhammad suffer; they killed him before he could have any male descendants.

Another teacher gave a lesson on "How the Jews betrayed the Prophet Muhammad." They'd promised to help protect him while he was in Mecca, but behind his back, they plotted to kill the Prophet. As a result, he said, we should never trust a Jew. A Jew's word is no good. When the hour came to a close, the room was silent. "The Jews are foxes," our teacher said. "Even if they seem good, they're always hiding something."

I hated Jews. Hated them without question.

At home and at the mosque, religious leaders denounced these people. Jews ate pork. Jews engaged in constant fornication. Jews drank alcohol. The Jews took the word of Allah and distorted it. The imam cited a hadith that said, "The Day of Resurrection will not arrive until the Moslems make war against the Jews and kill them, and until a Jew hiding behind a rock and tree, and the rock and tree will say: 'Oh Moslem, oh servant of Allah, there is a Jew behind me, come and kill him!'"

I pored over the Quran, and it seemed to say the same thing: "But on account of their breaking their covenant, we cursed them and made their hearts hard. They altered the words from their place and they neglected a portion of what they were reminded of; and you shall always discover treachery in them excepting a few of them; so pardon them and turn away, surely Allah loves those who do good to others." This passage confirmed it. Allah said these words. I couldn't test this characterization. I didn't know any Jews personally, but the words were law.

I was no judge, not formally like my grandfather, but the evidence seemed strong. And soon it would prove to be incontrovertible.

◇◇◇◇◇

The late September sun leaked from beneath the drawn window blinds and puddled on the classroom floor. Our teacher, Abdelsalam, had yet to enter the classroom. It was the final year of our primary education, and at thirteen and fourteen years old, we'd matured. We waited, silently; no longer was anyone assigned to take down the names of those who were misbehaving. I sat and looked over at a boy named Ahmed. He'd once been my fiercest academic rival, but we'd bonded over the fact that we both had fathers who demanded excellence at school and quiet at home. I took out my notes on a chapter from our science text that we would cover in the next week. Sooner was better than later.

I had just finished reviewing a bit about potential energy when our teacher came into the classroom. Generally a stern man whose smiles came less frequently than the full moon, he looked particularly fierce today. His normally hawkish appearance was enhanced by a pair of bushy eyebrows narrowing to a sharp V above his nose. Without saying a word, he stood in front of the class, his fists trembling.

"Everyone," he said, his voice catching momentarily, "there is something you need to know. Something you need to see. When you go home, watch your televisions. Learn from this."

On the screen that evening, every channel broadcast an image of two figures pressed up against a stone wall, huddling behind some curved protrusion. The picture, a grainy mix of whites and blues, was static. The volume on the set was too low for me to hear. The words beneath the image were clear: *Israeli soldiers shoot Palestinian boy in violence on the Gaza Strip.* I looked closer and saw that the pair was a boy, slightly younger than me, and a man. The boy was crying, his mouth open in anguish and fear, while the man (his father, I would later learn) held the child's arm, trying to keep him pressed flat and out of harm's way.

The next day, before classes began, Abdelsalam stood in front of us, still shaking, still overwrought.

"This is what they do," he said. "They murder the innocent. What had this boy done? Why did he have to die? Because he is Palestinian? Because he is a Muslim? Because Jews have no mercy? Yes. Yes. Yes."

I cast a glance at Ahmed. His eyes wide, his mouth half slack, he sat shaking his head slowly, imperceptibly, registering the disquiet that we all felt.

That boy could have been us.

I'd heard for years that the Jews in Israel killed children indiscriminately if it advanced their aims. Just two days before, on September 28, 2000, the Second Intifada had commenced. I'd sat with my father and watched as Ariel Sharon, Israel's prime minister, had, in an act of provocation, visited the Temple Mount in the Old City of Jerusalem. This was one of the holiest sites for Muslims. Why had that horrible man chosen to go there when he knew that with tensions this high, the gesture could only mean one thing: an insult. Protests followed; rioting ensued.

Now my classmates and I sat together, fighting back tears. I covered my face, not wanting anyone to see me. I'd been taught not to cry. Crying was for girls. But when I stole a look to my side, I saw that we were all hiding behind our books to cover our tears.

I would come to learn more about the boy, Muhammad al-Durrah. He was just two years younger than me. Like me, he loved cars. He'd gone out with his father that day because the elder al-Durrah had just sold his 1974 Fiat at a car auction. Muhammad didn't come back home.

When I returned to my house that afternoon, my mother greeted me at the door. She held me in her arms for a long while, ran the back of her fingers over my temples and through my hair, reassuring herself and me. That night, my father sat in front of the television set as he usually did, but he gathered the rest of us around him, his expression alternating between horrified and angry.

Everywhere we went for the next few days, people stopped and spoke of Muhammad al-Durrah. The crossroads at which he was killed was known locally as al-Shohada: martyr's junction. The father, Jamal, was a hardworking carpenter, a good and decent man. They weren't part of the protests, the rioting; they were minding their own business. Victims. If it could happen there, it could happen here. The dogs.

A few days later, I sat in the classroom again. Three representatives of the Muslim Brotherhood stood at the head of the class. They wanted to speak to us. As we knew, Yemen was the poorest country in the region, but we were told we ranked first when it came to financial support for our Muslim brothers in Palestine. The Emiratis, the Saudis, Kuwaitis, Qataris—they had much more, but we were told that they didn't give like we did.

Founded in Egypt in 1928 by Sunni members of the intellectual elite, the Muslim Brotherhood began as a secret society that aimed to return the Muslim world to the Muslims. The first step was establishing an Islamic government in Egypt and cutting ties with the West—an immoral and corrupting influence that caused all the world's problems.

Since at the time Egypt was still under the influence of the British, the Muslim Brothers were forced to exist as an underground organization. Many of its members fled to other countries in the region where they spread their message through hundreds of secret chapters and splinter groups. In 1987, for instance, they established Hamas, a militant anti-Israeli organization.

As fellow Sunnis, the Brotherhood gained support and funding from Saudi Arabia. And as a result, the group became a powerful force in spreading Islamist thought around the region. Which is why, by the time the Muslim Brotherhood representatives came to visit our classroom, we embraced them as a legitimate and mainstream organization, and a source of pride—even though they were Sunni and we were Zaidi Shia.

In a sense, this was a simpler time in Yemen, and though Sunnis primarily lived in the south and Shia primarily lived in the north, most people swept the historic Sunni-Shia conflict under our shared prayer rugs. In my community, we all simply identified as Muslim. There was no such thing as a Shia mosque, or a Sunni shop; we all ate together, talked together, and followed Allah together. Everyone prayed five times a day, fasted during Ramadan, and learned the Quran in school. Religion united us, as did groups like the Brotherhood. Even if there were doctrinal differences, the Brotherhood was committed to charitable work and supporting Muslims across the region.

As the representatives from the Brotherhood stood in front of the classroom, they told us that fighting the enemy was just one type of jihad. Giving money was another. Supporting the fighters was jihad.

We may not have been able to take up arms for the word of God, but we could help with money.

I reached into my pocket. I'd just gotten my allowance for lunch for the week. When the small basket came to me, I handed it all over, feeling like I had to. No. I wanted to. That could have been me. The Jews must be stopped. Israel could not win.

That afternoon when I returned home I told my mother that I was hungry. She looked confused, so I explained why I had skipped lunch. She hugged me, radiant. When my father came home, I heard them talking somewhere above me. A moment later, my father and mother came into my room. I sat and looked at them, frightened. My father never came to my room; we were always summoned to his level.

"Mohammed, I heard what you did," he said, standing in front of me, nodding, his eyes never leaving mine.

"You should have this," my mother added, handing me a small stack of bills. "Because you gave, you shouldn't go without."

"Double," my father said. "He acted like a man, he should be rewarded like a man." With that, he left the room.

My mother and I exchanged smiles.

That night, I lay in bed after I'd turned out the lights. I imagined walking through the war-torn streets of Jerusalem. I carried a machine gun. Smoke, sparks, and bullets flew around me. I was like a figure from my *Deus Ex* video game.

"Show no mercy," I whispered to myself. "Show no mercy. Give them what they deserve."

I fell into a deep and untroubled sleep.

Muhammad al-Durrah's death served as a catalyst for many in the Arab world. For years afterward, on the anniversary of his death, we watched television broadcasts and read headlines that offered some variation on this theme: "Today Muhammad al-Durrah would have been thirteen years old"; "Today Muhammad al-Durrah would have been fourteen years old" . . . Like concrete, anger continued to set and grow harder over time.

For years, I fantasized. I pieced together the different books I'd read:

histories of warriors, epics of heroes, tragedies of martyrdom. Faced with the enemy, would I be an evangelist or a conqueror? Would I be a soldier or a captain? Would I be strong or stronger? Would I smite him or rise above and show mercy? As one of the hadiths states:

> *Whosoever removes a worldly grief from a believer, Allah will remove from him one of the griefs of the Day of Judgment. Whosoever alleviates the lot of a needy person, Allah will alleviate his lot in this world and the next. Whosoever shields a Muslim, Allah will shield him in this world and the next. Allah will aid a slave of His so long as the slave aids his brother.*

◇◇◇◇◇

In secondary school, I began spending time at the hospital with my father, organizing his schedule and helping pick up the slack. I felt useful, and I told myself this was good job experience, despite the hours with nothing to do. One day, while waiting for my father to finish, I was walking down the hall when I saw two men in dark Western suits and white shirts. Each man had a black, disc-shaped headpiece on, and tendrils of hair dangled alongside their bearded faces.

Jews.

I stared at them.

Foxes come to prey on the sick and the weak.

One of the men draped his arm around the shoulder of the other, his Adam's apple bobbing up and down. Only seven little vertebrae connected his head to his body. A small, thin set of bones. My left hand clenched into a fist. I thought of charging them, tackling them to the ground. But instead of grabbing the nearest surgical blade, I went into lockdown mode. My tongue stuck to the roof of my mouth, my throat closed, and my arms froze to my sides. I watched helplessly as they turned down a corridor. And when I managed to dislodge my feet to peer around the corner, they were gone. Disappeared, as if by sorcery.

On high alert, I went to my father's office and collapsed into a chair. Who let them into the military hospital? Would any of our doctors treat them? And, more important, had I wasted my only opportunity to prove myself? I had had my chance, and I had done nothing.

I knew that there were a couple hundred Jews still living in Yemen, somewhere, hidden away. But could I get to them?

CHAPTER 4

◇◇◇

RINSE AND REPEAT

Arab rider of Yemen, circa 1787

W hile I was falling down a rabbit hole of revenge fantasies, my older brother, Hussain, was falling in love with a woman who was half Egyptian and half Yemeni. The woman wasn't a Zaidi like we were. And even though Sunni and Shia wasn't a distinction that played a role in our lives, maintaining the Zaidi bloodlines was important to my parents, perhaps because of their own mixed marriage.

My mother and my father were a couple that broke all traditional and social conventions. The Al Samawi family was well respected, dating its lineage back to the Prophet Muhammad. For generations, the Al Samawis served as judges, lawyers, and engineers. They were highly educated, highly esteemed, and highly insular when it came to picking a spouse. My father, excellent in school and determined to become a doctor, was a perfect catch for any Yemeni mother seeking a good match for her daughter. But before he could be married off, he left to study medicine in the Soviet Union. This gave his mother a bit more time to secure a respectable Zaidi bride from the north.

At the time, Yemen was carved into two countries: the Yemen Arab Republic in the north and the People's Democratic Republic of Yemen in the south. The division, though short-lived, was born out of thousands of years of history. Since 5000 BCE, people have occupied the coastal plains and interior mountains of the southwest Arabian Peninsula, and since then, a trade route between European and Asian civilizations passed around and through Yemen. Control of and access to this route was of great value to the entire world. The Ottomans understood this, and when the sultan of the Ottoman Empire expanded through the Arabian Peninsula to the Muslim holy cities of Mecca and Medina, he became not only a source of religious authority but also the key to this very trade route between Europe and India. But his army stopped before they got to Aden—a fact that ultimately contributed to the empire's downfall.

For a while, the Ottomans had control of regional trade, but by the fifteenth century the Europeans were pushing against their restraints. In 1497, Portuguese explorer Vasco da Gama set out to discover a new sea route from the mainland to India, and he realized that if the Portuguese could control Aden—along with Muscat in Oman and Diu in India—they could finally bypass the Ottoman Empire entirely. The Portuguese fought the Ottomans for control of the region—and the sea route—throughout the early sixteenth century. Though the dates seem to differ, the Portuguese did at some point capture parts of Aden, and in doing so, threatened to cut the Ottomans out of the spice trade entirely.

In 1548, the Ottomans retook the land, but it wasn't enough to save their empire. With a weakening trade route, and the resultant loss of power and wealth, the empire began to rapidly decline. This left a hole for a new superpower: the British. The global shift of power was illustrated in 1839, when the British moved into southern Yemen and took Aden for themselves. Their control of the city tightened in 1869, after the opening of the Suez Canal, which ran through Egypt. Though the Egyptian government and private French financiers initially owned the canal, the Brits took advantage of Egypt's financial distress and bought nearly fifty percent of the shares from the government. Before long, the Suez Canal became the key to all trade between the Mediterranean and the Indian Ocean.

But here was the catch: in order for ships to pass from one body of water to the other, they had to get not only through the Suez Canal but also through the Bab el Mandeb strait, control of which was split between Africa and the Arabian Peninsula—that is, Yemen. Thus, in order to secure control of the Suez trade route, the British needed to formalize their control of Aden, which was why in 1874 they established the Aden Protectorate along the southern coast.

By 1922, the Ottoman Empire, one of the largest empires in history, had been dissolved, delivering a huge blow to the Arab world, and to Sunni Muslims in particular. Not only was this a political collapse, but also a collapse of the Sunni religious authority. The northern lands of Yemen became the Shia Mutawakkilite Kingdom of Yemen with its capital city of Sana'a, while the southern lands remained the Aden Protectorate, under British control.

While the north and south grew up together, the countries were as different as two siblings could be. The north was more populous and economically developed, while the south—outside of Aden—was geographically inhospitable and more sparsely populated. Not to mention that the north had a large concentration of Shia Muslims, while the south was overwhelmingly Sunni.

My father's family, the Al Samawis, were from the north, and we prospered through education and hard work. The woman he would marry, my mother, was from the south. She, unlike my father, grew up very poor; every day, she and her four brothers and three sisters scavenged to find food. Despite the grinding poverty, she had more freedom in the Aden Protectorate, and then the People's Democratic Republic of Yemen, than she would have had in the north. Islamic law wasn't as strictly enforced, so my mother wore Western-style clothes, and exposed her head and hair. She went to school, and even though her family didn't have money to pay for a private education, she wasn't forced to drop out and marry young. Instead, she juggled her responsibilities at home with her own professional dreams, both caring for her siblings and keeping up with her studies.

When my mother was old enough, she went against all odds and societal expectations and traveled to Ukraine to train as a pediatrician and gynecologist. Enjoying the freedom to do whatever she wanted, she took a short trip to the capital of the Soviet Union, where she met a striking young urologist. Needless to say, she ended up with more than a postcard and fond memories. A courtship began, which was followed by a marriage proposal, which was followed by a fit of disapproval. My mother wasn't from the Al Samawi family! She wasn't from the north! She wasn't even a Zaidi Shia! Did my father not understand what that meant?

The oldest branch of Shia Islam, Zaidi materialized all the way back in the middle of the eighth century. Born out of the pursuit of justice and morality, and a questioning of leadership and law, Zaidi was a religion of social action. Early on, I was taught that Zaidis are "unable to live in their own houses," because of their need to get out and take a stand against any kind of injustice. This was literally part of the Al Samawi DNA. And yet when my father brought my mother home from the Soviet Union, there was a distinct feeling that *she* was unable to live in *their* house.

More than reluctant to embrace a southern girl with darker skin and significantly fewer resources, my father's family begged him to reconsider. They picked at my mother, but she had practice surviving far worse, and gradually they had to give in. She became pregnant, and it was clear that she would be the mother of their grandchildren. The ice thawed, though the relationship never quite warmed. But through years of tense family gatherings and not-quite-whispered critiques, my father remained loyal. Even though, according to Islamic law, he could have married up to four women, he chose my mother, and he chose us.

His commitment to monogamy cannot be overstated. I went to school with two brothers, Hadi and Hatem, about whom the only thing similar was their names. They looked nothing alike, weren't twins, but were in the same grade, only six months apart. At first I didn't really question it. They called themselves brothers, so I figured they must have been brothers. But when I thought to do the math, it just didn't work out. After much consideration, it dawned on me that they had different mothers. No wonder they were so dissimilar! I asked Hadi and Hatem about it, and they said the families all lived together in the same house, but even though the two of them got along okay, tension always existed between their mothers. They didn't like to talk about it, which only led me to ask more questions. I may have had trouble with a soccer ball, but I had no trouble chasing answers.

When I was in eighth grade, my teacher, Iqbal Zain Haj, led us through a passage in the Quran that mentioned Muslim men taking multiple wives. I raised my hand.

"Please, can you explain to me the reason why Allah allows this?"

"It is of use in spreading His word, Mohammed. If a man has more than one wife, he can have many children. The more children he has, the more children God has."

Iqbal Zain Haj looked back at his book, but before he could begin again, I said, "Yes, that makes some sense. But is there a reason that women have to suffer the burden?"

"They don't suffer. They are taken care of," he snapped, closing the conversation.

"But what is their reward in heaven for having done this?" I pressed on. "They will become one of the seventy-two maidens that a man killed in jihad will be rewarded with? Instead of sharing with three other women, they have to share with—"

I didn't get to finish my point.

"Mohammed, close the door from the outside. Now!"

I slid out of my desk and shuffled unsteadily into the hallway. I'd never been asked to leave the classroom before.

That evening, over dinner, I told my parents the story of my banishment.

My father continued chewing as if he hadn't heard what I'd said, and my mother looked at me and rolled her eyes as if to say, *Don't you know better by now?*

I looked back down at my plate and moved my fork without conviction. After a minute of silence, my father delivered his verdict.

"One wife is enough for any man," he said, his tone and expression completely neutral.

My brothers, sisters, and I all leaned forward in silent respect, chins tilted toward our chests, eyes raised. We looked at one another, silently asking, *What does he mean? Is he joking?*

My father lowered his head as well, but only to meet his fork. He took another bite of his dinner.

I was about to ask another question when I felt my mother's hand on mine.

"I have ordered the lamb for Eid al-Adha," she said. "I got a good price."

My father nodded absently. The holiday was approaching, and with it the ritual slaughter and preparation of a lamb. The women would cook the meal, and then they would clean up after us. We men would be well cared for.

◇◇◇◇◇◇

Even though my father chose my mother in defiance of his family, that didn't mean he wanted his children to follow in his footsteps. He took great pride in the Al Samawi lineage, as demonstrated by the large family tree that adorned the wall of the main living area. Anyone entering the house would have to contend with our towering ancestry, and my brothers and I were taught to list our forebears centuries back.

But much like my father at his age, Hussain didn't care. He was twenty-four, a fully grown man. He didn't ask permission so much as announce his intention to marry this half-Egyptian woman of no notable family background. And so at eighteen years old, fresh out of high school, I witnessed an acute example of history repeating itself. In a storm of sound and fury, my father refused to share the same room with Hussain, and my mother couldn't breathe without weeping. I hated to watch my mother suffer, but I would have bought a ticket and some popcorn to watch Hussain squirm.

Over the years, the temperature of my relationship with my older brother had plummeted. The breaking point came just months before this, when Hussain was home from university on a break. I rarely got to see him, and when I did, I tried my best to give him space. But one evening, I needed a ride, so I asked him to drive me to meet up with my buddy Ahmed.

Ahmed and I had met in the seventh grade. He was bright and from a good family, and I was bright and from a good family, so we did the only thing we could think of: we became rivals. Whenever we had an exam, we raced to finish first; and whenever the teacher asked a question, we corrected one another's response. After school, I'd pore over my homework, eager to do better than Ahmed. And when I'd finish, I'd crank up my music and open a book, so I would know more than Ahmed. I'd spend day after day by myself, with Michael Jackson, the Backstreet Boys, and Britney Spears cheering me on to beat Ahmed.

My classmates couldn't have cared less about this battle of the brains, but to me it was everything. I was locked in an intellectual tug-of-war, and neither Ahmed nor I would let go of the rope. Until an unexpected solution presented itself: we could join forces. We both felt like we were up against the world, so using the age-old wisdom that the enemy of my enemy is my friend, we shelved our personal competition and become a united front. Finally, an ally! It was a dream come true. Billiards and table tennis were much more enjoyable with a partner.

On the afternoon in question, I buzzed around Hussain until he reluctantly agreed to drive me to meet Ahmed. He ignored me as we climbed into my father's Toyota Land Cruiser, and as our gate opened, he turned on the radio and slammed his foot on the gas. Yemen's traffic laws are very simple—do what you want and let the strongest and fastest survive. I'd already pushed Hussain to his limit, so I didn't bother shouting at him to slow down; not that he would have heard me over the pumping bass line of NWA's "Gangsta Gangsta." The lyrics meant almost nothing to me, and less to Hussain, who didn't have any real command of English, but he bobbed his head to the beat as he wove through the crowded streets of Sana'a.

At one point, he cut in front of a car. The driver had to slam on his brakes to avoid a collision. I sat with my good hand pressed against the dashboard, horrified as the other driver pulled up alongside our car and gestured to Hussain to pull over. I watched as Hussain hit the brakes and turned the wheel.

He got out of the car, shouting and screaming at a man who was shouting and screaming right back. The two of them engaged in a kind of long-distance dance, several feet apart from one another, circling and testing out their jabs, like boxers in a ring.

I was afraid that they would run out of words and start to use their fists—or worse. Most men in Yemen carried guns . . .

"Please! Stop!" I called out. "My brother was wrong. He apologizes."

The two men froze and stared at me. Next, I felt a sharp sting across my cheek. Then another. A more direct hit rocked me back on my heels.

Hussain stood screaming at me, his eyes ablaze. I was so stunned that I couldn't hear what he was saying. I curled up and put my hands over my head, but nothing happened. When I looked up, I saw that the other driver had grabbed my brother and was yelling at him to calm down.

I never said a word to my parents about what happened, and Hussain and I never spoke about it again. But after that, there wasn't much left between us but resentment. So, now that he'd proposed to the woman he loved and felt the blows of the Al Samawi judgment, I couldn't help but find a little to smile about.

Eventually my father relented and gave Hussain his blessing. Perhaps he recognized some of himself in his oldest child. Perhaps he voted with his heart and not his head. Or perhaps this was yet another way to show the rest of the extended family that he and his children wouldn't bow down to every bit of tradition. I'll never know, because I knew better than to ask.

Regardless, peace was restored. Until it wasn't. Three months after we celebrated his marriage, Hussain was back at home explaining that he had been wrong, that my parents had been right. This woman wasn't the woman for him. Months of negotiations and drama ensued, until finally my parents disentangled Hussain from the marriage and the mess he'd made. Head between his hands, he agreed to entrust my parents with his future, and a few months later we attended another wedding. This time to the woman my mother had chosen.

Hussain seemed happy. His bride was from a good Zaidi family.

◇◇◇◇◇◇

While all this was happening, I looked like a paragon of virtue. At home, I performed the role of the perfect child, kissing my father's head at the dinner table, and helping my mother tidy the rooms. At school, I'd entered my first year at Sana'a University and was studying business administration. Even though I was nineteen years old, I still lived in the same room I grew up in and obeyed my curfew (10:00 P.M.). I told my parents everything that I did, where I went, and who I was with. I distinguished myself with good grades, and I kept out of trouble.

My biggest extravagance was the Sana'a International Book Fair. First held in 1984, it was the second-largest book exposition in the Arab world, with only the Cairo Book Fair besting it in terms of sales, participation, and demand. Ever since I was a child, I'd save some of my allowance money and attend, coming home with a huge bag of books. Novels opened up entirely new worlds—as did my collection of American television shows.

When my eyes hurt from reading, I went to the store to purchase DVDs and videocassettes. The films were dubbed into Arabic, or had Arabic subtitles, and they were edited to eliminate all nudity and physical contact between men and women (or men and men)—except when it came to violence.

At least once a week, I would go to the neighborhood video store and browse the shelves, or I'd dive deeper, into the black market. One afternoon I was looking through a bin of DVDs in search of the latest unedited action films when a cover caught my eye. It had a photograph of a man, running, his coat spread out behind him like a cape, and a beautiful woman peering around the door. The title, *Unfaithful,* didn't tell me much, so when I got home, I started watching . . .

The film told the story of a man who discovered that his wife was having an affair. He became obsessed and started tracking her, and at several points he saw her having sex with another man. I'd never seen a woman's naked body—and there it was, on the screen! I shut off the screen and hid the DVD with my schoolbooks. What had I done?

Sexual education wasn't a course in Yemen, and even though my parents were doctors, I'd never seen an anatomy book. Of course, we all whispered and joked and pretended to know about sex, and some of the boys at my secondary school even bragged about having been with girls, but they weren't any more specific than that. The only real instruction we received about sexuality was that we should avoid it at all costs.

In ninth grade, a teacher compared Muslim women to a perfect red apple. The red skin, he said, is beautiful and unblemished. But what happens when you take a bite out of that apple and expose the white flesh beneath it? After a short time, it grows brown. After a longer time, it shrivels up and rots. Why? Because it is exposed to bacteria that start the decaying process. If that skin hadn't been broken, the apple would have remained a beautiful thing for a very long time. That's why women need to be covered—to avoid exposure to the elements that would harm them. By extension, any woman who didn't remain covered was less beautiful, less desirable, because that process of decay had already begun. I accepted this logic, as did everyone around me, but the rationale felt thin when my sisters came in crying that a taxi driver had cursed them because their hijabs left their hair and faces exposed. I tried to remind myself that they needed to remain covered for their own protection, but who or what exactly were they being protected against?

The West, of course. We were all taught that the West was the corrupting influence. Our imams and teachers lectured that Western society was a failure and Christianity a sham. They used the television cartoon *SpongeBob Squarepants* as an example of American hedonism—this Bob wore no clothes! It seemed an odd example, since "pants" was part of his name, but who was I to question? I'd never seen the show. Our teachers presented clips of nude scenes from various foreign films, mostly American, with the offending body parts blacked out, while speakers warned that Western attire contributed to the proliferation of pornography, and a decaying civilization. Western women, they concluded, were little better than, and in many cases actually were, prostitutes. Worse, they were trying to spread their influence around the world.

Of course, the number one offender was Israel. I grew up hearing that Jewish women were out of control. All they wanted to do was fornicate, drink alcohol, and go to parties. We were taught to hate them, while most of the boys secretly wished we could live in a place where women acted that way. And in those unfiltered moments of the film *Unfaithful,* I finally understood why.

◇◇◇

CHAPTER 5

THE ECONOMICS OF LOVE

King Solomon and the Queen of Sheba, who some say ruled in the land that is now Yemen

I sat waiting for my classmates to clear out of the lecture hall. "The Principles of Macroeconomics" was a well-attended class, but I made it a rule to be the last one out the door. There was no need to parade down the aisle and put myself on display.

A small cluster of students gathered at the exit. A tall, slender young man stood in the center—the nucleus around which the others seemed to orbit, magnetized by his confidence. Their unguarded laughter echoed through the room. I could have joined them; I knew that. The novelty of putting me down had worn off, and besides, I'd learned to laugh at myself first. Not to mention, everyone knew I had the best DVD collection in Sana'a. I had friends, like Ahmed, and there were a handful of girls who confided in me. But despite all that, I still felt like an outsider. The downside of all my reading and high-minded posturing was that I came across as a kind of elder statesman, a trusted uncle—not one of the gang.

As the guys slapped each other on the back, I tried to look busy, shuffling my papers and reviewing my notes. But after a fifty-minute lecture on the required reserve ratio, my brain was as numb as my backside.

When the last of the stragglers was out of sight, I pushed myself up and hoisted on my backpack, nearly toppling over from the weight of my textbooks. A last-second grab at another desk saved me, the screech of the metal feet against the tile floor sounding an alarm for no one but me. I took a few steps toward the door and then heard the patter of quick, soft footfalls.

"I'm so glad you're here."

I looked up into a pair of dark eyes. In the fluorescent light, they shimmered like pools of India ink.

"Of all days," she said, more to herself than to me. She paused and took a deep breath, her shoulders rising and falling under her hijab.

She scanned the floor as if she'd lost something. I followed her lead, but only saw a couple of scuff marks that reminded me of the Arabic letters *raá* and *daal*.

"Are you okay?" I asked finally. My mind raced to likely scenarios—a sick family member, an argument with a boyfriend, an insolent cab-driver.

"I am. I am. Thank you for asking, Mohammed."

I grinned at the sound of my own name coming out of her mouth. Her gaze left the floor and settled on my face. I could feel the heat rush to my cheeks.

"May I ask a favor of you?"

My head bobbled up and down like a broken toy. "Sure. Absolutely. Yeah. However I can help. What can I do for you?"

Gratefully, she ended my string of assurances.

"I missed the lecture," she said, sighing, raising her palms to the sky. "May I borrow your notes?"

"Sure. Absolutely. However I can help. I'm happy to do it." As I spoke, I shrugged out of my backpack and slung it around to my chest. With my good hand, I tugged at the zipper, pulling at it ineffectually for a few moments before its teeth clicked open. An inexpert magician, I finally produced the notebook.

"I'll return it to you as soon as possible," she said. "Thank you so much. You have no idea."

I smiled; she was right. I had absolutely no idea—who she was.

As if reading my mind, she said to me, "Oh, sorry. My name is Ahlam. I should have begun with that, I know."

She glanced over my shoulder at the clock on the wall. I turned as well.

"As soon as I can," she said. "And thank you."

And with that, she was gone.

I'd be a liar if I said I didn't think about that encounter for the next day. Why did she choose me? Maybe she knew I was a good student. She must have noticed me taking notes, hunched and contorted in my right-handed desk as I tried to keep my left elbow from shoving me out of my seat. I tried to think nothing more of it. She'd approached me out of desperation, nothing more.

When Ahlam returned my notebook to me two days later, I kept my eyes down the entire time. But when I flipped through the pages to find my place, I stopped short. There, in the margin, alongside my ink-smeared scrawl, rested Ahlam's delicate script. Her words looked like a series of beautiful women reclining on an elegant sofa.

Thank you so much. ☺

That smiley face might as well have been written in gold, formed out of clouds, accompanied by the soft strains of Michael Jackson's "You Are My Life." It was nearly as bold as Ahlam walking to the front of the lecture hall and tossing her hijab to the side. A smile on a page in a notebook may not seem like much, but in Yemen, where a woman cannot overtly express her interest in a man, it was as if Ahlam were openly saying, *I like you*. It was brazen; it was dangerous. If a Muslim woman in Yemen couldn't even show her hair or her skin, what did it mean if she exposed something even deeper than that? What kind of woman expressed her emotions and desires? We lived in a world where a smile was much more than a smile.

My mind raced with possibilities. I didn't know Ahlam at all. Until two days earlier, I didn't even know her name. But the boldness she displayed by initiating anything at all between us was thrilling. I didn't spend much time weighing my choices. I was more concerned with not letting the opportunity slip away on leather slippers. I tore a piece of paper from the notebook and hastily wrote out my phone number. Before the lecture began, I followed after her, down the aisle, past my classmates, toward the back of the enormous room where she sat.

"Ahlam," I said, worried that I'd shouted. I looked around. No one had noticed. "I have something for you." I held out the crumpled scrap of paper. "In case you have any questions about other lectures . . ." I said, my courage trailing off with my voice.

Ahlam took the paper in her long, slender fingers. The light brown of her skin made it seem as if she was wearing fine, soft gloves.

"Thank you," she said, her voice bright, cheery, lilting. "That's so kind."

And *wallah*, swear to God, my heart felt like a fish, flopping around in my empty chest.

I took notes in starts and stops, interrupted by visions of Ahlam's hand so close to my own, the sound of her voice. The only thing that kept me from abandoning the enterprise entirely was the thought that she might need help with the day's lecture. Perhaps I could win her over with my mastery of macroeconomics.

I spent the rest of that afternoon trying to will my mind to behave. It didn't. Every rustle of feet, every whisper of wind made me look around. But Ahlam wasn't there. Every sneeze, every car horn made me jump. But Ahlam wasn't there. Finally, I returned home, to the clatter of dishes and the buzz of the television. And when the phone rang, I took a deep breath. I waited another two rings, and answered in my most casual-but-manly voice. This time I knew; Ahlam was there.

When I heard her voice, I felt myself floating on air. My clumsy body disappeared, and my reality was reduced to the melody of Ahlam's laughter. I clung to the sound of her breath, the way she said "Mohammed." I let each character of her name roll off my tongue, through my lips. Her name was like a sigh, like a feeling of comfort, *Ahlam*. Her voice turned her words into song lyrics, and I felt like a plucked string, vibrating in harmony with the world.

We spoke about school and classes, favorite foods and hobbies. Macroeconomics never came up.

For the next two weeks or so, Ahlam and I spent hours on the phone. She'd tease me, telling me that a lot of other girls liked me. I'd laugh. I'd seen enough movies to know that I was the sidekick, the best friend, the one whom the leads came to for advice. I wasn't the heartthrob.

She'd tell me how good I looked and how popular I was. And then, inevitably, she'd say, "Now what about me? Do people like me?"

"Yes," I said. "Yes, they do." I named the football star Wayne Rooney, the singer John Mayer. Leonardo DiCaprio.

But that wasn't enough for her. Then she'd ask, "And how about you? How do *you* like me?"

I felt like I was in a Hollywood movie! For the first time in my life, I had the chance to be the romantic lead. I wasn't sure how I truly felt about Ahlam, but I knew she made me happier than I'd ever been. After another week, I said three of the most dangerous words a man can say.

"I love you," I blurted out.

Hardly a heartbeat passed before she said, "I love you, too."

Ana hemar. I hadn't planned on saying that. I was just caught up in the moment! But as soon as the words came out of my mouth, I be-lieved them to be true. Not that I really knew what it felt like to be in love. I'd never been alone in a room with a woman, let alone on a date with one. But this was euphoria, and I was following the only script I knew.

I was twenty-two, but—like most Yemeni men my age—I was more familiar with romantic comedies than real-life romantic conversations with women who weren't part of my family. Respectable ladies didn't socialize with men in closed settings. That just didn't happen. People didn't go to movies together, didn't share meals out at restaurants to-gether, didn't hang out at one or the other's apartment together, didn't go to parties together . . . And while we attended the same schools and sat in the same classrooms, males and females were segregated most of the time. This was even true of two people who were about to be mar-ried. On the day of their wedding—the males had one celebration and the females another.

But now I had a secret phone line to a woman, and apparently we were in love! Emboldened by our own daring, I gathered my courage and said something even more audacious. "Ahlam," I said, gathering my courage. "I would like to see your face."

At this, she paused. I felt my heart thudding in my chest as the mo-ment stretched on. Time distorted itself, like a dripping Dalí clock.

"Meet me fifteen minutes before economics class," she said, the trill in her voice a bit tighter. "The room isn't used then and should be empty. I will show you my face."

I was thrilled; I was terrified; I was going to throw up. I arrived in the designated room thirty minutes early and collapsed into a chair, my left foot tap, tap, tapping like the shots of a distant machine gun. Suddenly the door swung open, and there was Ahlam. She marched up to me, and without an ounce of hesitation, she showed me her face.

Simply put, Ahlam was beautiful. Breathtaking. Her almond eyes sat in an oval face that came to a delicate point at her finely carved chin. Her full lips were the color of desert roses, and when they parted into a smile, I felt my mouth go dry. After a few seconds, she drew the curtain of her niqab back across her face and marched back out.

As I sat alone, the image of her face played like a movie in my mind. I thought about the space between her lips, about the crinkle at the corner of her eyes . . . I was young, drunk on flirtation, and caught up in the playacting of courtship. Marriage hadn't crossed my mind, and I certainly hadn't considered what this naïve dare might have meant for Ahlam.

Later that week, my phone rang and I rushed to pick it up. It was Ahlam. I felt bubbles in my chest. She told me she had seen me at lunch, and that she was jealous of the people who got to sit near me. She said she wished she could sit with me, but of course, this wasn't possible. Then she said, "What would you do if I was near you right now?"

I held the phone close and said, "I would hug you."

The words had just barely stopped vibrating in the air when I saw my mother looming in the doorway, her face pinched into a question mark. *Ana hemar*, I thought. *Donkey, donkey, donkey.*

"Who are you speaking with?" my mother demanded.

"No one, no one," I said, Ahlam still on the line.

"No," she said. "I heard you speaking with a woman. Who is it?"

I quickly hung up the phone.

My mother saw this and started to cry, swatting at me. "Who is it, who is it? I heard you speaking sexy words!"

"No one," I insisted, never having been so ashamed in my life.

She wheedled and coaxed, and finally I told my mother I was speaking with a girl from the university. Suddenly she smiled, like a little girl.

"Do you love her?" she asked.

"I don't know," I said.

"Do you want to marry her?" she asked.

"I don't know," I said.

Then she went completely still. "Did you do anything sexual with her?"

"No!" I said. "I've just been speaking with her for a couple weeks. I'm not sure what's happening."

All the light disappeared from my mother's eyes and she started crying again, calling for my father, shouting and shouting. I begged her to keep this between the two of us, but she said no, my father needed to know. She ran upstairs. Seconds later, my father started shouting, wary, frustrated that there was a conflict that needed mediation.

My mother screamed, "Mohammed was speaking with a girl and they were speaking sexy words!"

"What?" he roared.

Next thing I knew, my sisters were running into my room, yelling, "What happened, what happened?"

The bubbles burst somewhere in my throat and came out as a hiccup. This wasn't fun anymore. This wasn't how a leading man's role was supposed to be played. I sat on the edge of my bed and pressed the flats of my palms into my eyes, a field of stars dotting the blackness. Hiccup.

I explained the situation to Lial and Nuha, and they shook their heads knowingly.

"Whatever you do," Lial said, "do not go upstairs. Don't get him started. You know there's no calming him down then."

I nodded slowly—hiccup—and they skipped off together, arms around each other, giggling.

Within two minutes Nuha ran back in. She sat next to me and gently whispered, "Father wants to speak with you." That was enough to scare the hiccups right out of me.

My mind blanked until I found myself standing before my father in his study.

"Your mother told me you were speaking with a girl," he said. "Do you love her?"

"I just met her," I said.

"Is she Zaidi?" he asked, his tone neutral, expression unreadable.

"I'm not sure. I think so."

He nodded. "Give your mother her full name and she'll ask about her family. We don't want you to make the same mistake as your brother. If she's a good person, you need to do this in the right way. You can't speak with a girl like this without being engaged first. You need to know who she is. What kind of girl she is."

My ears burned with embarrassment as I studied the space between my shoes. I'd been so enamored with my own daring that I'd forgotten there could be real consequences for Ahlam. Flirting before an engagement wouldn't affect me in any way, but it could destroy her. For a single woman, even an innocent conversation could lead to a "reputation." A man could have hundreds of relationships and still find a good match, but for a woman . . .

For years I'd heard whispers of girls who'd been ruined, who were condemned to lives as spinsters or childless "aunties." I remembered a male classmate of mine who was caught kissing a girl. His parents pulled him out of school at the age of fifteen and arranged a marriage for him with someone else—someone they approved of. He had a big wedding and celebrated with his friends: now that he was married, he could sleep with his wife as much as he wanted and not get into any kind of trouble. In fact, he could marry three other women, and sleep with them all, and still be an honorable man. I didn't think much of it at the time, but now I wondered, *What happened to the girl?*

Fear twined with a new sense of responsibility. I'd told Ahlam that I loved her; I'd asked to see her face. All of this implied that my intentions were serious. I'd tried to be the leading man, but I wasn't playacting. These were our real lives. I thought of the hours I'd spent speaking with Ahlam on the phone, the freedom I'd felt to joke around. To let go. To be myself. I'd never felt as whole with anyone else before, other than my little sister Nuha.

I gave my mother Ahlam's name and address. I was ready to do the right thing.

The next day at university, I told Ahlam that my parents were looking into her. She practically danced out of her shoes. This was a clear indication that we were in the process of getting engaged. Her delicate hands clapped together, and I couldn't help but smile. I wondered what kind of jewelry I might buy her to celebrate our engagement.

When I returned home, my mother sat me down. This was the conversation I'd been waiting for; it was only a matter of minutes before I'd officially have a betrothed. Her eyes flicked to mine, and I tried to communicate that it was okay—that I was ready for this. She got straight to business. My mother had asked around and found out that Ahlam was Zaidi, which was a good thing, but her parents were divorced, which was not. Her family had a lot of issues, she said, shaking her head. They didn't have money, means, or connections. My mother's eyes pinned me to my seat. Ahlam knew I was from the Al Samawi family, she said, that we had money. I was an easy target because of my disability. "She's poor. She's trying to take advantage. You're naïve."

Without ceremony, she stood up and left. Her words hit me harder than Hussain ever had.

I stayed in my room, dumbstruck, until my father called me to him. In a trance, I went, my mind as paralyzed as my body. He repeated everything my mother had told me and gave his final judgment: Ahlam wasn't the right girl for me. He pointed to Hussain and said, "Do you see how happy your brother is now because of the arranged marriage?"

I shook my head, unable to speak. Unwilling to give him this victory.

I sat in silence as I considered my next move. But before I could make a play, my father made his: "If you let me choose a wife for you, I will give you a car. I will give you a job in the military hospital. Even if you stay at the university and don't go to work, I will make sure the hospital puts you on payroll and that you receive your own salary."

My father, the director of the urology department, wielded that much power.

"No," I said, reaching to find the right words. "I like Ahlam."

My father flinched, as if an insect had flown near his eye. A nearly imperceptible loss of control. "Think about it," he said. Cool, restrained. "Then come back to me."

That evening I went out with Ahmed. We drove through the valley, weaving our way through the densely packed houses, spinning through dusty roads that were built centuries ago for camels and donkeys. I told him what had happened with my father, and he put one hand on my shoulder, grinning, wide-eyed.

"That's amazing!" He shook me. He whistled through his teeth and looked to the sky. "If you take the deal, you'll be so far ahead of the game. You'll have a job, an apartment, and your parents will set you up with a wife. You won't have to spend a single rial!"

This was not the reaction I expected. I wasn't thinking about expenses; I was thinking about love! And honor! What did I care if I needed to pay Ahlam's family the equivalent of $10,000 USD as a dowry? I had an average monthly salary of $100–$200. It might take a long time to save up, but wasn't it worth it? Sure, there would be additional expenses. After the initial costs, I'd have to pay for the wedding, her dresses, our children, the entire household . . .

"And"—Ahmed gave me a sidelong look—"you'll have sex every single day. It will be amazing!"

I tried to summon my noble indignation, but before I knew it, I was laughing along with him. As the spices of the marketplace filled my head, and the clear white light of the moon cracked through the windshield, my father's offer didn't seem so bad. I hardly knew Ahlam. She didn't love me. I was naïve. An easy target. Maybe I wasn't strong enough to find my own wife. Maybe I needed assistance.

When I got home that night, I told my father I would agree to his terms. He clasped my arm. "Okay," he said. "Your mother will handle this."

◇◇◇◇◇

I ignored Ahlam. I stopped picking up the phone when she called, and I avoided eye contact at the university. When I saw her walking down the hall, I started up a conversation with the closest person at hand. I talked to people I'd never talked to before. They laughed at my jokes. I created my own shell, a protective orbit.

The one time Ahlam broke through, I told her I was sick and having problems with my parents. She asked if there was anything she could do, and whether or not we were going to get engaged. I didn't say anything. I was weak. I didn't want to hurt her, and so I hurt her a hundred times more. Once it became clear that there would be no engagement, Ahlam took a leave of absence from the university.

Did I take this as proof of her affection? No. I told myself she was upset at her loss of fortune, that she didn't want to spend time at a place that would remind her of how her scheme had failed. And thank goodness it had! My parents had saved me from disaster. I'd tried to fly in the face of tradition and expectations, but I wasn't strong enough to prove the exception. A love marriage hadn't worked for Hussain, and it wouldn't work for me. I thought I'd wanted a partner in life, but my parents were right. I needed a caretaker.

If nothing else, I understood economics. Risk and reward. I chose the latter. My parents found a wife for me, and the two of us married. We were very different people, but we came together to build a life. I won't say more about it, as that is her story. All you need to know is this: I had a family, and then I lost everything.

CHAPTER 6

◇◇◇

THE BOOK OF LUKE

A late-nineteenth-century engraving
depicting a man reading the Quran

If life were a romantic comedy, Ahlam and I would have reached for
the same pencil. If life were a tragedy, we would have reached
for the same sword. But life was just life, and it went on without a
single montage or vial of poison. I continued going to school, and the
march of progress played on.

In early September 2009, I enrolled in evening classes at the Canadian
Institute in Sana'a. After several years of studying business administration, I was comfortable conversing in the language of numbers and
economic theory. But if I was going to succeed in the corporate world, I was
going to have to master the language of consumerism: English. Sana'a
University was a top institution in Yemen, but the Canadian Institute

offered courses in basic conversational English, specialized courses in business terminology and practices, and a Teaching English to Speakers of Other Languages (TESOL) certification. If I wanted to open my own business one day, this would be a critical step.

On the first night of the semester, I walked into a classroom to find the tallest man I'd ever seen. He looked like a giant, straight out of one of the fantasy books of my youth. I stared straight up at him, until he saw me gawking, and then I looked away.

"My name is Luke," he said. "And you are?"

"Mohammed Al Samawi," I said. "I'm happy to have meeting with you."

He smiled and ran his hand through his white hair. "Welcome to the class. I'm eager to learn more about you."

"Thank you," I said, and took the nearest seat, throwing a smile to anyone who caught our exchange, which had been *in English.* The days of folding up into the smallest version of myself were behind me.

I waited as the rest of the students trickled in. Luke tried greeting a couple, but most responded with smiles, nods, and quick dashes to their seats. English was as scary to them as swimming was to me. When everyone settled in, Luke stood in front of his desk and formally introduced himself, along with the course. I tried to focus my attention on the strange English words, but the most foreign thing about Luke wasn't the language he was speaking, it was the way he looked. He was completely different from any teacher I'd ever seen. Whereas all the professors at Sana'a University carefully maintained their scholarly beards, Luke was completely clean-shaven. Instead of wearing a standard suit and tie, he wore a T-shirt. The temperature outside had dropped to the mid-70s. I was freezing, but it didn't seem to bother Luke at all. *Canadian fortitude,* I thought to myself, admiring his manly regard. Luke, it turned out, was from England.

As the class progressed, it was clear that most of the students were too unfamiliar with English to understand even the basics. And so Luke was forced to resort to stilted Arabic. He slipped up many times, misusing words like *Mashi,* which means "I agree" in Egypt, "no" in Sana'a, and "walking" in Aden. But he laughed at his own mistakes.

This was something new—a teacher who didn't need to be correct all the time, who didn't mind looking foolish. He was, after all, learning right along with us. The next time Luke stammered, I helped him finish his sentence. We exchanged a smile and a nod, and like that, I became the unofficial translator. In a matter of just a few classes, I was filling in the blanks and rerouting misused phrases. English, it turned out, was pretty easy for me—a gift I owed to my father.

When I was a child, and when the schoolyard tyranny left my eyes as puffy as the storm clouds in the sky, my father told me I had a choice. I could either give in, or I could do something that would make me feel special in my own right. I couldn't play soccer—so what? There was more than one way to stand out. There was more than one muscle to exercise. Under his tutelage, I started to train my brain; I took up the study of languages. My father placed pieces of paper with English words on objects around our house. *Lamp. Chair. Plate.* My mother, who'd learned Russian while studying abroad, quizzed me on Slavic vocabulary. I pored over language books and foreign magazines that my father brought home from the hospital, and spent entire days in my windowless room studying *The Green Park* series—an Arabic book with English on one page and Arabic on the other. My self-imposed exile was set against a backdrop of Japanese cartoons with English subtitles and tapes of American television series I'd bought with the money I'd saved up from my birthday and Eid al-Fitr, the end of Ramadan.

Still, I knew I'd never get better at English if I didn't get to speak it. Within years, I'd outpaced my father and mother, and it became clear that Ahmed was more interested in the flywheel of his car than with the illogical logic of American grammar. I tried speaking out loud to myself, but I could only talk to myself for so long without going crazy. I asked my father if I could study abroad, like my brothers and sisters. Like Ahmed, who was going to study in Malaysia. Might I go to Germany? I asked. My request was brushed aside due to my "limitations," and the weight of injustice was heavier than a backpack filled with bricks. But who was I to stand against my parents? Ever obedient, I continued attending Sana'a University, where lectures were three hundred to five hundred people, and people cared more about chewing qat than chewing on foreign words.

Now, finally, I had the opportunity to put myself to the test. Luke encouraged a new kind of intellectual curiosity. He pushed me to mess up, and, following his example, I found I didn't mind reaching for a new bit of vocabulary and landing somewhere between nonsense and baby talk. Instead of racing to finish the assignments and sitting in silence with a smug sense of satisfaction, I helped Luke by helping my classmates. Within weeks, I realized I was learning more than I would have otherwise. I got to play a new part. For the first time, I was the person offering help instead of the person in need. For the first time, I understood I had something to give.

Luke and I developed a routine. We chatted before class, and exchanged pleasantries on the way out. We continued at an agreeable distance until he stopped me, just as I was leaving. He asked if I would like to join him on a walk around the Old City of Sana'a. I looked for the joke in his eyes; he had to be kidding. Recently, Sana'a had become unsafe for foreigners. Several Yemeni tribes had taken to kidnapping westerners and holding them for ransom. They'd set up a pretty good trade. To avoid capture, foreigners either took to dressing as locals, or only went out with Yemeni bodyguards. Six feet tall and white as *mahalabia* pudding, Luke certainly wasn't going to blend in. But did he think I would be able to protect him from a marauding gang? I could barely protect myself!

I was about to make some excuse in hopes of avoiding an embarrassing explanation, but Luke was already out the door. So I grabbed my backpack and followed him into the night. Some thirty years older than me, Luke was deliberate yet calm amid the frenzied pace of the city. He eased through the streets in the same unhurried way that he spoke. We started discussing sports, wound around to movies, and ended up back on the football pitch, back at the Canadian Institute, right where we'd started. Luke hadn't asked me to be his bodyguard; he'd asked me to be his companion.

After that first meeting, we fell into step. Every Friday evening we walked and talked. I confessed to Luke that I dreamed of traveling the world, and he told me he'd admired Yemeni culture for years and finally took the opportunity to come to work here. He went on about how he loved the Old City, how he was fascinated by Yemeni culture, and how the Muslim people held such an important place in world history—and in Christian history. I matched my stride with his, and I felt a quiet pride blossom with the sunset. The buildings reflected the dripping light, and as the sun dipped, they changed from red ochre to brown to black.

Luke stopped to admire the stonework. He said that the ornate, geometric trimwork, mostly done in white gypsum, reminded him of frosted cakes from back home in the UK. I told him that some of the buildings dated back as far as twenty-five hundred years.

"It's amazing," he said, placing the palm of his hand against a wall. A chorus of car horns and screeching tires pulled him out of his reverie. Luke smiled and shook his head. "And it's just as amazing that the traffic laws are the same today as they were back then." I laughed as we approached an intersection where pedestrians waded through a mess of vehicles.

"It's not like this in England?"

"Not at all," he said, and then corrected himself. "Well, not unless a soccer match lets out." He gave me a wink. "The thing is, there are rules in the UK. Maybe a few too many. Perhaps we should export some to Yemen."

I thought this over, this joke pickled with truth. Could Yemen use more rules? No, certainly not. I'd grown up with more than enough of them. But perhaps that wasn't the right question. Perhaps the question was, Could Yemen use *different* rules? This was something new; questioning the system. I'd always relied on the wisdom of authority, the stability of the establishment. And yet . . . Maybe Yemen could benefit from change. Maybe *I* could benefit from change.

I looked around at the cobblestone streets. The dust, the dirt baked into the cracks, all of it could date back to the seventh and eighth centuries. We were standing outside a mosque—one of thirteen hundred scattered around the city. Its minaret rose straight to the sky, a weather vane without wings, unable to change directions with the wind.

◇◇◇◇◇◇

In late spring of 2010, Luke pulled me aside after class and told me he was going to be leaving Yemen. I didn't know what to say. Was his contract up? Did his visa expire? Or had he grown too homesick to continue living in a country that both fascinated and frustrated him? I didn't ask, and he didn't explain. In the end, it didn't matter. He was leaving in a few months' time, and I wasn't ready to say goodbye. Luke was somewhat like my father. Luke was nothing like my father. Luke was the man I'd wished my father would be.

I went home from class that night and decided that I had to do something for this person whose friendship had changed my understanding of the world. By the time I got into bed, I'd developed a plan. I would buy something for Luke that was symbolic of Yemeni culture. I would visit the local craftspeople, the jewelry makers. I would find him a traditional ring. *Aqeeq* set in silver. It was said that the Prophet Mohammed wore an *aqeeq* ring, and that in ancient times, soldiers used these semiprecious gems to strengthen their shields. I would never be able to serve as Luke's security detail, but at the very least I could bolster his defenses.

I closed my eyes, pleased with my decision, and then sat bolt upright. I was overcome by a troubling thought. Luke was going to hell. He was a good man, but he wasn't a Muslim, which meant he was doomed to an afterlife of eternal misery. Every bit of religious instruction I'd received had stressed this point. As a nonbeliever, his fate was sealed. He couldn't enter *Jannah* unless he followed the path of Islam. This was a problem. I liked Luke; I couldn't let him suffer the pits of *Jahannam*, the boiling water that would be poured over him after his flesh had been seared from his bones by the fire. As the Quran says, "Fear the fire whose fuel is men and stones—which is for those who reject faith" (2:24).

Suddenly, a ring seemed like the silliest idea in the world. How could I waste time on colored gemstones when there were other types of stones to consider? So much more was at stake! Hell was a place for "[men] whom Allah hath cursed. And those whom Allah hath cursed, thou wilt find, have no one to help" (4:52). But Luke didn't have "no one to help." He had me. It was my duty as a Muslim to call him to follow the path of *da'wah*. But I had to get to him before he left Yemen—before it was too late.

I knew that I didn't want to approach Luke with a fire-and-brimstone sermon. I didn't want to scare him into being a Muslim; I wanted to convert him with the beauty and blessings of the religion. For every description of the damned Tree of Zaqqum, with its devil-shaped fruit stalks, there were dozens of images of the fresh fruits of heaven. I wanted him to know, as I did, that God's mercy embraces all things. "Do they not see the birds controlled in the atmosphere of the sky? None holds them up except Allah. Indeed, in that are signs for a people who believe" (16:79).

The next day, I went to the bookstore and purchased an English-language translation of the Quran. I was so eager to save Luke's soul that I watched the clock that entire day. I had to remind myself that Allah rewards those who are patient. At the conclusion of class that night, when everyone else had left the room, I approached Luke.

"I'm surprised that you're leaving. A little bit sad, too," I said with as little emotion as possible. The way I'd been raised.

"I understand." He sighed, sitting on the edge of his desk. "I agree that leaving will be sad."

I shifted my weight from my heel to my toe, trying to find my center. "I want to give you something," I said, swinging my backpack onto the desk. "I value our friendship, a lot. I want you to remember me and the time we spent together." In my head, I cursed my own formality, but words seemed to be scattering from my mind like startled birds. I busied myself with the zipper of my backpack, taking a moment to pull myself together. When I stood up, I met his eyes with mine. "I also want you to read this. If we are friends, you will do this for me and for yourself."

I handed Luke the Quran.

He held it in one hand, the spine of it resting in his palm. He spread his hand and the book fanned open. He ran a finger down the page, and then read aloud, "And if whatever trees upon the earth were pens and the sea [was ink], replenished thereafter by seven [more] seas, the words of Allah would not be exhausted. Indeed, Allah is Exalted in Might and Wise" (31:27). He pursed his lips for a moment, then raised his eyebrows.

"There must be a lot of words in this, then?" He smiled.

"Yes. Many. I like the metaphor a lot."

"As do I."

He sighed and looked away, lost in thought, leaving me waiting, wondering if I'd done something wrong.

"I know this is a gift and you want me to read it. Gifts should be given, and accepted, freely. But I want you to do something in exchange. I want to give you something as well. I'll have it for you on Friday. We can talk about our bargain then. Agreed?"

"Of course," I said. "I can't wait."

"Good. It's nice to have something to look forward to."

Two days later, I sat in a teashop across from Luke, who handed me a red plastic bag. I reached inside and pulled out an English edition of the Christian Bible. Emblazoned on its green cover were the words "The Book of Life." It was the first time I'd ever touched a Bible. The words inside might threaten my entrance into heaven, and presently, they might threaten my very existence. I stuffed the book back into the bag. If anyone saw him, or me, walking down the street holding a Bible, we would be in grave danger.

A small thrill coursed through me. I felt like a spy who'd just been given sensitive information. No one I knew had ever read a single word of this book in front of me. We'd been taught that the Christian Bible was a holy work, but that over time Jewish scholars had altered it. Rabbis and false prophets believed that they had the power to change the word of God. They removed the Prophet Muhammad from the Bible, and they tried to erase Allah. The truth was right there for them to see, in the Quran. All they needed to do was to accept it, but they chose not to. They rejected paradise for the fiery pits of hell.

Part of me wanted to throw the bag to the ground, but I couldn't stop myself from holding it to my chest. This was my chance to set myself apart. My father's words echoed like a mantra. *I couldn't play soccer—so what? There was more than one way to stand out.* This was my chance to get up from the bench and go down a new, unique path. I scanned the room. No one was looking our way.

"So," Luke said, taking out the Quran. "You read your gift and I read mine. Fair?"

I ran my finger around the rim of my cup and felt my skin catch at an invisible chip.

"Yes," I said. "I do think that this is fair."

I would take Luke up on his challenge, and, with luck, I would save his soul and preserve my own. As it said in the book that Luke now held in his hands, "Be open-minded and promote freedom of expression; listen to all views and follow the best" (39:18). Like a good Muslim, I would follow the Quran's teachings. What harm could come from that?

Now that I owned a Bible, I needed to figure out what to do with it. I tucked the bag inside my shirt and hurried home, pretending there wasn't a jagged corner sticking out of my stomach. I eased open the front door. The house was quiet; lights were on in some of the rooms on other floors, but I didn't hear any movement. I went into one of the smaller, lesser-used rooms off the main hall, a few doors away from my bedroom. There, I settled into a chair and took out Luke's gift. I held it on my lap for a minute, then two minutes, then ten. I couldn't decide what to do. But time was passing, and I didn't know how long I'd be left alone, so with a do-or-die recklessness, I opened the cover. *This is it,* I thought. *I'm about to read the Christian holy book.* This was my one opportunity to find evidence to convince Luke that Christianity was flawed and Islam was the one true path.

I took a breath and began. *In the beginning . . .* I made my way through the first five days of creation, and then I ran into a wall. "Then God said, 'Let us make humankind in our image, according to our likeness; and let them have dominion over the fish of the sea, and over the birds of the air, and over the cattle, and over all the wild animals of the earth, and over every creeping thing that creeps upon the earth.'" This was so different from what I knew to be true. As a Muslim, I knew that Allah and his appearance or likeness was something I could never understand, should never even have an image of. We couldn't, and shouldn't, have known what God looked like. Now this Bible was telling me that God looked like the rest of us humans? He had a face, a nose, eyes, and a mouth? How could that be? Why would God create a copy of Himself? Was He lacking in imagination?

I made a mental note to challenge Luke with these questions. Then I kept going. A few paragraphs on, I read that after God created the world in six days, He needed to rest on the seventh. This didn't make any sense. God was all-powerful. Why would He need rest?

Certainly, Luke would see the inconsistencies and agree that the Bible offered more confusion than it did real answers. The more I read, the longer my list of questions grew. But as the minutes flew by, I realized that I was no longer reading to find mistakes, I was reading to understand. When I got to the story of Adam and Eve, I lost track of time. I knew this story! This was in the Quran. God created Adam first, and because Adam had no one to assist him, God created Eve.

In school, we learned that Adam didn't truly need Eve, but she needed him. This was used to explain the fact that women were naturally less capable than men—that a woman's brain capacity was lower than that of a man. The boys all slapped each other on the back, but I knew that my mother and my sister Lial—both physicians—were as smart and capable as any man.

Suddenly I heard my father's car pull into the driveway. I closed the book, wrapped it back in its red bag, and hid it under my mattress. This Bible raised a lot of questions. But—so did the Quran. Why did the Prophet have to marry twelve women? Did He really need to marry a member of each of the twelve tribes to spread the faith as quickly and as widely as possible? Was I to believe that this was the only way to spread the word of Allah? Questions dating back to secondary school rushed back to me. The Quran encouraged reason, but when I'd pressed my teachers for answers, I was sent out of the room. This was an inherent contradiction. As Muslims, we were supposed to question all things, but to question any single thing was to be a bad Muslim. For years, I'd tucked my questions into the darkest corners of my mind. But that didn't mean they weren't there.

◇◇◇◇◇◇

One week later, I leaned in, elbows on the table, gripping my right hand with my left, trying to keep still.

"The book is an amazing book," I began, failing to moderate my enthusiasm.

Luke nodded, his composure at direct odds with my own.

I tried to rein myself in, but my curiosity, already chomping at the bit, broke loose. The words flew out of my mouth, straight to a gallop. The stories were so similar to the ones in the Quran! The account of Adam and Eve was familiar, and was this the same Noah from the Quran? It had to be. He was a prophet, a very old man, had three sons, and preached to the people to turn away from their wicked ways. As a child I'd learned, "Allah did choose Adam and Noah, the family of Abraham, and family of Imran above all people." I recognized so much, but where did the truth end?

"What does the book mean when it says, 'God created human beings in His image'? Does that mean our faces look like God? Does that make God a man? Do you think God is a He or a She? When God created Adam in the Garden of Eden, was Eden on earth or in heaven?"

I was between breaths when Luke cut me off—

"No, no, no. You read the Old Testament?"

"I read what you gave me."

"From the beginning?"

"Of course." I began, "'In the beginning, God created the heavens and the earth.'"

Luke pursed his lips and expelled a deep breath. "I wanted you to begin in the middle with the Christian Bible, the New Testament."

The middle, I thought. *Who reads a book from the middle?*

"Then what have I been reading?" I asked.

"The Torah," he said. "The Jewish Bible."

My jaw went slack, like a broken rubber band. I saw Luke's mouth forming words, but I couldn't compute what he was saying. My mind was in lockdown mode, managing and containing a level-one emergency. Sound wasn't allowed in or out. No one had ever told me there were two parts to the Bible. Why had no one ever mentioned that the Christian Bible began with the Jewish Bible? The lights felt too bright, too hot. I needed water. I'd been reading the book of the enemy, of the infidels.

I'd spent my entire life hearing about the Jewish agenda. As a child, I'd heard the name Hitler in school. I asked about him in class, but the teacher said that he was part of World War II, Western history. All we needed to know was that Hitler was a hero for killing many Jews and burning their literature. We'd been taught their books were dirty, amoral, sinful, impure, demonic. And yet I'd liked this book. There was nothing impure about it. Was I being rational, or was I being seduced by its spell?

I returned home and tore the Bible out of the bag, determined to learn the truth. I stumbled through, sentence by sentence. "Don't kill human beings"; "Give money to the poor"; "Help those in need"; "Respect your parents"; "You shall not take vengeance or bear a grudge against your kinsfolk"; Love your neighbor as yourself." It was so similar to a hadith from the Prophet Muhammad! "Not one of you truly believes until you wish for your brother what you wish for yourself." How could this be? Why hadn't I been told that these similarities existed? I heard my mother come home, and Nuha run to greet her, but I couldn't get up from my chair.

My mind felt swollen. Everything I thought I knew, my entire basis of good and evil, was being thrown into question. From the time I could talk, I'd been taught that Islam was light and Judaism was dark; that

Islam was day and Judaism night. My teachers and imams, the most educated people in my community, had all agreed on this point. But what if their conception of right and wrong had been as muddled as their judgment of right and left? What if the angel Gabriel had given the Prophet Muhammad the same exact stories and teachings that he'd given the Jews?

Cain and Abel; the Tower of Babel; Abraham's sacrifice of his son Isaac; Moses and Pharaoh; King David and Solomon; the angel Gabriel; the Jewish woman Rebekah who covered herself with a veil when she saw Isaac, just like a Muslim woman wearing a hijab . . . I had been taught that the Quran was the one true word, along with the hadiths, but the very same words appeared in the Torah. How could the one true word be split in two?

I thought again of the creation story. I'd been taught that Allah had created the world in six days. He had done this, despite possessing the capability of doing so instantly, in order to teach human beings a lesson about patience and persistence. I had taken such issue with the idea of the Jewish God resting on the seventh day, interpreting this as a sign of weakness. But what if this was another way of presenting the same message? What if both books chronicled the exact same events but in different words? What if we could only get a full picture of each by putting all the lines together?

I developed a routine. Every day I read the Bible right before bed. I kept a piece of paper by my side, along with a pen, and every time I had a question, I wrote it down so that I could bring it up with Luke, so that we could discuss it together after class. The us-and-them dichotomy, the scaffolding of my moral convictions, was collapsing on itself.

A few weeks into my study of the Bible, my mother came to me, the thick book in her hands. "What are you doing with this?" she demanded.

I choked on my breath. "Where did you get it?" I coughed, fully aware of the answer.

"I was cleaning your room," she said, defiant. This was a long-standing battle: the fight between my desire for privacy and her desire for order.

"It is the Jewish and Christian Bible," I offered with casual indifference, as if she'd asked me for the time. The parry didn't work.

"Why are you reading it?" She looked at me with laser focus. I wouldn't be able to brush this off.

"I just want to understand better," I said, thinking fast. "I'm looking for ways that show how the Quran is superior. If I am to follow the path of *da'wah*, I need to understand what we're up against."

She nodded, neutralized. "I see."

With that, she turned and walked away. It was true. I did want to convert other people to Islam. As the hadith says, "Advance cautiously, until you reach their open space, then invite [the Jews] to Islam, and tell them of their duties before Allah. By Allah, if Allah were to guide one man through you, that would be better for you than having red camels." But was that all I wanted to do?

My mother returned to the subject several more times that week. She would stop me in the hall, or in my room, as if she'd just remembered to ask me to pick up milk from the corner store. "Are you still reading *that book*?" she'd say, an offhand comment folded into a crease of worry. I would say yes, and she would say, "Please keep praying. Please keep reading the Quran."

In response, I would nod with such vigor that I'd find myself nearly bowing to her request. "Of course," I'd say. "Of course."

It was only a matter of time before news of my endeavor reached my father. His devotion to Islam had continued to deepen over the years, and he approved of my dedication to spreading the true word. With his blessing, I no longer had to hide the Bible in a bag, in a drawer, under a layer of socks. I could now leave it out in the open, a testament to my piety.

In a sense, my parents had nothing to worry about. As the days passed, my faith didn't diminish. I wasn't about to reject the basics of my belief system. I was challenging the methodology of the instruction, but not the words or the lessons themselves. I trusted God. It's just that I was beginning to have doubts about some of the people He created.

One Friday after class, Luke suggested something new. The two of us had started to feel a bit insecure discussing the Bible in public, in the marketplace, so he asked if instead of going to a café or walking the streets of the Old City, I'd like to come to his apartment that weekend. He said he'd told his wife all about me, and she was eager to put a face to a name. Or, in other words, how was this Mohammed different than the millions of Mohammeds roaming the streets of Yemen? I accepted his invitation immediately, and then I immediately regretted it. I'd never been to a westerner's home. Would I know how to behave properly? Would they be offended if I took off my shoes at the door, as is our custom? How was I to address his wife? Was Luke trying to convert me? Was he enlisting his wife in some kind of double-agent spy scenario?

The following day, I readied myself, sick to my stomach. Going to a westerner's home to speak about the Bible was a terrible idea. My mother and father would never have approved, so instead of asking Taha to drive me, I called a taxi. We wove through the city toward the university, and I got out at an apartment building that was typical for the neighborhood—a very plain steel-and-stone rectangle. The cool concrete kept out the heat, and I wrapped my arms around my body. *It's freezing,* I told myself, trying to excuse a quiver for a chill. I stood, petrified, unable to take another step forward, and watched a small spider crawl between the beige carpet and the wall. This, I convinced myself, was enough adventure for one day. Nature at its finest! *Well, I saw a spider. Now I can return home for dinner, perfectly content.* Relieved that I'd come to this conclusion, that I no longer had to face the possibility of mortification or entrapment, I turned around. Whereupon I tripped over my foot, knocked my elbow against the door, and inelegantly righted myself as the door handle turned.

There was Luke, smiling broadly as he stepped to the side to allow me in. I smiled sheepishly and looked down at his feet. His shoes were on, so I left mine on as well. As he led me through the hallway, I saw framed photos of the Old City of Sana'a and of Socotra, one of the four islands that formed an archipelago in the Arabian Sea off the southern edge of Yemen.

"I read somewhere that Socotra is considered one of the most alien places in the world. Seven hundred different species of its fauna are found nowhere else in the world."

"I didn't know that," I said, looking at a picture of the island's most distinctive feature, the dragon tree.

"Ninety percent of its reptiles are endemic as well. Everyone knows about the Galápagos Islands, but no one talks about Yemen. It's a shame. Or maybe that's a good thing? Leaves it unspoiled."

Broccoli, I decided. The trees looked like florets of broccoli.

Luke escorted me into the living area. A moment later a woman walked in holding a tray with cups and saucers and a platter of what Luke called biscuits and I called cookies. The woman wore a Western blouse and a pair of trousers, but her hair was wrapped in a light blue hijab.

"Hello, Mohammed," she said as she set the tray down and sat on the couch, opposite me. "Welcome. My name is Linda."

I matched my voice to hers and returned the greeting. Neither of us made any move to shake hands. I appreciated her respect for my culture, and when I told her this, she laughed softly.

"Of course. We are your guests here in Yemen, even if you are in our flat." I liked the way she spoke. Her accent was somehow different from Luke's, the sounds clearer, cleaner.

We spent the next hour going over the Bible. I addressed my questions to Luke, but he wasn't always the one who answered. Sometimes Linda spoke instead of Luke, expressing her opinion, and even suggesting that maybe Luke's perspective wasn't always the best one. As she spoke, I tried to maintain eye contact, but my eyes kept floating over to Luke. Why didn't he look displeased that his wife spoke over him? Why did he smile when she disagreed, and shrug when she corrected him? If I had been at the home of a Yemeni friend, a woman wouldn't likely be in the room with us, and if one was and she made the mistake of speaking up? A verbal attack would have followed, at the very least.

But here the air was light and laughter made ripples in our tea. Was this how it could be between a man and his wife? I'd seen this kind of thing in movies, but everyone knew Hollywood wasn't real. Could it be that the novels I'd read had more truth than I'd realized?

When I returned home, my father was on one floor, and my mother was on another with my sisters. Different wasn't always better. But sometimes, maybe, it was worth the exploration. I returned to Luke's home two or three times, until the day that he had to move back to the UK. When I went to say goodbye, he offered me his old laptop; I declined. So he offered me his old car, which I also declined. Instead, he gave me a small postcard that said *"Maa al-salamah,"* farewell.

In exchange, I gave Luke a small bauble and promised him that I would make him proud. I would finish reading his book, and I would try to live the kind of life he did. Luke had immense curiosity and appreciation for countries and cultures that weren't his own. He had enormous empathy for other people and their ways of life. He didn't love Yemen blindly or uncritically, but he expressed faith in its future and its people.

I committed to reading at least a page of the Bible a night. A month turned into two, and I finally finished the Old Testament. *This is for Luke,* I thought, as I began again, this time in the middle. The exercise of comparing the Bible to the Quran was no longer purely academic. My questions were no longer contained to the page. Why did my teachers tell us that Jews, and to an extent, Christians, were unrelentingly evil? Why were we being treated like children, too immature to read the words for ourselves and make our own judgments? Did anyone else see that the truth was far more complicated than we had been led to believe, or had we been spinning the same fiction for so long that no one knew it was even fiction? It seemed as if, despite all the memorization examinations we were forced to take, no one wanted to truly test our faith.

What began as a mission to save a friend's soul had turned into something else entirely. As I said, my story begins and ends with a book. This, right here, is another beginning.

CHAPTER 7

◇◇◇

THE FOX HUNT

Me in my father's house, wearing a
jambiya in my belt

L ife turned between the pages of two different, too-similar stories.
I held dueling realities in my mind, somehow accepting the
lessons of my youth while completely dismantling them. Which
books were correct? My textbooks? The book of the enemy? What was
the truth? Who could I trust? An author wasn't necessarily an authority. Words, even Allah's, were subject to human interpretation. Pages of
explanation were no longer enough; I needed to get to the source itself.

I needed to track down a Jew.

It was July 2010. I'd recently graduated from Sana'a University and
started working full-time for my father. From 8:30 A.M. to 1:00 P.M.
I served as his clerk at the hospital, and from 5:00 P.M. to 8:00 P.M. I

worked as his office manager at his clinic. It wasn't thrilling. I'd been working for my father part-time since secondary school and the novelty had worn off. Every day, I checked inventory, ordered supplies, scheduled patients, and dealt with a series of overly aggressive men with urinary infections and enlarged prostates.

I also felt the pain of having given up my dream of being a doctor. My disability, my hand in particular, made it nearly impossible for me to do what every one of my siblings was able to. Working for my father, I was in a medical environment, that was true, but it was like I was backstage handing out towels to the actors, cleaning up after those who were starring in the film. Unglamorous didn't begin to describe it.

I created a kind of game for myself. After every forty-five minutes of work, I would take fifteen minutes to find information about Jews in Yemen. I didn't dare buy too many books on the subject, but with the help of the Internet, I figured I could piece together an overview. In between adding an appointment to my father's calendar and saying farewell to a patient, I opened a new window. I typed in "Jews" + "Yemen," but was quickly overwhelmed by the search results. Modern-day Judaism was just as complicated as modern-day Islam! A Jew wasn't a Jew wasn't a Jew. I thought that all Jews were created equal (and equally bad), but there were Ashkenazi Jews from Germany, France, and Eastern Europe, and Sephardi Jews from the Arabian Peninsula, North Africa, and the Middle East. To make things even more complicated, there was a discrete group known as Yemeni Jews, or Yemenite Jews, who were considered to be part of the Mizrahi Jews, who descended from Babylonian and Mountain Jews from today's Iraq, Syria, Iran, and other Eastern countries. But all their histories were different.

I heard my name and looked up. A slight man with yellowish eyes needed me to schedule his next appointment. I pretended I didn't know he suffered from an overactive bladder, and when I returned to my computer screen, I typed in a new search: "Jews" + "Yemen" + "History." I started clicking and reading, clicking and reading. According to some sites, the Jews fled Jerusalem and arrived in Yemen in 629 BCE, after

Jeremiah predicted the destruction of the Temple; according to others, the Queen of Sheba brought Jewish artisans to Yemen to help her glorify the kingdom. Some said that the Jews came from Judea with King Solomon's trading and naval operations in 900 BCE; but still other reputable sources pointed to archaeological evidence that Jewish merchants entered Yemen around 200 CE in conjunction with the spice trade. They all seemed plausible to me, and as the stories competed for attention, one thing became clear: the Jews had been in Yemen for a long, long time.

In fact, they were such a fixture that at the end of 400 CE, the Himyarite king converted *to* Judaism, as did Zar'a Yusuf, who took power in 518 CE when he drove the Axumite Ethiopians out of Yemen. Though its reign was brief, Judaism was the religion of the land until 525 CE, when the Christians from Ethiopia took over. It wasn't until about a hundred years *later,* at the end of the Prophet Muhammad's life, that Islam first came to Yemen.

I stared at my computer screen. The Jews were in Yemen before the Muslims? The Jews had *ruled* Yemen before the Muslims? How had we never learned any of this in school? I returned to my search window in need of answers. How did the Jews go from having everything to having nothing? As I read, the pieces started fitting together, like evidence from a crime scene.

In the seventh century CE, the Muslims took power in Yemen, and everything changed. Under sharia law, the Jews and Christians—fellow "People of the Book"—were technically safeguarded. They became *dhimmis,* protected people, who paid special taxes in exchange for residency. The Jews were allowed to follow their own religious rules and operate their own religious courts—under certain conditions. They were barred from political office and armed service; forbidden from touching a Muslim woman; banned from riding horses or camels; required to sit sidesaddle when riding a donkey or mule; mandated to walk barefoot when in the Muslim quarter; and restricted from defending themselves against a Muslim in court. They were left in peace—so long as they didn't insult or offend a Muslim in myriad

subtle and unknowable ways, on pain of death. They suffered daily
degradations, such as the Orphans' Decree, which stated that Jewish and Christian orphans should be forcibly converted to Islam. But
despite the inequality, there was a relative state of calm through the
tenth century. The Jews who kept to themselves were left to themselves, and they took the jobs that their fellow Muslims eschewed.
Which meant that the Jews became the only silversmiths, potters,
masons, blacksmiths, tailors, and so on in the entire country. Though
they weren't exactly welcome, they'd made themselves essential.

I fumbled around my desk for a bottle of water. I took a gulp, completely oblivious to the line that had formed in front of my desk. When
my father charged out of his office to subdue the mayhem, I quickly
minimized my browser and clocked another hour of work. Then, as a
reward to myself, I opened up a web page.

In the tenth century, the Zaidi Shiites—my people!—took power.
Over the next several centuries, Yemen changed hands from the Ra-
suliden dynasty to the Tahiride dynasty, and then from the Ottomans
back to the Zaidi tribesmen in 1636. I felt a swell of pride for my an-
cestors, but was soon choking on my own arrogance. Al-Mutawakkil
Isma'il, a man I knew as a righteous leader and honored warrior, was
brutal to the Jews. He determined that they had to either convert to
Islam or leave, and his successor, Al-Mahdi—known to me as "the pu-
rity of religion"—carried out the edict. He banished the Jews from all
the cities and towns, sending them to the inhospitable banks of the
Red Sea. Men, women, and children died on the way, and disease and
starvation plagued them in Mawza. But, ironically, the Jewish people
weren't the only ones to suffer. Without its artisans and craftspeople,
Yemen's economy started to fall apart. And so only a year after the Jews
were kicked out, they were invited back. They returned to find their
homes gone, destroyed and resettled. They tried to rebuild, but they
were stopped and sent outside the city, to "hyena's field."

These were the actions of my people; these were the crimes of the
Zaidis. I'd prided myself on following a religion that taught tolerance
and reason, but how could I square this circle? Over and over again,

the cycle of gaining and losing repeated: when the Imamics came to power and then lost power in the nineteenth century, when the Turks took control in 1872 and then barred the Jews from leaving in 1883. Throughout history, the Jews were to one degree or another repressed and killed in large numbers. The Jews were not the aggressors; the Muslims were.

I felt my nails digging into the soft flesh of my palm. The destruction was too massive for me to wrap my mind around, but the sense of hypocrisy and guilt was acute. The displacement, the destruction, the massacres . . . Weren't these the crimes of the Jewish people? Of Israel? From childhood, I'd been armed with a quiver of accusations, but what if I was aiming at the wrong target?

My anger turned to denial, an inside-out progression of grief. This couldn't be true. This must be a Jewish conspiracy. Who wrote these articles, anyway? The Internet was full of garbage. Everyone knew that. And the Jews controlled the media; surely this was Jewish propaganda. The writers ignored all the stories about how the Jews had been deceitful, how they'd been drunkards and fornicators. They must have been a moral cancer; why else would the Zaidi imams have forced them out when they were such an important part of the economy? Wasn't that proof enough?

I searched and searched for answers, but the Internet could only take me so far.

I needed to make contact with a Jew.

◇◇◇◇◇

Every morning, when I arrived at the hospital, I tried to figure out a way to find a Jew. But there were too many patients, and not enough time, and by the end of every day, my brain was soggy from hours of filing, organizing, ordering, scheduling, making copies, and juggling people with malfunctioning reproductive organs. I wanted to tell my father I needed a new job, but I couldn't abandon him without a good reason. I needed to build my case.

After weeks of thinking and digging through the Quran, I found just what I needed. I told my father that I wanted to work at an NGO, that Allah placed a higher value on being of service to others than on anything else. "And as for those who strive in Our path—We will surely guide them in Our ways. And indeed, Allah is with those who are of service to others" (29:70). He agreed, but he reminded me that I also needed money in order to be of service to others, and that salaries at nonprofits weren't very high. Essentially, he sent me off with "Wait and see." I think that he believed that I would outgrow my idealism. I didn't.

One evening, after spending my break studying the Bible, I decided it was time. It was my turn to make a difference, to change someone's world, as Luke had changed mine. I opened up a web page and typed in www.yemenHR.com, scouring the site to find a job at an NGO. I found an organization called Partner Aid. Based in Germany, it was a non-denominational Christian organization that wanted to ensure every human could live free of poverty by having access to three resources: health, water, and nutrition. I had no idea what "nondenominational Christian" meant, but I assumed I was one of the only people in Sana'a who'd read the Bible, which I hoped counted for something. I submitted an application for a position as a project assistant, and soon after was called in for an interview.

I started reading websites on how to behave in an interview. Eye contact, that was a big one. Turning weaknesses into strengths. I reviewed some sample practice questions. What is your weakness? *I'm a workaholic.* I put on a tie and a suit, and despite the climbing temperatures, I hoped the jacket would hide my right hand. At the office, a young German man greeted me and introduced himself as Lukas. *Good*, I thought. *I'm good with Lukes.* We spoke in English, and apparently that was enough, because at the end of the interview, Lukas told me that the job was mine. I felt like Nicolas Cage, or Sylvester Stallone. Then I thought about my father.

"Lukas, that's very great. I'm pleased. But can it be possible for me to work with you only part of the day?"

Lukas looked confused. "But the posting clearly states that it is a full-time job."

I went on to explain that I hoped I might still be able to work with my father at least a few hours a day. I could disappoint him a little, but not completely.

Lukas bobbed his head and told me he understood, but there was nothing he could do. The job was as described.

I wanted this job with Partner Aid. But I needed to explain the situation to my father carefully, strategically. When I got home that evening, I pulled out a Quran. Then I quietly entered my father's room and pointed to a passage that I hoped would help him see things my way: "And when he reached his age of full strength and attained maturity, We gave him wisdom and knowledge; and thus do We reward those who do good" (28:14).

My father couldn't argue with Allah. I might not have been of full strength, but I had attained maturity, and at twenty-three years old, I'd succeeded in securing employment on my own. I'd be earning roughly the equivalent of $700 USD a month, nearly double what my father had been paying me, and I'd have the opportunity to do good works. What that meant long-term wasn't yet clear. But I'd figure things out as I went along.

I arrived at my new job eager to discuss the Bible with my new Christian colleagues, but I quickly found out that Lukas was not a mirror image of Luke. When I tried to broach the topic, I was told to focus on our current project: getting water and sanitation for the Akhdam.

Which meant I was back to relying on books and articles. I was spinning in circles, reading myself in and out of a hole. I'd never understand anything if I continued with these secondary sources. I needed to dig deeper. I needed to speak with a Jew. But how? From 1948 to 1950, some 50,000 Jews had been airlifted to the newly created state of Israel in a secret mission known as Operation Magic Carpet, and in 2009 the U.S. State Department had evacuated much of the remaining Jewish population. Now there were some 435,000 descendants of Yemeni Jews in Israel, 80,000 in the United States, 10,000 in the UK, and in all likelihood fewer than 250 Jews in Yemen itself. Those remaining had banded together and moved to fortified communities in the mountainous regions of the north, in Sa'dah or in Rada'a. I couldn't very well call them on the phone to ask them questions about their faith. I'd seen what had happened to them when Muslims came knocking. They'd think I was a government agent, or worse. I needed to be creative. But first I needed to order more paper clips.

◇◇◇◇◇◇

I opened up a browser and decided to try something new: Facebook. Social media had been around since my days at university, but I didn't use it. The networks were too slow, and besides, why did I need to see my friends online when I saw them every day in real life?

But here was an opportunity to expand my social circle; to contact people I might otherwise never meet; to get in touch with Jews. I created a profile—my name, location, and little else—and began my quest. I wanted to meet Jews, so where was the best place to look for them?

Israel.

I typed that one word into the search box, and the results showed up. I almost fell out of my chair in surprise. In Yemen, the government blocked sites relating to Israel. This meant I had no access to Israeli newspapers, Israeli media, or Israeli citizens. This also meant I'd never seen pictures of Israeli women.

I scanned the profiles, telling myself that this was research. I found Nathalie from Tel Aviv, a beautiful woman with a picture of herself riding a horse in a stream. I sent her a friend request. Next was a young woman named Leen, a student at Tel Aviv University, and her classmate, Ruba. I spent a few hours sending off requests. Then I waited . . . and waited . . . and not a single person (woman) accepted my friend request.

I was about to give up when I received my first new message. It was from a man reaching out to *me*. He wrote, "If Muslims don't follow Zionists' ways, they will go to hell. When the Messiah comes, all gentiles will serve the Jews."

Had a Jew made contact?

Eager to engage, I typed, "What does hell mean for you?"

I waited, staring at the cursor as it blinked in time to my heartbeat.

Had he been joking? Was I missing some sarcasm? I sat with my good hand poised over the keyboard, my bad hand curled in my lap, twitching. Was this a test? I wanted to show him the true and peaceful Islam, but he didn't respond.

"That's very interesting," I typed. "Thank you."

From somewhere inside the house, I heard my mother calling my name. I shut my laptop.

I hurried to her—she wanted to know if there was anything special I needed from the market—and when I returned to my room, I opened my laptop again. I had a new notification! One of the Israeli girls had responded to my friend request! We started to chat, and then she began attacking me for how women were treated in Yemen. I couldn't disagree, but I couldn't shoulder the blame for the entire country, could I?

I looked at my screen. No other messages. No other notifications. The only thing that was moving was the clock in the top right corner.

I needed to take a new approach. I typed up a quick message: "Greetings from Yemen! My name is Mohammed Al Samawi and I am a Muslim living in Yemen. What do you think of Islam? What do you think of Muslims? What do you think of Yemenis?" Then I clicked send, send, send, over and over again.

No one answered. And who could blame them? People probably thought it was a scam, like a Nigerian prince asking for a million dollars.

Disappointment squeezed the hope out of my body. I'd been so close to finding someone who could answer my pileup of questions. Had I been rejected because I was a Muslim? In Yemen, if I was walking through the Old City of Sana'a and I passed by a teahouse and an older man was sitting by himself, he'd wave me over and ask me to join him. He'd buy me a cup of tea and we'd talk about life. He'd have no inhibitions. In Internet-land, things were different; people had no issue walking past me, no matter how hard I waved.

Maybe I shouldn't have indicated that I was from Yemen? But that was the whole point of this. I didn't want to misrepresent myself. With no answers in sight, I gave up for the night. I had to be at work the next morning, and it was already well after midnight.

The following morning, nothing. The following evening, I raced home, rushed through dinner with as much composure as possible, and then retreated to my room to log on to Facebook. Nothing. No one had responded. The same thing happened the next morning, and the night after. I was about to give up on Facebook altogether when I received a message from a man named Nimrod Ben Ze'ev—an Israeli. A Jew. My fingers twitched over the keyboard, and then I carefully typed out my first question, in English: *Why is it that Arabs and Israelis hate each other so much?* I watched the screen, and within minutes there was a response. *There are a lot more Jews and Arabs who get along than don't get along. You just don't hear or read about them. You shouldn't believe everything you read in the news.* Each sentence seemed more ridiculous than the one before. Was I supposed to believe a Jew in Israel over the newspapers in Yemen?

I paused. And yet . . . these same government-approved sources taught that the Jewish Bible was evil, and yet it was so similar to the Quran. I'd been taught that westerners were only interested in destroying our way of life, and yet Luke was so respectful of our culture. The teachers, the imams, the news—they'd all been wrong about that. Could it be that they were wrong about the Jews, too?

I took a leap of faith.

I asked Nimrod where I could find these Muslims and Jews who got along, and in an instant, he replied: YaLa Young Leaders, a new Facebook group where Jews and Arabs gathered to discuss and promote peace between our peoples. Without further questions, I typed "YaLa Young Leaders" into the search box on my profile page. If what Nimrod said was true, this would be the key to my yearlong pursuit. If it wasn't, I'd prove, once and for all, that Israelis were liars and tricksters. Either way, I'd find my answers.

A web page blinked onto my screen, and my eyes ran over a mix of English, Hebrew, and Arabic. *Ya ilahi.* Nimrod was telling the truth. This group was real.

All of a sudden, a new series of concerns came crashing down on me. Was I ready to reveal my activities to others? If I joined the group, if I posted on the wall or liked a picture, would it send an alert to my entire network? I felt like any action would leave me completely exposed, and as someone who'd spent a lifetime trying to be invisible, I wasn't sure I wanted to be public. What if my sisters found out what I was doing and told my parents? What if my friends from school read my questions and comments? What would they think of me? How much trouble would I be in?

I deleted the half-formed comment I was about to post on the YaLa Facebook wall, and instead drafted a private message. There were some fifty thousand participants in the group, which meant I had a lot of messages to send.

The more I participated in the group, the less overwhelming it seemed. A core group of perhaps forty to fifty people took shape. These were the men and women who posted regularly, and were the most likely to respond to my messages. In time, I came to understand that YaLa was more than a place where we could virtually hang out. As its mission stated, it was a place to "Unite the Region Through Knowledge." I began to get a sense of who was there to discuss larger issues related to the Muslim/Arab–Israeli conflict, and who was there to share their viewpoints on music, movies, television shows, and books. I also figured out whose posts to ignore entirely after reading a comment that spilled the entire plot of the last James Bond movie, *Quantum of Solace*, including the ending (spoiler alerts are a universal courtesy).

While I loved having a place to read about things like Vladimir Nabokov, I was most interested in understanding Torah passages, and why Muslims and Jews hated one another when their religions were, in so many ways, so similar. When I managed to build up the courage, I asked questions, carefully, selecting and supplying quotations from the Bible and the Quran. I may have been from Yemen, but I wanted to prove I'd spent time in the trenches—or at least in the library. The response was overwhelmingly positive. People were liking my posts, writing comments saying, "Thank you so much," and even sending me friend requests.

I met a young Palestinian woman named Ferozah who had been diagnosed with multiple sclerosis. The treatments were extremely expensive, and she and her family couldn't afford them. They were about to give up, but then the Israeli government stepped in and provided her with medications and doctors' supervision at no cost. How could I balance such generosity with the violence I'd heard about my entire life?

In time, whatever reticence I felt around these onetime strangers disappeared. This was the only place in my life where I could openly express my opinions, my confusions, and my concerns without fear of rebuke. Though I was at my desk in my parents' house within a traditional Muslim community, I had access to the entire world. And what I saw threw everything that I thought I knew into question. My focus had been so restricted, narrowed down to one small point: the Jews were the cause of our troubles. But now I was using the great gift that Allah had provided me—my ability to make judgments and analyze evidence for myself.

I was like Saul from the New Testament. Initially, he intensely persecuted the disciples of Jesus. But then, when he was traveling to Damascus, Jesus appeared before him and struck him blind. Saul suffered for three days, and only after he accepted Jesus was his vision restored. Like Saul, I had sinned. I was lying to my mother, fooling my father, and I didn't know if I'd ever get over what I'd done to Ahlam. But now, *inshallah,* God willing, my world was expanding. I felt unlimited, and enrolled in several online peace-building classes offered through YaLa. I was ready to be the change in the world I wanted to see—and I wasn't the only one. It was the summer of 2011, and revolution was in the air.

Across the Arab world, reformers were taking to the streets. Back in December 2010, Mohamed Bouazizi had set himself on fire and ignited protests in Tunisia and later Algeria. The Arab region seemed primed to make legitimate and lasting social and political advances. By January 2011, protests had spread to Yemen, Syria, Egypt, and Morocco. Then

Tunisia's old-line repressive regime fell, and next went Hosni Mubarak in Egypt, who resigned from the presidency and turned over control of the government to the Supreme Council of the Armed Forces. This was just the beginning.

Now, in the late summer of 2011, we the people were using Facebook and Twitter to come together, transform our countries, and take control of our fate—peacefully. Violence no longer seemed justifiable. Online communities were accomplishing more through protests than through in-person guerrilla attacks. There were reports of violence—an antitank missile was fired out of Gaza and hit a school bus in Israel; a Jewish family of five was murdered in the West Bank town of Itamar; six civilians were killed and forty more injured in a cross-border attack in Eilat—but it made so little sense to me. There was another way to justice, and I would be a part of it—at least through my computer.

As autumn flew by, the air was filled with jasmine and a sense of possibility. A book had once again changed the course of my life, only this time it was Facebook.

◇◇◇◇◇◇

The deeper I got into my double life, the more daring I became. I started smuggling books and articles into my house. I figured if my mother had accepted finding a Bible in my sock drawer, she'd accept anything. I was wrong.

"Mohammed!" I heard as soon as I came home from work one day.

My mother marched to the door carrying two thick books. One was a critique of the Quran, and the other was a history of Christianity. *Astaghfirullah!*

"I want to speak with you," she said with iron in her voice. "Later, after your father has gone to sleep."

I went straight to my room and tried to divert my mind with a movie. But even 007 couldn't distract me. Sure, he had to fight the Russians, but he didn't have to deal with my mom. A few hours and a handful of gray hairs later, she came to my room, hands behind her back. I looked at her, eyebrows raised. She followed suit, head tilted to one side in an all-too-familiar posture of indignation. Her nostrils were the only things that moved.

"And what is this?" she said, her voice even and low. She held out the book about the Quran, her face as hard as the cover.

"I can explain," I blurted out.

And I did. I gave the best explanation I could think of; but the best isn't always the most accurate.

I told her that everything I was reading, all the time I spent studying, was in service of one thing: I was trying to amass evidence to show that the Quran was truly the one and only inviolate word of Allah, the legitimate God. I told her about Luke, and my attempt to save his soul. And I told her that even though the process had been trickier than I'd intended, I hadn't given up. I would do whatever I needed to do to show the infidels the way to the *sirat,* the straight path.

My mother watched me closely, and after a minute, she accepted my three-quarters truth. Her face broke into a beatific smile and she apologized for doubting me. She'd make it up to me, she promised.

The next morning my mother cooked me a special breakfast, but I felt sick to my stomach. Was *I* even on the straight path anymore? I wanted to share the truth, but my mother would never forgive me. She'd tell my father, and he'd kick me out. What was the point of giving myself such a headache and hurting my mother so deeply? I couldn't do that. For her sake and mine.

◇◇◇◇◇◇

Without the stress of sneaking around my own house, I was able to redouble my efforts in YaLa. My commitment materialized in a surge of posts. I was relentless. I outflanked my fellow commenters and charged ahead—question after question. I moved from the outer circle of YaLa to the inner sanctum, and it was only a matter of time before I was asked to take on a leadership position. I was told that I was the only person from Yemen in the entire group of fifty thousand, and so the leadership believed I might have unique insights into the challenges of living in a closed Muslim society. The idea was that I could help build bridges and train peace advocates in remote areas like my own. It would be my job to subtly introduce the similarities and differences between Islam and Judeo-Christianity, and from there move on to conflict resolution. Before I knew it, I was part of the YaLa Core Team, one of the people who helped administer the Facebook group and partner with others to expand its reach.

In theory, this was terrific; in reality, I was having some difficulty with the "partnering" aspect. Nobody in Yemen knew what I was doing. I was going to work in the mornings, and spending a lot of time at home, in my room. My mother thought I was a Muslim evangelist, and my friends thought I was tied up at the office. No one knew I was studying the materials YaLa had prepared and posting to private groups. I was electrified but unplugged from all the people in my real life. *The classic Clark Kent dilemma,* I thought to myself.

My community moved online. Via Facebook, I debated the nuances of international relations, and only found myself entrenched when it came to the ever-heated debate on who invented hummus (we did). We built our own ecosystem, and in it, peace and understanding seemed like the most basic principles.

At least until hostilities between Israel and Palestine flared up again.

In the spring of 2012, Gaza militants launched more than three hundred missiles and mortar rounds into southern Israel, wounding twenty-three Israeli civilians. The Israeli government responded with a show of force, and twenty-two Palestinians lost their lives in the reprisals. In retaliation, an Israeli soldier was shot and killed in September. In November, the situation escalated and Israel initiated Operation Pillar of Defense: fifteen hundred missiles were launched at strategic sites in Gaza.

I learned these facts through Facebook. The only thing that flooded the airwaves in Yemen were the numbers: 133 Palestinians killed, 840 wounded. Ahmed Jabari, second in command of the Hamas military, was reported dead. Hamas struck back, firing missiles at Jerusalem and Tel Aviv for the first time since the Gulf War. On and on it went. Who was keeping score? Was there a winner or a loser? Whose lives mattered more?

YaLa Online Academy was in chaos. The friendships we'd made broke up as lines of loyalty were quickly redrawn. The world outside these bits and bytes was chewing itself apart; we weren't immune; no firewalls could protect us. A young Palestinian in the group sent me a private message: "You think the Jews and Israelis are good people, but that's just because they're hiding behind a computer screen. If you met them in real life you'd see the truth."

I stared at my computer screen in shock. I'd been devoting myself to the YaLa online community. I'd been completely open and honest, and expected the same in turn. But what if I was wrong? Why did I expect the truth from a group of strangers when I wouldn't even give it to my mother? What if I'd mistaken online interactions for the real thing? What if this young man was right, and all this was just a trick, a scheme? What if YaLa was no more than a sophisticated video game and we were all just playing roles?

I needed to meet a Jew in real life to find out for myself. But the question, once again, was *how*?

◇◇◇

CHAPTER 8

UP, UP, AND AWAY

At the Muslim Jewish Conference in Bosnia, where I met Daniel Pincus

I knew I couldn't get to a Jew in Yemen, which meant I had to go outside of Yemen. My first opportunity to leave the country came in March 2013, with Boehncke Business Information, a company I'd started to work with as a freelance researcher at the end of 2012. As one of the few local staff with anything approaching fluency in English, I found myself accepting more and more responsibility, and soon I was directed to report on the state of health care in Sudan. This required an on-the-ground investigation, which meant I needed to relocate to Sudan for three months. This was my chance! Surely I could find a Jew in Sudan! I just needed to quit Partner Aid, and tell my father I would be moving. Easy.

The conversation with Lukas went well. He said he understood that I needed to move on, and that if I ever wanted to return to humanitarian work, he would have a position for me. Then I consumed my body weight in antacid tablets and waited for the perfect moment to speak with my father. At breakfast over *kebda*? Would lamb liver give me the strength I needed to overcome his fierce overprotectiveness? After the evening news on Yemen TV? Would a report of international violence make him more afraid for me to travel alone? Before afternoon prayers on Friday? Would God see things my way?

The days passed, along with my openings. My boss pressed me for a firm commitment, and finally I was forced to take action. As soon as my father returned home from the clinic, I ambushed him, the timing about as far from ideal as possible. I planted my feet, ready for the blowback, and presented the situation. My father sucked air through his teeth and shook his head. And then he told me, in the firmest possible terms, that I couldn't miss this opportunity.

My eyelids fluttered, freezing the moment at a shutter speed of a thousandth of a second. My father actually *wanted* me to go! He had many friends in Khartoum and Darfur, he went on. They were all doctors. They would look out for my safety and assist me with my research. I couldn't believe my luck: I would be going to Sudan—with my father's blessing. And with that, I readied for my first international trip since I was a toddler, since I'd gotten an intimate tour of the operating rooms of hospitals as far-flung as India, Egypt, Jordan, and Syria.

I arrived in Sudan in a blur of heat and haze. A driver took me into the city of Khartoum, where traffic seemed less chaotic than in Sana'a, and cars stayed more or less in their lanes. The air was dry, and the sun, cresting the horizon, blazed across a modern city of concrete and glass. As I sat in the air-conditioned seat, I saw men in Western clothes, and others in traditional jalabiyas, women covered up in black hijabs, as well as others in brightly colored thawbs. What I didn't see? A single man in a skullcap. I opened a window on my phone and searched "Jews" + "Sudan." Link after link confirmed the worst. The once-vibrant Jewish community in Sudan had ceased to exist by 1973. After Sudan declared its independence in 1956, violence against the Jews had become so extreme that Jewish people abandoned everything they owned and fled to America, the UK, and, of course, Israel. Oops.

I checked my phone and saw a new message from Mohamed Abubakr, my Sudanese friend from YaLa Young Leaders. He welcomed me to his country, and apologized that he had to miss me. He was away on holiday in Ethiopia, but his two good friends would be happy to show me around and help me get to meetings and appointments. With their help, and with the assistance of my father's friends, I was a very efficient researcher. But after working at an NGO, the work felt hollow.

I realized that the sooner I finished the job, the sooner I could return to humanitarian work, so though I'd been allotted twelve weeks for this assignment, I finished my report in just four. I saved Boehncke two months' room and board, and booked a ticket for my flight home. As a bonus, they offered me the full twelve-week stipend I'd been given for daily expenses. I took the money and tendered my resignation. I wanted to make an impact, and I knew that the research I was doing wasn't the most immediate way to make a difference.

I returned to Yemen on a high. I'd proven that I could travel alone. I'd completed my work—and far more efficiently than anyone had expected. And I'd been paid better than I'd ever been in my life. But still, I hadn't had the opportunity to meet a single Jew. I sat at my computer and thought . . . and thought . . . Then I pecked in a new search: "Muslim" + "Jewish" + "Conference."

What do you know, the first hit that came up was for something called the Muslim Jewish Conference. Logic had prevailed. But what exactly was this conference? I clicked around the site and learned that it was sponsored by a grassroots organization that promoted interfaith and cross-cultural dialogue. Exactly the thing I was looking for. Every year, they put on an annual conference for Jewish and Muslim leaders. The first retreat had taken place in 2010, in Vienna, and the following one took place in Kiev. According to the website and their Facebook page, they covered topics that included "Conflict Transformation,"

"Anti-Semitism and Islamophobia Through Cinema," "Introduction to Judaism and Islam," "Gender and Religion," "Hate Speech and Its Influence on Public Opinion," and "Education and the Effects of Historical Narrative." The next meet-up was to be held in Sarajevo, Bosnia and Herzegovina, from June 30 to July 5, 2013.

I had to go.

I'd been trying to immerse myself in an ocean of greater understanding, but it was more like I'd been spraying myself with a water gun. The stain of my childhood education still lingered, like one that had long ago faded into the fabric of a shirt. I hoped that by going to MJC, I'd be able to rid myself of that residue.

I knew I couldn't escape my past—nor did I want to. But there was something to the idea of going somewhere and building a new identity. To not having to be with the same small group of friends and family who always remembered me as the boy with the disability. The boy who had to be carried or wheeled around. The one whose independence was defined by how far others were willing to take him. I wanted to be understood while also being challenged. I wanted to fit in with my peers while setting myself apart.

I was twenty-six years old. The world was calling.

I filled out an application, and within weeks I received an email from the conference. I read the first sentence and jumped out of my chair: I'd been accepted! I punched the air around me in a kind of celebratory dance, and when I'd properly exhausted myself, I sank back into the chair. Then I had a moment of panic. What if I was mistaken? What if I'd mixed up the English words? I woke up my computer screen to see if I'd misunderstood, and this time I read the message from beginning to end. I had indeed been accepted, and the MJC would cover my hotel and my meals. But I was expected to pay for my own ticket and visa.

Suddenly I had to wonder: was it worth it? Obtaining a visa to another country from Yemen was a minefield of paperwork and fees. Boehncke had taken care of all that for me on my Sudan trip, but if I was going to spearhead this, I would have to navigate this process on my own. Before I made any decisions, I did what I always did: I went online. I searched for the Bosnian embassy in Yemen, and learned that Bosnia did not have an embassy in Yemen. This meant I would need to fly into another country with a Bosnian embassy without any guarantee that I'd get a visa, and then apply for the visa and hope to be accepted.

I looked at the money I'd saved up over the years, and knew this would take away a big chunk of it. But this was my chance, and I didn't know if I'd get another. So without another thought, I replied to the MJC confirming that I would be attending the conference. I had about two months to prepare, and I'd need every bit of it.

First step: finding a neighboring country with a Bosnian embassy. I started with Egypt. Yemen had an Egyptian embassy, so I could easily get a visa to Egypt; and Egypt had a Bosnian embassy, so I could apply for my Bosnian visa there. Perfect. I congratulated myself on a job well done—until I heard a rumor that the Egyptian visa process could take forever. I didn't have forever! Egypt was out. Next I tried Turkey. Turkey had an embassy in Yemen (check), and Bosnia had an embassy in Turkey (check). So this would be the plan.

With step one behind me, I moved on to phase two: telling my family. If working through governmental red tape was difficult, it was nothing compared to the Herculean effort of getting the go-ahead from my mother and father. I thought of one plan after another, and after three weeks of anxiety, I went with the simplest possible solution. I told my parents I would be attending something called the Muslim Jewish Conference. There I would finally have the opportunity to put my studies into action and convert Jews to Islam. My mother believed me, and with her help, my father signed on.

The final month flew by, and soon enough, I was flying, too—to Istanbul. I took a taxi to the Bosnian embassy and applied for a visa. Everyone was very friendly, but no one could guarantee that I'd get approved. I waited one day, two days, eight days . . . no luck. After ten days, I contacted the team at the MJC, and the founder stepped in and reached out to his contacts in the Bosnian government. They, in turn, contacted the Bosnian embassy in Turkey. With a little bit of diplomatic grease, I was in. Next stop, Sarajevo.

I arrived in the crowded baggage claim area, craning my neck to find a person holding an "MJC" sign. A few moments later, a woman emerged from the crowd, sign aloft. Her short dress revealed long dark legs that couldn't stand still. And her pinched brow and darting eyes made her look like an angry bird. I approached her and gave her my name. She scanned her clipboard and looked back up. "Fine."

I started to wander off in search of a chair, but I turned when I heard my name and saw the woman with the clipboard flapping an exquisite bare arm. "Wait, wait, wait," she said, and then she was gone. A few minutes later she fluttered back alongside a tall man with a deep tan and a floppy plumage of curly hair. He held out his hand.

I tried to shift my carry-on bag to attempt a makeshift handshake, but when he saw my struggle, he gripped my arm. "Corey," he said with a grin, pronouncing his *r*'s like a native Arab. I told him my name, and he laughed.

"Mohammed Al Samawi! I know you!"

My heart nearly stopped. Who was this man? Was this a trap?

"YaLa Young Leaders," he said, as if it were obvious.

The picture started coming into focus. This was the same Corey from Israel whom I'd been messaging with on Facebook for two years! I started pulling from my memory, trying to match old conversations with the person in front of me.

We made our way to the bus that was waiting for us, exchanging updates, laughing, and after we boarded, another man settled in beside us. I squirmed in my seat, hoping to sit as tall as possible.

"Josh Nason," he said, offering me his hand. "From Texas."

"Mohammed," I said, twisting my left hand to meet his. "Yemen. Sana'a, if you've heard of it."

"*Ana uhibb* Yemen," he said.

The way Josh pronounced each word in Arabic—*I love Yemen*—was excellent, tinged with Jordanian color around the edges. I suddenly worried that he might really be a spy. I stared, unsure how to proceed, and he laughed. He told me that he loved Yemen and that he was a graduate student at the Johns Hopkins School of Advanced International

Studies, getting his master's in international relations/Middle East studies. We spoke on and off for the rest of the ride to our hotel in Sarajevo, alternating between English and Arabic.

When we arrived at the hotel, the woman from the airport settled in behind the reception desk. "I'm Heba," she said. "Sorry I forgot to introduce myself. Things just get so crazy with pickups." I nodded, as if Sarajevo International Airport had anything on Sana'a International; Bosnia was positively systematic in comparison. Heba had a melody in her voice, and I asked where she was from. Vienna, she said, though her parents came from Sudan. My breath caught. Heba was Muslim? The geographical odds pointed to yes, but she wasn't wearing a hijab. Her eyes met mine and then returned to her computer screen. She brushed off my revelation as if it were dust on a window ledge. Her fingers clacked on the keys.

I started speaking to her in Arabic, hoping to make a deeper connection, but she stared back at me, blank. She couldn't understand a word.

"You'll have a roommate," she said, handing me a room key. "But he hasn't arrived yet."

I thanked her—in English—trying to hide my confusion. How could someone be a Muslim and not speak Arabic? How did she pray? How did she read the Quran? I knew that translations existed—I'd gotten one for Luke—but those were for foreigners. "Arabic" and "Muslim" were inseparable concepts.

I pulled my luggage through a cluster of men and women who were shaking hands, hugging, acting as if they'd known each other for their entire lives. There was such intimacy, such a public display of affection. Was I the only newcomer, the lone outsider? And did I even want to be part of a group like this?

My room was tidy, if a bit small. *At least there are fewer places to hide cameras,* I thought, and began to sweep the room. Even though Corey and Josh seemed perfectly nice, I couldn't erase the tape that had been playing in my head since I was five or six: *Jews are foxes. Even if they seem good, they're hiding something bad.* I pulled out my drawers,

looked up and down my closet, and inspected the bathroom. No sur-
veillance devices. Still, I felt uncertain.

I decided the best course of action was prayer. But in which direction was the Kaaba, in Mecca? I struggled to orient myself, but with no
sense of north, south, east, or west, I picked a spot at random, unrolled
the prayer rug my mother had given me, and knelt, waiting for the
sense of peace I was reaching for. Nothing. Back down to the lobby I
went.

Clusters of white and brown men and women congregated in groups.
I targeted a man who looked like he was from Pakistan and asked if he
could point me in the direction of Mecca. He asked me what side of
the hallway I was on, and told me to face the windows at the end of my
room. I thanked him, grateful to have an answer, and to know there
were other people here who were like me. He invited me to join the
group prayer session, but I was a private person, and even though my
imams had taught me that it was better to pray in a congregation than
at home by myself, I believed that what I had in my heart and mind was
for Allah alone, and not the others.

By the time I left my room, I felt a seed of peace buried deep within
my chest, but when I arrived at the official welcoming ceremony, that
seed had moved up my sternum, through my clavicle, and was lodged
in my larynx, cutting off airflow. As people trickled in, I drifted around
the edge of a group of Muslims, trying to emit a sense of confidence I
in no way felt.

Either my charisma or my desperation was strong enough to attract
a man who introduced himself as Moath. He was born in Yemen but
his family had moved to Norway. Unable to contain my excitement, I
burst out that I was from Yemen, too! He smiled and said, "Awesome.
But where are you *really* from?" He assumed I'd relocated to Europe,
like him. This, it seemed, was the trend. Most of the Muslims I met
no longer lived in the Middle East. They now held dual citizenship
in Europe or the United States. There were a few still living in Africa
and the Middle East, but not surprisingly, I was the only person in the
entire group who lived in Yemen.

When everyone arrived, we were asked to take our seats. A tall, rakish man with ice-blue eyes stood at the front of the room, waiting for silence. He smiled like a man who knew how to keep a secret, and introduced himself as MJC's founder and secretary-general, Ilja Sichrovsky. With a disarming mix of passion and recklessness, he commanded the room. And after a brief set of opening remarks, he introduced members of the MJC core team. *Heba Hazira, Daniel Pincus, Ben Rosen* . . . I tried to remember each name, but there were thirty-some people and I lost track.

After the formal remarks, we were encouraged to meet one another. I stepped outside to clear my head. The temperature had dropped to the mid-60s, but I found myself sweating through my chills. I looked around and saw people, clearly Muslims, openly drinking alcohol, and I started to wonder if I was in the right place. MJC was supposed to be for Muslim and Jewish leaders, the best of our people. But these men and women were desecrating Islam—and in front of Jews, no less. Did they invite just anyone to come here?

The following day was a whirlwind. We bustled from one seminar to another. Information was coming from all sides, and the lessons weren't always what the presenters had planned. At one point in the day, I happened to find myself next to a woman I'd seen the night before. She told me that she was Jewish, and a lesbian, as casually as if she'd said, "I had cereal for breakfast this morning." I didn't understand.

"Does Judaism accept homosexuality?" I asked. I knew there were gays in Yemen, but no one would openly admit to it.

She smiled wryly, but before she could answer, I followed up: "Can you be a lesbian *and* a Jew?"

"Well, I should hope so!" She laughed. "I don't even believe in God, and I'm still a Jew."

This was beyond my comprehension. "What? Hold on? How— Can you explain that to me? How can you call yourself a Jew but not believe in God?"

"Listen, Mohammed from Yemen," she said. "Judaism is more of an identity for me than a religion. It's kind of who I am. What my parents endured, and what my grandparents suffered during the Holocaust, that's a part of me. That's who I am. But it's not about religion for me."

I started to scramble for words, to tell her that I felt that Judaism was a great religion, that I'd even read the Torah. But I stopped myself. Was I doing a disservice to Islam by admitting this?

By the evening, my head was spinning. This was my first venture into face-to-face interfaith work, and one thing was crazier than the next: there were Jews, Jews who didn't even believe in Judaism, and openly gay men and women of all faiths. I wasn't in Yemen anymore. I was sitting at the dinner table trying to stab lettuce with a dull fork, wondering if anything would ever make sense again, when a burst of laughter pulled my attention. I glanced up to see a tall, lanky man who looked remarkably like a younger version of the actor Jeff Goldblum. He walked over to my table, and as he got closer, I recognized him from the opening ceremony, when the founder of MJC praised him for his hard work. Slender and fit, with a pair of metal-framed glasses that highlighted his angular face, Daniel Pincus had seemed so at ease in front of a crowd. And now, as he stood in front of me, I understood why: people were drawn to him.

One of the men at my table rose unsteadily and waved. "Daniel, *habibi*! My friend. I love you, man."

Daniel's eyes widened, and he walked over to clap the man on his back. They talked for a while before he turned to me, his blue-gray eyes glittering in the fluorescent light. "You're from Yemen?"

I nodded, honored that one of the leaders of the conference remembered who I was. "That's right," I said.

"We're so happy you're here."

"I'm happy to be here."

"Are you enjoying yourself? Tonight? At the conference?"

"Yes—"

Before I could say more, a chorus of people began shouting: "Dance! Dance! Dance!"

He looked up, surprised by the attention, though it seemed so naturally his. His eyebrows wiggled as he studied his feet. What was the expression passing over his face? Doubt, embarrassment, pride, and then a kind of reckless "why not?" that I admired. A few seconds later he was on the floor, spinning on his head, breakdancing. I'd only ever seen these moves in videos.

The table wobbled, the beer glasses tipped precariously, and I sat there thinking, *This is what it must mean when people say that their world has been rocked.* Who was this Daniel Pincus?

◇◇◇◇◇◇

Being the only one from Yemen, I felt an intense pressure to represent my country well, to demonstrate that Yemen was not just a closed society. The responsibility situated itself squarely on my tongue, and I couldn't bring myself to speak to anyone. By the middle of the week, I started to loosen up. I began to participate in the sessions, and I tried to adopt an edge of the devil-may-care recklessness I'd seen in Daniel Pincus.

Before I knew it, I'd visited a synagogue and put on a yarmulke and witnessed Jews at prayer. I started to make new friendships. A woman who looked like she'd just stepped out of a shampoo advertisement came up to me and introduced herself as Tina Steinmetz from Austria. She asked me what I did, and I started to tell her about my peace activities. I told her I wanted to do something with Muslims and Jews in Yemen, and she told me she was researching for a book about a Muslim cleric who helped the Jews—could I help her out? Sure, I said. I could do that.

Soon after this encounter, Tina introduced me to a friend of hers named Alexis Frankel. She worked for the American Jewish Committee, and was super friendly all around. She invited me out for a drink, and after we got to the bar and she ordered for herself, she asked, "Do you drink alcohol?" I said I didn't. Mortified, she returned her own drink to the bartender and profusely apologized. I told her that wasn't necessary, but I appreciated the thoughtfulness of the gesture.

Over water, she told me that she grew up in a family who worked in the Foreign Service and was active in assisting Soviet Jews. Consequently, she'd traveled and lived in many places around the world, mostly in Africa. She'd developed a global view, knew people of various religions and backgrounds, and had even married a Bosnian man. This led into a conversation about Bosnia, and the many peoples fleeing persecution, including the Jews.

I also got to know Corey as a person, not just as an online avatar. He was a peace activist who worked with a Palestinian woman, and together they went around with a video camera and interviewed people, asking them some of the very same questions I'd posed on Facebook. *What do you think of Jews? What do you think of Muslims?* They recorded the responses and put them up on YouTube. Some clips were sad. Some were silly. Some were angry. But all them were undeniably human.

As we came to know one another, Corey told me that he was gay, and I told him he was my first three-in-one: Jewish, Israeli, and gay! He handled my bumbling idiocy with an ease that I wished I possessed, and he talked about his partner with such warmth that I blushed inwardly.

I met a woman named Ruth from Hungary who asked me if I ever ate *jachnun*. I looked at her googly-eyed and said, "How do you know about that?"

"I have it in Israel all the time when I visit. I love it."

"Amazing."

"And you chew qat in Yemen?" another woman asked.

"Yes. We do. How did you know?"

"People chew qat in Israel, too."

It was a miracle—the Israelis knew so much about my culture and my religion. I'd been involved in interfaith activities for more than a year, but I knew so little about Israel. I knew there was a city called Tel Aviv, but I had no concept of day-to-day life there—besides a vague idea of the Zionists plotting to destroy the Arab world and murder Palestinian babies in their sleep.

In MJC's committee session on "Islamophobia and Anti-Semitism," I learned how restrictive our media in Yemen really was. Until I began poking around on Facebook, all I ever heard was how the Israelis had killed or wounded Palestinians. I'd heard that Jews didn't allow their children to interact with Palestinians, that all they did was teach them to hate us. I found out that Hamas restricted the Palestinians in a similar way.

An Israeli named Yovav Kalifon, who'd created a program called Walk for Peace, in which Israelis and Palestinians literally hold hands and walk down the streets together, explained that he hoped to break through this messaging. Hamas recruited children and teens, he explained, reaching them before they were old enough to think clearly. I thought of how I'd been influenced by the killing of Palestinian children like Muhammad al-Durrah, how my revenge fantasies had played out in my head. I was young. I was impressionable. I'd believed what my leaders and the media presented to me.

But now I had questions. I asked him about the response I'd gotten on Facebook that non-Jews would end up being servants to God's chosen people. He told me that there was a brief mention of this in the Talmud, but no one he knew truly believed those words to be the literal truth. They were just a few words among thousands. You could choose to focus on those and make a judgment or you could look at the bigger picture. I nodded. I could say the exact same thing about the Quran and the hadiths.

I had a conversation with a mixed-faith couple. I learned about dietary laws, and the similarities and differences between kosher and halal. I reflected on Walter White's transformation from mild-mannered schoolteacher to murderer, wondered how Don Draper could take his marriage vows for granted, and debated the merits of Miley Cyrus, Lady Gaga, and Katy Perry.

Near the end of the conference, a man named Mohammed (there are a lot of us) asked me to take a walk with him near the hotel. He was a Muslim, he said, who was born in India and moved to South Africa. Despite his long, full, imamic beard, he treated me as an equal. When we talked about interfaith issues, he seemed not to take sides.

We'd both read the Bible. We'd both read the Torah. We both wanted to understand both perspectives. We lived thousands of miles from one another, but in very real ways were on the same path.

I wondered if I could have honest conversations like this with anyone I knew in Yemen, much less a stranger. What would happen to me? What would they say if I encouraged them to speak to Israelis? Would I be shut down, shut out, or worse? Or might somebody say okay and see what I'd seen?

On the final night of the conference, we all posed for a group photo. Then we gathered our bags, crammed into the buses, and headed toward the airport. I boarded a plane to Turkey, and saw that someone had posted the farewell picture to Facebook. Everyone had their arms locked around one another's shoulders, their smiles free and natural. I stood there, stiff and posed, inches away from the closest person. It was as if someone had taken two pictures, and cut and pasted me into the first.

But still, I had been there.

And I was closer to becoming the kind of person I truly wanted to be.

CHAPTER 9

✧✧✧

CONSEQUENCES

Working with World Relief

I flew home on the wings of a dream. There was a world in which people wore niqabs, burqas, chadors, and hijabs and others walked among them in jeans, shorts, T-shirts, and skirts of every length and style. Where women and men could dress the same, act the same, and love the same—or not. Where borders were just as fluid as the Bosporus, the strait dividing Europe and Asia. Someday those imaginary lines might not matter so much. But that utopian future wouldn't happen on its own.

My mother welcomed me back with chicken and lamb. She cooked all my favorite dishes, and asked how many nonbelievers I'd managed to convert to the one true Word. I could feel my trachea close; the food on my fork dangled impotently. My voice squeaked out, a thin reed of an explanation. As I spoke, my mother organized her face into a picture of patience, but when I mentioned Israel, it slid into a series of creases. Her lips pressed together, tighter and tighter, and when her mouth could shrink no smaller, it popped open with a surge of indignation.

I might have stayed quiet and retreated to my room, but curiosity won over cowardice. Why, I asked, was it that Yemenis, who'd never suffered any attacks from Israel, hated the Israelis so much? "Our Palestinian brothers!" she screamed. "Have you forgotten them?"

But that answer was no longer enough. I pushed on. I understood the Palestinians were suffering. I had pain for them. But why were they our only brothers who mattered? Why didn't we unite against the Saudis when they beheaded their own people? Or the Syrians, when Bashar al-Assad massacred innocent men and women? Why did we *only* care about Palestine at the expense of everything else?

She shook her head sadly, the wind pushed out of her. "If you have to ask, you will never understand," she said, walking away.

Next I tried Ahmed. Buzzing with energy, I invited him over and told him about my experiences in Sarajevo. But my enthusiasm was met with a blank stare and a shrug of indifference. He didn't want to hear about the conference, or conflict resolution. When I explained that we were brainwashed by the media, that it was one-sided and biased, he fidgeted with the radio. The only time he perked up was at the mention of a woman's name: Was she good-looking? Did you talk to her? Do you have pictures?

"Pictures?" I picked up the thread. "Why just have pictures? You could talk to these women yourself. I could arrange that."

His attention popped like a pricked balloon.

"Why would I do that? What's the point? Looking would be good, but that's enough."

When he returned home, I was more convinced than ever that I needed to build bridges between Yemeni Muslims and Jews. But once again I was plagued by the age-old question: *How?* I stared at my computer. A notification popped up: one new friend request.

I had an idea.

I created a new Facebook group called "Jews Muslim Friendship."

Then I scrolled through my contacts and invited people to join the group. I chose five of my Yemeni friends, my brother Hussain, my sisters, Lial and Nuha, and a longer list of Jews I'd met at MJC. This was going to be good. A fresh start. A new approach.

My phone rang. It was Ahmed.

"How could you do that? Are you crazy? You put my name out there like that? If you'd kept this between us, that might be okay. But now everyone knows."

He went on for a few minutes, fuming, saying more of the same, punctuating his fury with the same question, again and again: *Are you crazy?*

Finally, I cut in. "I'm sorry," I said. "You're right. I was stupid."

I looked back at the screen. A number of the Jews had accepted the invitation, but not one of the Yemenis had. Ahmed's call had sobered me up. Maybe Yemen wasn't the best place to make interfaith inroads. If something as innocent as a Facebook group could inspire such an extreme reaction from one of my closest friends, what would happen if I tried anything more? I didn't have long to consider.

"MOHAMMED! Come here!"

I flinched as my father's voice thundered from the floor above me.

Ana hemar!

My father had recently suffered a mild heart attack, and everyone had been tiptoeing around him, trying to keep him calm. This—this was not good. I scrambled upstairs as quickly as I could, and when I found him, both of us were nearly out of breath, me from exertion, him from anger.

"What are you doing with this shit thing, this Facebook?"

"What do you mean?"

"Don't question me! Hussain told me that you are forming some group there. Something with Jews and Muslims. Are you crazy? What are you trying to do? I have a son! I have a man! You're not five years old playing games. No more! No more Facebook!"

I held my anger in my fists. I'd come home from Bosnia and Herzegovina feeling like I was finally becoming who I wanted to be, that

I had a direction for my life. And now I was a child again—a child of twenty-six whose father was punishing him by taking away his favorite toy.

I couldn't argue back; for all I knew, that could push my father's heart to the limit. His anger was like the electrical power in Yemen, unpredictable in its surges and outages. I bobbed my head once and exited his room in silence.

I am a child, I thought, as I walked past my sisters and my mother, like a prisoner on the long march to solitary confinement. As I sat on my bed, I took down my Facebook group; it didn't even make it a full twenty-four hours. Maybe starting with my family and friends hadn't been the best idea.

I messaged Mohamed Abubakr from YaLa Young Leaders. I told him that after returning from the Muslim Jewish Conference, I was inspired to do interfaith work but didn't know how to begin. He mentioned an organization that he was working with that partnered with major tech companies and teaching organizations to help ninth- and tenth-grade students in the Middle East and North Africa region prepare for the professional world, while promoting tolerance and understanding. The organization was looking to expand, he said—why not give them a try? Mohamed introduced me to one of their staff, who said, "We mainly work with Palestinian and Israeli organizations. Is it safe for you to do this work in Yemen?" I assured him that it was, and that I was very passionate. And with pushing from both me and Mohamed Abubakr, he finally relented.

◇◇◇◇◇

I knew I wasn't allowed to use Facebook, but my father hadn't said anything about Skype. A plan formed. What if, instead of approaching the issue of peace-building head-on, I took an indirect approach and partnered with this new organization? What if I used the same method that had been used on me? When I was younger, I tried to distinguish myself by learning English. English had led me to Luke, to my job at Partner Aid, and to MJC. English, once again, could be my key.

Holed up in my room, I called a friend of mine who over the years had started to look up to me. When I worked at an NGO, he wanted to work at an NGO. When I worked as a researcher, he decided he wanted to work as a researcher. So when I told him about my idea to compile a group of teenagers to practice their English over Skype, he told me he'd do everything he could to help. He spoke with his sixteen-year-old cousin, who invited two relatives, who brought along a couple of friends.

Since the entire group was made up of relatives or close friends, it was all right for them to hang out together in public. So I invited them to an Internet café on the pretense of practicing their English with fluent speakers of the language. We gathered around my laptop, and I opened up Skype. We watched the connection fade in and out, listened as the bubble-like dial tones played on repeat. I tried to keep my cool, but with every failed attempt, I got one step closer to abandoning the plan altogether.

At last I connected with the director of the program, who'd gathered a group of Jewish teenagers. She'd agreed to set up this series of Skype conversations, but I hadn't shared the context. I didn't want to implicate anyone else in my scheme.

The conversation began with stilted introductions. The Yemeni teenagers had only a basic grasp of English, so their questions were all innocent enough. "How old are you?" "What is your favorite color?" "Do you have a dog?" Things were going well! Until one of the girls asked, "Where do you live?"

One of the girls on the other side answered, "I'm in Hebron. In Israel."

I closed my eyes and wished for the connection to drop, or the screen to freeze, but when I opened my eyes, the only things that had frozen were the expressions on the children's faces.

"So," asked a girl named Muna, "how many Palestinians did you kill today?" Her voice dripped with venom.

The line went silent. I didn't know what to say. I considered letting the conversation take its natural course, but I knew this likely wasn't wise. So I quickly ended the call and eyed Muna, who was laughing with her friends, tipping her chair back and extending a palm for a high five. The first and last session was over in less than five minutes.

I slinked home, kept my head down—literally—and retreated to my room to regroup. The tension crept up from my shoulders to my neck to my temples. I pressed the flats of my palms into each eye, hoping to erase the images of this most recent failure. What was I to do now?

The next day passed without incident. I kept to myself and stayed off my computer. I couldn't risk another misfire. I lay down on my bed thinking about making a Plan C, when my father burst through the front door.

"Where is that dog? Where is that stupid dog?" His voice thundered off the walls. I shot up like a bolt. I knew I was the beast in question. *Ana hemar,* I thought, pinching the bridge of my nose. I really was a donkey.

I edged my way down the hallway. When I made it to the entryway, my father was still shouting and my mother was still trying to calm him. She stood before him, leaning forward as if fighting a stiff wind. One hand was on my father's chest, holding him back, and the other was waving at me furiously, signaling that I should retreat.

"There he is!" His voice vibrated through my body. "I give you every freedom, every opportunity in the world, and you spit on it. You spit on me. This is what you do?" My father's rage had turned his face the color of an eggplant.

"What has he done? What could be so bad that you act like this?" my mother wheezed, nearly out of breath. "Why don't you talk to him? Let him explain."

"He won't explain. I'll kill him—"

I retreated to my room, moving as swiftly as I could. I sat on the edge of my bed, too scared to move, chewing at my lips. When my mother finally approached, tears were streaming down her face. I stood and spread my arms to hug her, but instead of embracing me, she struck my chest and arms with her fists. The pain that followed wasn't from the blows; it was from seeing my mother helpless, confused, scared, livid.

"What have you done?" she said in time with her punches. Over and over she repeated the words. I stood there with my arms at my sides, my head tilted up as if I could get my tears to drain back into my eyes.

"I don't know," I told her. "I honestly don't know."

I thought of my efforts over the past few days, wondered what my father might have heard. She collapsed onto my bed, a battery without charge. And gingerly, I sat next to her. Minutes passed in silence as my father's shouts dissipated into an angry clamor of silverware against ceramics.

"I will go," she said with finality. "I will speak with him. We will figure this out, *inshallah*."

"*Inshallah*," I whispered.

The last time there was this amount of upset in our house was when my mother caught me speaking on the phone with Ahlam. That seemed like a lifetime ago. Who would have thought I'd look back on that period as a pleasant one?

A rolling growl made its way up the stairs as my father and mother spoke. I made out the words "Israel" and "Mossad." I tiptoed to the door to listen, but when my father unleashed a few more "dogs," I knew I'd be hearing from my mother again shortly. She appeared a few minutes later, looking shrunken and stooped, more like her mother, Shafika, than her usual self. As she sat down beside me, I noticed the creases that had spread from the corners of her eyes. I wished that I could wash them away.

"Listen closely," she began. "Your father says that he was at the hospital. A colleague came to him, Muna's father. He said that you tried recruiting his daughter for the Mossad. That you are an Israeli agent."

Like James Bond in *Die Another Day*, I'd put my trust in the wrong girl. I nearly laughed at the ridiculousness of the accusation, but then I realized that the accusation was not ridiculous—not at all. The penalty for such a crime was death. If there was even the appearance that this allegation had merit, I would be in grave trouble. And not only me. The consequences of this charge would encircle everyone around me. The mere assertion, whether true or not, could bring great dishonor to the Al Samawi family. To my father, that was a fate worse than death. No matter what happened to me, my actions had essentially murdered my entire family.

My mother could no longer contain her anger. Words spilled out of her, words that she'd likely held back for years. She spoke of my ingratitude, her sacrifices, my betrayal, my lies, my stupidity, my self-ishness. She'd quit her job as a doctor to take care of me, and how did I repay her? By wasting every opportunity they'd provided for me. I sat and took it, my head bowing lower with each indictment. Everything she said was true. Never had the desire to run been greater; but I couldn't.

"Did you do that? Do you work with Mossad?"

"No, *wallah*. I swear to God." The firmness of my response was equal only to my fear. By now, everyone knew I'd gone to Sarajevo to attend a Muslim-Jewish gathering. A case could easily be made against me. "You have to believe me." My resolve crumbled. "Please. Please. Please." It didn't take much to imagine my body shot through with bullets, burning in the eternal flames of hell.

My mother drew her hands together as if in prayer. "Do not go near your father. I fear that he will kill you or that you will kill him. His heart is not well. He needs to heal. Let him. Don't think so much of yourself and what *you* want. Promise me."

I didn't even want to use the word "I," so I just said, "Yes."

I barely noticed my mother leave. I sat there like a zombie, and when I looked up again, I saw my sisters, Lial and Nuha. I looked them in the eyes, one after the other.

"Hussain believes that you are up to nothing good," Lial began.

"I'm not surprised," I said and cleared my throat. "I've been a burden to him my whole life."

Lial exhaled sharply. "Don't pity yourself. This is not just about you. You've put us all in danger."

Nuha sat beside me. "I'm worried about you."

Her tenderness pierced what was left of my will. "I'm sorry," I mumbled. "I don't want to worry you. I don't want to worry any of you—"

"Don't go near Baba," Lial cut me off. "I mean it." Her tone allowed no contradiction.

"Baba loves you," Nuha said. "He doesn't want to see you hurt. None of us do."

My melancholy calcified until I couldn't even move my mouth. I wanted to change the world like I wanted to ride a bike. Neither would ever happen; both were fantasies. At best, I'd waste my time; at worst, I'd hurt myself along with anyone ignorant enough to get close to me. I'd been naïve and stupid. I'd been posting things on Facebook, on a public profile. I'd told my friends about my interfaith activities and encouraged them to speak with Israelis. I trusted them; but by saddling them with my secrets, I implicated them as well. If they made even a casual remark that was overheard, I could be in trouble—and so could they. "Mohammed spoke with Israelis" could turn into "Mohammad spoke with *the* Israelis." And who were *the* Israelis? The Mossad, of course, the bogeymen, the alpha fox, the devil bent on destroying us.

I needed to figure out a way to protect my family without sacrificing my conscience. By the next morning, I had restricted my Facebook profile, and deleted any friends who might be identifiable as Israeli or Jewish. I asked Nuha to give my siblings that update, to act as a kind of goodwill ambassador. I stayed in my room and hoped against hope that I'd done enough to save us all.

That evening, I logged on to Facebook, and had a momentary pang of regret at my reduced friend count. *Ah, well,* I thought to myself, as I opened my one new message.

We know what you're doing and we're going to kill you.

◇◇◇◇◇◇

I ran to the bathroom and heaved over the toilet. Pain shot through my body, but my stomach, my chest, my heart were empty. I felt my throat close, as my muscles contracted, pushing out air and little else. Was this what it felt like to be choked? Was this how it would feel while I knelt on the ground and heard a sword scything through the air before everything gave way to darkness? I knelt in unholy prayer in front of the toilet. The water stared back at me, unmoved.

From somewhere above me, I heard the sounds of the rest of our household. I thought of my mother. I couldn't say anything to her. Not only had I put myself at risk, but I'd jeopardized her well-being. I'd endangered sweet little Nuha. The blame was all on me.

A jolt of anger replaced my crippling self-pity, and I pushed myself up. Why would these people threaten me? What had I done that was so bad? What kind of people would respond to peace and understanding with violence and hatred?

I returned to my room and called the only person who might understand: Mohamed Abubakr. He'd spent his entire life committed to peace-building in a conflict zone. He'd repeatedly broken with tradition, and the law, by organizing secret swaps of banned books, and in recent years by championing women's rights and LGBT rights in Sudan, a country that, like Yemen, punished sodomy with death. He'd been jailed before. Surely he knew how to handle death threats.

He saw through my pretense of calm immediately and asked me what had me so worked up. Grateful that I could be fully honest, I let all my anxiety spill out of me.

"I've received these things," he said, his voice measured out, like a prescription. "Many times. Don't be afraid. It's the Internet. People feel safe making others feel unsafe. They think that by making their profile pictures Osama bin Laden and posting threats they are martyrs."

His steady logic, the easy tone in his voice, were like medicine. With each breath I took I told myself he was right. He understood the situation; he was even able to intuit that the threat had come from a Facebook member using a photo of bin Laden as their profile picture. My friend had experienced this exact same scenario, and he was still alive. That boded well for me.

"They aren't serious," he concluded. "Just stupid."

I thanked him and rested easier. I didn't share the news of this death threat—or the ones that came after it—with anyone in the family. There was no need to worry them. Instead, I took care of the situation.

I stopped posting anything on Facebook or on YaLa Young Leaders. When Jewish people reached out to me, I didn't respond.

I called Lukas, my former boss from Partner Aid, and told him that I'd thought about his offer and would really like to return to work in the humanitarian field. I asked if Partner Aid might have an opening, and he said it didn't exist anymore. In fact, he'd moved to Germany and started working at a new organization called World Relief—an NGO that partnered with local churches to provide aid to the needy and build sustainable communities. He offered me a job on the spot, and I accepted the position of Senior Logistics and Procurement Officer.

Day by day, I focused on my job and stayed away from controversy, and soon enough I became a normal person again, worrying about myself and little else. My family seemed safe, and I slept at night. But I felt hollow, like a reed that the wind had once whistled through, playing a tuneless less-than song.

In Arabic, we have an expression that describes what I'd become. I was a zero on the left. A nothing. I wanted to be a zero on the right, a real number—a whole number—but that wasn't my lot. As ever, I lived on the left and dreamed of being on the right.

◇◇◇

CHAPTER 10

IF AT FIRST YOU DON'T SUCCEED . . .

With Megan Hallahan, whom I met in person at the YaLa leadership program

At home, there was a new normal. My mother prayed for me, but my father didn't waste his breath. He believed I was damned. I ate at his table. I kissed him on the top of his head whenever I saw him. But he either ignored me completely or said one thing only: *Khalik rejal,* be a man. Take responsibility for yourself and your family.

I wanted to make him proud, but by following his advice, I felt less and less like a man. I retreated into my shell, and let emails and requests ricochet off my back. But all that changed when I received an email from YaLa MENA Leaders for Change (MLC). Megan Hallahan, an American living in Israel and one of the consultants at YaLa, had recommended me for YaLa's leadership program, and the first conference was about to take place in Jordan in October 2013.

This was my chance to pursue my mission. More than two months had passed since the Skype situation. Surely people were on to the next scandal. Surely I could now continue advancing my cause without putting my family in jeopardy. And besides, I hadn't sought out this opportunity. I hadn't put myself out into the world or instigated new relationships. What harm was there in working within the network I'd already created?

Eventually, I wrestled my logic into shape. I contacted Megan and Mohamed Abubakr to let them both know that I would be attending the conference. Confident that this was the correct decision, I approached my mother. I told her I would be attending a two-day conference, which was true, and that I was going to network with other young leaders who worked in the same field as I did. Technically, this was also true. I explained that the conference wouldn't cost me anything but time— airfare, hotels, and even a per diem would be made available—and I wouldn't have to get tangled up in visa issues either. Simple.

"*T'me jak al,*" she said, giving me a look I'd become much too familiar with. *Think clearly.*

"I am," I replied.

"You're not. Why are you doing this again?"

"This is different."

She didn't say yes, and she didn't say no.

Then I went to speak with my father. I found him in his usual spot, seated in front of the television watching Yemen TV. Though we'd

barely spoken for weeks, I bowed my head, a man reduced to school-
boy fears. I presented my case, and without wasting a moment on
dramatic suspense, he delivered his verdict. He wouldn't let me travel.
I explained to him that I needed this trip, that it was indispensable to
my career advancement.

"You have a mustache," he said. "You already made up your mind.
Go."

He tapped me away like ash on the end of a cigarette.

◇◇◇◇◇◇

I'd gotten over the first hurdle, but the second obstacle caught me off
guard. When I arrived at the airport, I realized that the materials I had
on me for the conference were written in English and Hebrew. Even
worse, my ticket had been purchased by YaLa, an Israeli organization.
Anything that had to do with Israel would put the Yemeni security on
high alert. If anyone stopped me, I had no exit strategy. I tried to act
normal, but as soon as I thought to *act normal,* I realized I didn't know
what "normal" was, or why I needed to "act" that way to begin with. At
a loss, I stuck my hands in my pockets and walked as quickly as possible to the front desk. I gave the man my passport. He asked me what
business I had in Jordan, and I said, "A conference." He let me through,
no questions asked.

But when I arrived in Jordan, a security guard stopped me at immigration. "Wait here," he said. After a minute, he came back and instructed me to follow him. I tried to remember to breathe and swallow
as I entered a small room where a police officer was waiting.

"You're a single male from Yemen," he began. "Why are you coming to Jordan?" One question followed the last. *Why are you traveling
alone? What is your business here? Do you have connections in the military? Do you know Al Qaeda?*

On the one hand, I was relieved. This man knew nothing about my
interfaith work. On the other, I was furious. These men suspected me
of being a good-for-nothing criminal just because I came from Yemen.
It was humiliating. Demeaning. I wanted to sit him down and give him

a history lesson. Yemen wasn't some backwater nation filled with terrorists; it was one of the oldest civilizations on earth.

I wanted to yell: *My people are not defined by small men with bombs on their backs. Yemen has made and destroyed empires!*

But I didn't say that. Instead, I answered the policeman's questions with as much humility and dignity as I could muster. But even that wasn't good enough. After fifteen minutes, he still wouldn't let me go. Gritting my teeth, I texted Megan Hallahan and Mohamed Abubakr asking if either could help. Megan made a few calls, and I was released. *Crazy,* I thought, glancing behind me as I walked. *One call from an American can have so much power.*

In baggage claim, I spotted a driver with a sign for YaLa Young Leaders. He took me straight to the hotel, and before I could head up to my room, an extremely tall man loped through the front door into the lobby. It could only be Mohamed Abubakr. Even though we'd never met in person, I knew him from his Facebook pictures, and I could see the same easy spirit I'd gotten to know over the phone and through emails. When he reached out and embraced me, I felt like I was being wrapped up in the arms of a gentle giant.

He asked me if everything had been cleared up at the airport, and I brushed off his concern. I wanted to make a good impression. Instead, I started fussing over him, suggesting that he lie down and nap since he must be tired from the long flight; I offered to get him some water or anything else he needed to be comfortable.

Mohamed laughed with warmth and tranquility I wished I could share. "That's so nice of you. Relax. Sit down. Let's talk. How was MJC?"

A few minutes later, Megan walked through the door. Any worries I had left floated away in a cloud of dust particles. Megan, my point person at YaLa Young Leaders, moved with the grace and solidity of a former athlete, and when I mentioned that to her, she laughed and said, "That's because I am." She'd spent her childhood wanting to be like the American gymnast Mary Lou Retton, and had gotten the same haircut to prove it—but injuries ended that dream. So she picked up volleyball and soccer (a female footballer!) and was strong enough to get some scholarship offers to different universities. But she was never good enough to become a professional athlete, she said, and besides, she hadn't wanted that life. Her heart was in social action.

As we were talking, Corey arrived, his crooked grin animating his entire face. Later, we all ate together and I presented Megan with a small bottle of perfume and Corey and Abubakr with T-shirts. Abubakr held his up, and we all giggled; it would barely reach his waist. I explained that this was the very least I could do to show how much of an impact they'd made on my life, that seeing them was worth all the anger and resentment I faced from my family.

Megan thanked me warmly for the gift, and soon the conversation turned to activism. She mentioned an organization called Seeds of Peace and suggested I check them out. They worked to foster economic, social, and political change, she said, with a particular emphasis on Middle Eastern relations. They even ran a summer camp in the United States, where they brought together kids from all around the world and tried to break down barriers. The program was designed to educate young people to become leaders. But they also needed leaders to help teach and conduct the workshops and seminars.

"Sounds like something I'd love to do in Yemen."

"That would be amazing," she said, "but I'm not sure Yemen is ready for Seeds of Peace. Maybe you could be an administrator of a Facebook group or something like that?"

"I've been thinking that I want to be more involved in doing things beyond the Internet."

"That's wonderful, Mo. But I have to be honest. I'm worried about you. Things are tough in Yemen, right?"

"No more than usual," I said, and smiled as much to convince myself as her. "Besides, I have faith we'll turn things around. That's why we're here, isn't it? Because we believe that things can be better."

CHAPTER II

YOU SAY YOU WANT
A REVOLUTION

Protests in Sana'a as part of the Youth Revolution

I returned to Yemen after the conference, and continued to keep a low profile through the rest of 2013. I remained cautious about my activities, and felt (relatively) protected by the (relatively) functional government—until I started to receive death threats on my personal cell phone.

In January 2014, the Houthis, the Zaidi Shia–led militia in the north of Yemen, began to mobilize. They trekked down toward Sana'a, and by August they were in the capital, protesting in the streets, pressuring the

Sunni president, Abdrabbuh Mansour Hadi, to step down. The rebels became increasingly vocal, and in September events reached a breaking point. The military fired on demonstrators, killing a handful of them, and in retaliation, the Houthis stormed the city. Within days, the rebel fighters had taken over the military headquarters, government buildings, and the television station.

Despite the unrest, my own life didn't change very much. The fighting was along religious sectarian lines, and my family was Shia, as were the Houthis. Further, President Hadi—who still retained power—struck a deal with the Houthis and declared a cease-fire. Things settled down and life resumed. My father went to the hospital every day; I went to the offices of World Relief; and the markets were open for business. But while the streets seemed calm, old north-south resentments stuck like shadows.

After the Ottoman Empire fell, there were competing philosophies of governance in the Arab world: tribal royalty, theocracy, and military dictatorship. For instance, the Kingdom of Egypt, a puppet state of Great Britain, was overthrown in 1953 by a military coup; and in 1956, an officer in the Egyptian army, Gamal Abdel Nasser, became president. A secular autocrat and pan-Arabist, he sought to reunite the Arab world against its old enemies—namely, Europe.

Immediately after taking power, Nasser nationalized the Suez Canal, evicting Britain and France, its majority owners. But Nasser wasn't satisfied; he wanted complete control over the shipping route that connected the Mediterranean Sea to the Indian Ocean and Persian Gulf—Europe's major source of oil. This route included the Bab el Mandeb Strait, the choke point to the Red Sea, part of which was in Yemen—a land that was still divided into the Mutawakkilite Kingdom in the north and the British-controlled Aden Protectorate in the south. Nasser's economic strategy aligned with his pan-Arabist, anti-European, and anti-royalist ideologies, and in 1962 he sponsored a revolution in Yemen, helping rebels in the north overthrow the new king/imam of the Mutawakkilite Kingdom. As a result of this, the north became the Yemen Arab Republic, and the deposed royalists fled south to the Aden Protectorate.

While the age of European colonialism was cooling down, the Cold War was heating up. The United States and Soviet Union supplanted the Europeans as the major external players in the Middle East, and both countries inserted themselves in regional issues to pursue their own agendas, including access to oil and the spread of political ideology (capitalism versus communism). Players in the Middle East picked sides, as well. A complicated web of alliances formed across the sometimes mismatched religious, political, and economic lines. The United States, for instance, had oil interests in Saudi Arabia, while the Soviets shared common interests with the Egyptians. In 1967, the Egyptians supported the Yemeni nationalists who revolted against the British, thereby toppling the Aden Protectorate. The south formed its own country, later called the People's Democratic Republic of Yemen, which was embraced by the Soviets.

For the next thirty years, the Yemen Arab Republic in the north and the People's Democratic Republic of Yemen in the south lived in relative peace, despite the occasional conflagration and resultant politicking. The next big shift in power came in 1990. With the imminent fall of the USSR, South Yemen lost a crucial ally and found itself vulnerable. North Yemen pressed its advantage and forced a weakened South Yemen into unification. Ali Abdullah Saleh, a Zaidi Shia Muslim who'd led North Yemen since 1978, became the president of the newly established Republic of Yemen.

Very little changed for people from the north, where three-quarters of the population lived. But anger festered in the south. While the northerners had become more industrial over the years, the south, outside of Aden, continued to have a greater reliance on agriculture and oil. Under the communist regime, the resources had been the property of the state, and profits had been shared with the citizens. But now, under President Saleh, privatization was the name of the game, and the elites in the north—including the Al Samawi family—gobbled up the land and the profits that came along with it. We were the robber barons of Yemen. And to rub salt in the wound, we were Shia while most in the south were Sunni.

The inequality was unsustainable, and in 1994 another civil war broke out but failed to split the country. Yemen remained united, and for the next seven years it was one of the least considered and least prosperous of the Arab countries. While the rest of the Middle East was tearing itself apart, Yemen rejected formalized sectarian divisions and remained largely free of the conflicts that had its neighbors fighting among themselves and choosing sides. But though we had a stable political climate, and though we had the only republic with free elections in the Arab world, we soon became known for something else. A group of rebels had begun to coalesce in the south. Many of them had returned home from fighting the Soviet occupation in Afghanistan, and they rejected unification and the rule of the Shia. They might have faded away, but they pledged allegiance to another militant organization that was based across the Red Sea, in Sudan. This group called itself Al Qaeda.

Al Qaeda committed a major terrorist attack against U.S. servicemen at the Gold Mohur Hotel in Aden in 1992, and then in 2000 they bombed the USS *Cole* in the port of Aden. But it was after September 11, 2001, that Al Qaeda became public enemy number one. The United States, which had a history of providing financial aid to Yemen, proposed a deal. It would continue to support President Saleh and his government, as long as Yemen opened itself to U.S. special forces and intelligence agents to fight and collect information on Al Qaeda. President Saleh accepted the terms; he didn't have much of a choice. Already one of the poorest countries in the world, Yemen had started to suffer from a new economic crisis: declining oil revenues. Foreign aid was essential.

The line between Saleh's counterterrorism measures and authoritarianism grew thinner and thinner. The United States essentially gave him license to exercise his power to the fullest. Over the next few years, he began clamping down on all fronts. Which, as Newton would say, produced an equal and opposite reaction. To the south, Al Qaeda; to the north, pockets of Zaidi Shia insurgents.

The Houthi rebellion began in earnest in 2004, with the death of the

Zaidi cleric Hussein Badreddin al-Houthi. As his name indicates, Hussein hailed from the Houthi clans, a group that lived in Sa'dah, a town along the Saudi border, which had been all but forgotten by the Yemeni government. The Houthis may have been suffering economically, but they were fattening themselves up ideologically. Their forebears, the former Zaidi imamate, had ruled Yemen for more than a millennium, even expelling the Ottomans in the 1630s (before they were pushed out again). And now the Houthis were on a mission to return to their former glory. They asserted their right to their heritage and reignited local tensions by pushing on pressure points that had existed since the civil war of the 1960s and criticizing the Saleh government for colluding with the United States.

On the opposite side of the country, in the south, people were also openly and loudly pushing against the status quo, questioning whether unification was necessary or desirable. A few years later, in 2007, the Southern Movement (al-Hirak al-Janoubi) took on serious secessionist overtones. They put on daily demonstrations to peacefully oppose the Saleh regime. At the same time, the southern pockets of Al Qaeda were stepping up their attacks on the government. They targeted the state, its security forces, so-called foreign interests, and minorities—Zaidis in particular. The government had enacted measures and compromises to keep the violence to a minimum, but with fresh men, both groups were gaining power. Saleh saw the growing threat, and by 2008 he had drawn a line in the sand. No more coddling the opposition.

As the two sides butted up against each other, there was another group bubbling to the surface. In January 2011, Yemeni youth "suddenly"—at least according to the three minutes of coverage international television news allocated to the story—took to the streets in pro-democratic demonstrations.

Previously, young people had confined their political discourse to tearooms and cafés where they sipped beverages or chewed qat. But after seeing what had transpired in Tunisia, there was a tidal shift and people felt empowered to broadcast their opinions in public places.

Fifteen thousand students from Sana'a University wore pink ties and formed a human wall to symbolize their commitment to a nonviolent solution. They called for the removal of President Saleh, a new constitution, and economic development, among other things, to equalize society and topple the tribal and family power structures. This was what came to be known in some circles as our own Jasmine Revolution, also known as the Youth Revolution—a carryover from events in Tunisia and Egypt.

The movement was intended to dismantle the apparatus that sustained the status quo. In place of tradition and heredity, we wanted to create more "professional" politicians who attained representative power based on skills and abilities, rather than family and finances, to allow true democracy to take hold in our republic. We believed in social action and the peaceful tools of conflict resolution—open dialogue, a truly free press, and independent elections. These concepts were very new, and very radical.

For centuries, the traditional apparatus was mainly religious. If an imam told us that God wanted things to be the way they were, we believed him. Yet for those months in 2011, a crack in that kind of thinking and blind obedience was widening. It began with just a few students at Sana'a University, but eventually involved many political parties and hundreds of thousands of Yemenis of all ages and affiliations. They had nothing to lose.

By 2011, the World Bank estimated that more than 8 million of the 24 million people in Yemen lived in poverty. Estimates of the unemployment rate ranged from 20 percent to 40 percent. Sixty-one percent of the population at the time was under the age of twenty-five. Combine all those factors and the unrest was not surprising.

President Saleh tried to neutralize the threat, and on February 2, 2011, facing the prospect of ongoing civil unrest, he announced that he would not seek reelection, but would serve out the remainder of his term, which would end in 2013. Two more years of oppression did not satisfy the protestors. From February 3 to February 19, vigils, marches, and protests continued. The language of resistance changed from re-form (*al-islah*), to change (*taghyir*), to overthrow (*isqat*). Men and women pointed to the founding fathers of modern Yemen—Ahmad Numan and Mahmud Az-Zubayri, heroes of the 1962 revolution that overthrew the imamate—as examples of liberal and progressive leaders. People held posters of Mahatma Gandhi and Nelson Mandela, while they rebranded the president as Imam Ali.

By the end of February, the protestors had organized. They created secure zones for demonstrators and searched every passerby to ensure that no one was bringing in weapons or explosives. They put up signs and banners that stated things like "Welcome to the First Kilometer of Dignity" and "Welcome to the Land of Freedom." This was now their territory, and the people within it had to operate according to their rules and social norms. The most important of which was pacifism. The no-weapons restriction wasn't enforced just with outsiders, but also with those within the boundaries.

Entire families camped out in the safe zones, and they built recreation areas for the kids. A stage for speakers and entertainment was set up. Families, friends, men, women, all intermingled and walked the encampment, buying and drinking "Freedom Tea" from vendors. Friday prayer sessions, at the peak of protests in March and April, reportedly had hundreds of thousands of attendees.

The movement was no longer just students. The unemployed, tribesmen, women and children, human rights activists, and artists all joined together. There was no single ideology or sectarian affiliation that united the people; they all protested under the mantle of the Youth Revolution despite age, gender, geographical, political, and social differences.

In addition to assigning these spaces, the organizing committee also set up and distributed a daily schedule, arranged public speakers on the main stage and at other venues, and provided infrastructure to support other events. The security committee remained vigilant, performing stop-and-search duties, while the media committee sent out press releases and circulated other information. They even organized cleanup days, held classes in civil disobedience, raised awareness of civil rights, and continually trumpeted a message of mutual respect and cooperation.

This was the kind of world I dreamed about. This was the kind of world I wanted to live in. The Youth Movement was working toward the same thing that I was. Hope and change perfumed the air. And then hope turned to horror.

Saleh, no longer amused, responded with force: rubber bullets, tear gas, clubs, tasers, automatic rifles, and *jambiya*. On March 18, fifty-seven people were reported killed and more than two hundred were injured in a horrific military attack now known as the Friday of Dignity Massacre. The backlash was phenomenal. Thirteen members of parliament from Saleh's own party resigned in indignation, as did Ali Muhsin al-Ahmar, a prominent general and Saleh's childhood friend. Ali Muhsin's betrayal could have been a critical turning point, but he was far from a hero. Rather than supporting human rights, he had a history of being one of the president's enforcers and arms dealers. He was such a bad guy that his picture was among those put on display by the protestors identifying the corrupt culprits who needed to be ousted. Still, the army was clearly divided.

As a result, Saleh's position was weakened and the opposition political parties moved in. This was no longer a student protest for change; the political future of the country and who would lead it was very much at stake. It was as if the young people were shunted aside and the adults took over. The Youth Revolution and all the hope it stood for would soon be replaced by war.

On March 22, the Gulf Cooperation Council (GCC) stepped in to mediate. This coalition of six Arab monarchies—Bahrain, Kuwait, Oman, Qatar, the United Arab Emirates, and Saudi Arabia—drafted an agreement that would outline a power transfer between Saleh and the opposition parties. Saleh refused to sign. On March 25, one hundred thousand people gathered at the university to demand his resignation. He gave a speech accusing the protestors of colluding with Israel. The Israeli Mossad, he said, was hoping to divide the nation. The women who were standing against him, he said, were "loose."

No one said a word about the accusations against Israel, but thousands of women marched through the streets to promote women's rights.

But Islamists—including the Muslim Brotherhood—had also been raising their voices, and they began to exert more and more control over the direction and focus of the movement. Radical preachers from al-Islah spoke regularly on the main stage at Change Square and led the Friday prayer sessions. They rejected the fight for gender equality, and insisted on separating the women from the men. At first, a single rope separated males from females in front of the central stage; this was replaced by a plastic tarp, and then, eventually, a wooden fence. And it wasn't just the Islamists pushing for this. Tribesmen and the members of the Houthi militia—all protestors—supported the efforts to restore gender order in the encampment. Religious restrictions took precedence over political and social freedoms. Too many people didn't see how these things were all intertwined.

◇◇◇◇◇◇

On April 23, 2011, under increasing pressure from the GCC and the United States, Saleh finally agreed to resign, following a thirty-day transition period. Under the terms of his agreement, he would not be criminally prosecuted, and he would handpick his successor (his brother-in-law). Protestors were outraged. They insisted that Saleh be tried for over 140 counts of murder, for each of the protestors his men had killed. They demanded that the deal be shredded. For better or worse, they got their way, because Saleh refused to sign the agreement. Fed up, the GCC recused itself from mediating any longer. The protests went on, and the situation turned increasingly violent.

In a week, 350 Yemenis were killed. In retaliation, on June 3, there was an explosion in the mosque where the president and several members of his entourage were praying. In total, 7 died and 87 were injured in the attack. The president sustained serious injuries and was airlifted to a hospital in Saudi Arabia. Saleh blamed the Muslim Brotherhood for the attack as well as those who had defected from his army.

In his absence, the vice president, Abdrabbuh Mansour Hadi, was appointed interim president. By the end of June, three hundred soldiers had defected to the opposition.

Saleh appeared on television, his arms swathed in bandages, and addressed the country. Reports indicated that the blast had collapsed one of his lungs and the resulting fire had burned more than 40 percent of his body. In his address, he promised to share power with the opposition groups. He also indicated that he would only do so within the legitimate framework of the existing constitution and laws. Instead of restoring peace, the address was seen as proof of a power vacuum, and militants, particularly those in the south, took over key cities.

By late September, Saleh had returned to Yemen. Eight hundred thousand people gathered to demonstrate against him, instability in the south increased, and pressure intensified for him to step down. Saleh seemed to remain defiant and determined, but on November 23 he flew to Riyadh to meet with the GCC, which had agreed to resume its mediation efforts. He said he would sign their agreement. Saleh would transfer power to Hadi, but he would retain his title and would receive immunity from prosecution. Elections for a new president would take place within ninety days. Hadi's position was anything but secure.

The Youth Movement was devastated—this was a deal between political elites! It did nothing to address their concerns. Meanwhile, the Islamist al-Islah party couldn't have been happier, and former president Saleh was off to the United States, where he would receive expert medical attention for his injuries.

Elections took place on February 21, 2012. Former vice president Hadi was the "consensual candidate"—the only one allowed on the ballot—so he of course won. President Barack Obama praised Yemen's first-ever "legitimate" and "peaceful" transfer of power, and awarded Yemen $500 million in weapons to strengthen the country's counter-terrorism efforts against the Sunni militia in the south, Al Qaeda in the Arabian Peninsula (AQAP). In hindsight, it was clear where this was going, but we all closed our eyes and bought yet another ticket to see a remake of the same old film—*Civil War III: The Return of the Houthi*.

Hadi, a southerner, had the support of our Big Sister, Saudi Arabia, but he was now set squarely in opposition to the northern Houthis and their Iranian backers.

Months dragged on, and little changed. It felt like the results of a promised but poorly executed renovation. After long anticipation, everything looked the same. A few drawers and cabinets had moved; cups, saucers, plates, and bowls had been put on different shelves. But there were no new floor plans, no structural innovation. Things seemed stuck in their original blueprints.

While all this was going on, I was barricaded in my room single-mindedly focusing on Muslim-Jewish-Christian relations. While others were trying to change Yemen from the top down, I was trying to work from the bottom up. I wasn't paying too much attention to the Western news sources, and so I had no idea that the Shia nationalists were plotting their revenge—at least until September 18, 2014, when the Houthis stormed Sana'a and took control of the city. The United Nations intervened and negotiated a cease-fire—which didn't prevent the Houthis from seizing Hodeidah, a key port city on the Red Sea, second only to Aden.

But that was far from the end of it. Fewer than a handful of months later, the Houthis were ready for a more drastic change. In January 2015, they surrounded President Hadi's palace and held him under house arrest. The cease-fire was over.

CHAPTER 12

◇◇◇

ARE YOU HOME?

The GATHER+962 conference in Jordan, where I met Natasha Westheimer and Justin Hefter (to my left)

On January 22, 2015, President Hadi announced his resignation. The government was in chaos, the police force dispersed. No one knew what would happen next. All we could do was proceed with our lives. For me that meant World Relief, YaLa Young Leaders, Seeds of Peace . . . I was an administrator for My Face for Peace; involved with an organization called MasterPeace, which brought people together through music, sports, and art; and helping Tina

Steinmetz from MJC with her book project. It was too dangerous to discuss any of these things with anyone within Yemen, but from my room, from my computer, I communicated with people in Egypt, Jordan, Sudan, Australia, America, and even Israel. I used incognito windows, and signed out of every account after I finished using it. I thought I was smart, safe.

I was in my office when I received the first call.

"*Salaam alaikum*," a man said pleasantly. "Is this Mohammed Al Samawi?"

"Yes," I replied.

"We know you are a Mossad agent converting Muslims to be Jews and Christians," he said. "We know where you live and we will kill you today."

"Who is this?" I demanded.

"You will know who we are," he replied.

I heard a click.

A chill ran through me from the inside out. I stared at the blank screen on my phone and tried to shrug it off. It had to be one of my friends playing a trick on me. Ahmed knew I was jumpy these days; this would be just like him. I looked around the office, wondering if someone was going to spring out from behind one of the low partitions. I took a few deep breaths, cleared my throat, and walked to the restroom. I washed my hands and daubed at my face with a wet paper towel. *It's nothing,* I told myself. *It's just a prank.* My eyes caught my face in the mirror; it looked skeptical.

That evening, when I returned home, I went straight to my room. I booted up my laptop, cleared my search history, and combed through all my recent Facebook activity. Over the beat of El Far3i, my phone rang again.

"Are you home?" a voice asked. No greeting; no hint of politeness.

"Who is this?" I asked.

"*Are you home?*" he repeated, yelling.

I hung up. This call was a world away from the nameless, faceless Facebook threats; this was real. One call might be nothing; but two?

How had they gotten my cell number? Why did he care if I was home or not? Did he already know where I lived?

I picked at my dinner, using a piece of flatbread to push around a chunk of lamb from the *fahsa* my sister Lial had made. I was thinking about my recent Facebook activity. I'd commented on the war in Syria. I said I was heartened to see that hospitals in Israel were treating victims. Ahmed asked me why I'd posted that information. Was I saying that Israel was a good place—that Israelis were good people? Maybe this crossed a line. I kept replaying the call in my mind. It was one thing to see words on a screen; it was far more troubling to nearly feel someone's breath in my ear.

My mother asked if everything was okay, and I waved it off, pleading a headache. When the dishes were cleared, I retreated to my room. I couldn't tell my family; to do so would have meant confessing to my activities. I couldn't go to the police; without a proper government in place, the police were negligible at best. Houthis had taken over everything. And what would I tell them when they asked the inevitable follow-up questions? I imagined the scenario would play out like this:

Why would someone want to do you harm?

Because I've befriended Jews; because I believe that Muslims and Jews should get along.

Follow me.

Where are we going?

To this cell.

I slept fitfully that night. I woke in the fetal position, wrapped around myself, stiff and sore and achy. My mother noticed my distress immediately. She put her hand on my forehead and brushed back my hair.

"A little fever. You should stay home today."

The word "home" sent a shock through my system. Was home even safe? Had I put my entire family at risk?

"I'm fine," I said, and walked out the door.

That morning I asked the driver to take a different route to work and drop me off a few blocks from the office. This was Hollywood survival 101. Disrupt the normal routine; don't let them catch you unaware. Each day I felt a creeping dread as the clock ticked toward late afternoon and I had to go home. I didn't want to be out after dark. I didn't want to be at home. If they, those nameless, faceless they, came for me at home, they wouldn't only kill me, they'd kill my family as well. I couldn't do this to them. There would be no recourse. The city was tense; violence was on the rise. Death was easily explained away and dismissed.

Rebels.

Militia.

Just another body, caught in the crossfire.

◇◇◇◇◇◇

Keeping these death threats to myself wasn't easy. I wanted to reach out to others but didn't dare. What if my phone had been tapped? What if I was being watched?

Unable to eat, sleep, or function properly at work, I resolved to do something. I decided I would ask World Relief if they could relocate me to their office in Aden. It would solve everything. Aden, a southern port city, was near where my mother was from. I had relatives there who could assist me. I could tell everyone back home that I'd been temporarily transferred to oversee a project; that I was so respected, so needed, that I had to go. I'd miss my family and friends, but in a couple of months, after the danger had passed, I would return. And then I'd be out from beneath the shadow of the sword that hung above me.

I called my boss, Nate Harper, who was living in Jordan due to visa issues. I didn't explain about the death threats. Instead, I told him I was looking for a change of pace. With all the unrest in Sana'a, I was hoping to escape for a bit, to see a different part of the country, to get more experience with the organization by working out of a different office. It was nothing personal; I liked it here, liked working for him. But it was the right move for me.

He paused before declining my request. Nate was an amazing boss, and a friend. But staff changes like these weren't easy at the best of times. And now with him out of the country? I was, in a very real sense, the one in charge of all our operations in Sana'a. I was the one who signed the checks and approved the reports. If I wasn't there, the office might grind to a halt, and he wasn't sure he could find someone to replace me, however temporarily. I was somewhat flattered, but a compliment had never been so serrated.

Desperate, I told him about the threats. I could hear the pain in his voice, but he said he still couldn't transfer me to Aden. He promised he'd help me in whatever way he could, and said he'd call back shortly with expert advice. Within the hour, he contacted me with four recommendations: change your phone number, take different routes to the office, don't socialize in public, and avoid going out at night. I'd already made those changes. I appreciated his concern, but it wasn't quite enough to make me feel secure.

I scrambled to find another out. I searched job boards and ransacked my email. Surely there was some loose thread I could follow up on . . . And then I found it. Tucked away in my inbox, I had an email from Megan Hallahan about a conference that would be taking place in Jordan between February 26 and March 1, 2015. It was called GATHER+962, hosted by Seeds of Peace. Would I like to attend as one of three YaLa representatives? My fingers stepped on each other as they rushed to reply to the email: YES, I would like to attend.

I quickly reached out to Megan, and she told me she would be attending as well. What a relief. In the time since we first met in person, Megan and I had grown closer. She'd reached out to me regularly to see how I was doing, and how my interfaith activities were going. She had a good grasp on the situation in Yemen and wanted to be certain that I was okay. I was eager to see her in person. Hamze, whom I'd also met in Jordan back in 2013, was also going. GATHER+962 was exactly what I needed.

By this point, my family had gotten used to the fact that I traveled for work. I told them the conference would help me improve professionally, and I took their silence as acquiescence. Then I packed a bag, careful to remove any documentation written in Hebrew, and flew to Jordan.

When I arrived, Megan rushed over to me. She was glowing like a little ball of light. I told her that she seemed to be so happy, that it seemed like a lot of stress had lifted off her shoulders.

"No kidding." She laughed.

"I'm sorry. I may not be saying this so well."

"No, no, it's true." She tucked a loose curl behind her ear. "For this conference, I'm here as a participant. Like you. Most of the time I'm busy running things, so it feels good to be here to just enjoy and not have to think of it as work-work." She tilted her head to the side and raised an eyebrow. "Do you know what I mean?"

"Yes," I said, confident that I really did. Months spent moderating online interfaith groups had improved my English tremendously.

She noticed someone across the room, and waved like a little girl who'd just found her long-lost friend. "I'm kind of playing hooky," she explained, "skipping school."

"Oh?" I said.

She smiled conspiratorially. "My boss is away and I couldn't contact him for permission to come. I came anyway. Figured I'd earned it!"

"Wow," I said in hushed awe. "I don't think I have that kind of freedom."

Over the course of the week, and a series of watered-down coffees and underbrewed teas, Megan and I started to get to know each other as people, not just activists. I learned that her family was Catholic, and that the role of charity had always figured large in her life. Her father worked as an organizer for the Laborers' International Union of North America, and after school she'd help him stuff envelopes and join him at rallies. That's when she first found that this kind of work was her calling. His office was in a poor part of the city, and it wasn't uncommon to see homeless people lingering on the streets with shopping carts and trash bags, trying to make a living from redeeming cans. On television, she saw victims of the 1984–85 famine in Ethiopia, images of tiny children with distended bellies, and she wondered why it was that the people she knew had so much while others lacked so much.

There was something fundamentally unfair about conditions in America, she explained. The haves and the have-nots.

The University of California at Santa Barbara extended her vision beyond the borders of the United States, and with a degree in political science and international relations, she explored various organizations and locations, but found a home in Israel working with YaLa Young Leaders.

I felt a real kinship with Megan; it was as if we were schoolmates who'd been in classes together for many years but never really spoken about anything but schoolwork. I thought about telling her the difficulty of my situation, to return her openness with my own, but when I looked up at her, I sensed that she was drifting away, her head someplace else.

"Are you all right?" I asked. "I mean, are things good with you?"

She sighed. "It's been a tough couple of months. I lost my grandfather . . . been in a not-so-good-for-me relationship . . . but that's all starting to feel like it's behind me. I'm with some nice people now."

I smiled at the compliment. "I'm sorry I didn't know about your troubles."

She shrugged. "How could you? I didn't say anything."

◇◇◇◇◇◇

The next morning, I found myself alone in the dining hall. Little constellations of men and women had formed, but I hadn't figured out the science of easing into someone else's orbit. I spotted an open seat next to a young man who looked about my age. He was dressed in Western clothes, and seemed approachable, so I plopped down and asked him if he liked football. He angled his head in a funny way, and I realized I should have commented on the weather, or asked about his night's sleep. But then he smiled, leaned closer, and whispered, "You a fan?"

I nodded.

"That's awesome. Yeah, I am, too." He scanned the room. "Probably not many of us here. Don't know why, but sports seem like they're either a guilty pleasure or a bit of torture for this crowd. By the way, I'm Justin."

We talked about the Premier League, and he seemed to know something about every team I mentioned. I decided to test him a bit and asked him about La Liga, if he thought that anybody stood a chance at all against Barça or Real Madrid. His answer was detailed, filled with names and statistics. Needless to say, he passed.

It turned out that Justin had played football (soccer, as he called it) in high school and dreamed of a pro soccer career—like me. But he didn't have it easy. The only Jew on his squad, he stuck out. He tried to pass off his darker skin and curly brown hair as Hispanic, but his teammates called him out with nicknames like "Torah Boy" and "Heil Hitler." He took the jabs in stride, and sloughed them off along with the hard tackles. "Not worth the sweat off my back," he said.

I knew what he meant.

"These days," he continued, "I'm focused on other types of games. Video games that promote peace."

He said he had founded a tech company, and one of the games he'd developed involved getting Palestinians and Israelis to work together. The only way either player could advance to the next level was through cooperation. He showed me a sample on his phone. It was incredible. I'd never met someone who could create such a thing. I told him so, and he shrugged and handed me a business card.

Bandura Games. Justin Hefter. CEO.

I handed him my card from World Relief, and we promised to stay in touch. As I tucked his card away, I considered telling him that the word *bandura* in Arabic means "tomato." But before I could say anything, he'd left the table and was immersed in another conversation.

I was out of my league. I hadn't even moved out of my parents' house and Justin had already started a company. But there was no time for self-pity. I was running late. So I grabbed my bag and headed to my first scheduled group discussion.

We'd each been given the same assignment: pick one issue in the world that you want to tackle. I chose water. Experts forecasted that

Yemen was going to run out of drinking water by 2020, which would lead to a nationwide catastrophe that would make the Houthi skirmishes seem like a warm-up act. The issue was exceedingly urgent—and it avoided contentious subjects like religion and politics. The last thing I needed was more enemies.

As I waited my turn to speak, a young woman with a thick head of red hair and glasses got up to make her presentation. Her name was Natasha Westheimer, and her issue was water. *What?* That was my issue! I was about to say something, when Natasha explained her background . . .

Born in Australia and raised in the United States, Natasha attended the University of Maryland, where she cofounded a nutritional education organization called SNAK—Spreading Nutrition Awareness to Kids. This eventually led her to the Clinton Global Initiative, which led to a three-month study-abroad semester in Israel. Like me, she'd been taught to organize the world through a simple equation, only hers was the inverse of mine: Palestinians = bad, Israelis = good. While in Israel, she became aware of the far more complicated reality.

Returning to Maryland, she changed to a double major in Jewish studies (specializing in the Israeli-Palestinian conflict) and international development and conflict management (specializing in transboundary water management in the Middle East). She was determined to make a difference. To date, she'd interned at the State Department, worked with the Arava Institute for Environmental Studies, and then segued to EcoPeace Middle East. Her next step would be attending Oxford University in the fall to pursue a master's degree in water science.

I bit my tongue. Water was most certainly *her* thing.

I listened to Natasha explain the importance of water (which I knew), and the strategies that Israel has employed to deal with its water shortages (which I didn't). Apparently in Israel there were desalination plants that turned seawater into potable water. As long as the sea existed, Israel would never have to worry about drought. My mind was spinning with possibilities—could we adopt a similar program in Yemen?

I was so caught up in my own fantasies that I thought I heard Natasha criticize the Israeli government and its positions on Palestinians and water rights. I reined in my focus. No—that's exactly what she'd said. She was calling her own government to task over its treatment of Palestinians. The lack of censorship was shocking. But her loyalty wasn't to one party over another; it was to humanity.

When my turn came around, I quickly switched my topic and instead spoke about the Akhdam people, a minority in Yemen. The singular form of the word *khadem* means "servant" in Arabic, and that's exactly how these people were treated. As part of my work at World Relief, I was working to assist the Akhdam. They existed on the lowest rung of Yemeni society, worked at menial jobs, didn't attend schools, and struggled to survive. Without an education, their children stood little chance of advancing socially or economically. I hadn't worked out all the details, but I believed that there could be an opportunity to improve living conditions for the Akhdam through some form of microfinancing. If I could help the Akhdam set up a business selling a low-cost commodity, like, say, coffee, then they could send their kids to school in exchange for the beans. Most of the people in the group had never heard of the Akhdam, but they encouraged me to pursue the idea, and I was energized by the reception and support.

The next two days passed in a series of discussions and debates. I learned about other organizations and their efforts around the globe, and spoke with Natasha about water conservation systems. I asked how she became such a strong activist, and she told me that she'd always been drawn to the underrepresented and underserved—something that she traced back to the legacy of the Holocaust. While her mother's family had lived in Australia for four generations, her father's mother was born in a European concentration camp and escaped to Australia when she was five. Raised among survivors, Natasha was imprinted with a sense of social obligation. This was the first time I'd really spoken with someone about the Holocaust. I made a note to myself to learn more about it.

The only disheartening conversation was the one about the Syrian crisis. We could all agree that Bashar al-Assad was an awful man. I shared the fact that Yemen had opened its arms to welcome refugees, but not many came. At World Relief we heard that many Syrians believed they were better off in their war-torn home country than in Yemen. I remembered what Megan had said about the haves and the have-nots and thought of Saudi Arabia. It is one of the wealthiest countries in the world, yet were they taking in any Syrians? What kind of aid were they providing?

This was a pressure point for me. The more I thought about it, the more I realized that Saudi Arabia was more like a bully than Yemen's Big Sister. Over the years, she'd played Yemen for access to its seaports, offering little in exchange.

But the kingdom didn't stop there. In addition to using our resources, she tried to control our minds. Growing out of Saudi Arabia was yet another major sect of Islam, Wahhabism, named after the early political and spiritual leader, al-Wahhab. In the early 1700s, in reaction to the spread and popularization of mystical Sunni practices, he decided to return Islam to a kind of puritanism. Muslims who integrated into the secular world, he said, weren't Muslims at all. He rejected the practice of venerating saints and visiting shrines, and believed that only God in heaven was to be honored, and solely through a strict interpretation of the Quran. He told his followers that the "best of times" was the period that the Prophet spent in Medina, and that all good Muslims should strive to replicate that state of being. Extreme and uncompromising, he envisioned a return to an ancient Islamic state, free of corruption; a pure Islam.

Al-Wahhab along with Muhammad Ibn Saud, the founder of the first Saudi state, worked together—Saud politically and al-Wahhab spiritually—to unite what had long been disparate tribes with individual interests. The House of Saud went in and out of power until the 1900s, when it consolidated control with the help of the religious authorities. From then on, Western influence was, in turns, rejected and embraced—and particularly when it came to currency in exchange for drilling rights, the Ibn Saud family didn't think twice. And thus the blessing and the curse of oil-rich territory created a division that Saudi

Arabia still lives with today—the tension between spiritual wealth and material wealth.

As much as the Saudi royal family preached a strict form of Islam, they enjoyed an unabashedly lavish lifestyle. But their own extravagance in no way dimmed their support for Wahhabism. Strict religious laws were put in place as flocks of teachers and imams shaped the country, and countries across the Arab world. They set up schools in economically depressed areas with little access to education, and they embedded themselves across Yemen's countryside. The government was too poor to oversee the remote rural areas and its schools, so the Saudi teachers and imams stepped in to fill the void. They pressed their advantage, preying on the large number of illiterate Yemenis and "converting" them to the Wahhabi ways.

Wahhabism spread to such a degree that it infiltrated politics, which added another group to the mix. Now the divide was not only between the Sunni and the Shia, but also the Wahhabi—perhaps the most radical of any of the groups.

I'd heard for so long that in the Arab world we were all of one blood. That together we would fight against the enemy. But more and more it seemed that we were our own enemy.

◇◇◇◇◇◇

The final night of the conference arrived, and everyone gathered in the dining room for a farewell dinner. After three days of lectures and conversations, I finally worked up the courage to ask Megan the thing that had been itching in the back of my mind.

"I like that there are people here from the U.S. State Department. They have interesting insights."

"They do. It's so easy to dismiss our governments. But they really do have reach."

"Do you know any of those people personally?"

"Not the ones here, but I have some contacts . . . Why?"

"I'm just thinking about things. Thinking ahead." I leaned back in my seat and folded my arms across my chest.

"Are you thinking of leaving Yemen?"

It was the first time that someone had said the words that I'd been struggling to get out.

"No. I don't know. It may come to that."

Megan's eyes made a quick calculation. "You know," she said, with a look of compassion, "I've been worried about you. I don't know if it's a good idea for you to go back right now. If I can help, Mohammed, just ask."

"Thank you," I said. "I hope it won't come to that."

She nodded. "Anyway, I'll check around a bit. See what I come up with."

Before we could move on to a lighter subject, a Jordanian Bedouin dance troupe took the stage. Dressed in their traditional white robes and red-checked headscarves, their chests crossed with red belts, they burst into song. One man played a stringed instrument, another was on a kind of bagpipe-like apparatus, and another was keeping time on the drums. The beat drew the hundred or so people to the dance floor, and I felt my foot tapping involuntarily.

I looked to my right and caught Megan smiling, her eyes closed, head nodding. I smiled, and felt a nudge at my other side. Natasha was there, arms raised, alternately snapping her fingers and clapping her hands. A wide grin split her upturned face.

"Why aren't you dancing?" she called to me.

I shrugged and smiled. How could I explain to her about my leg, how clumsy it made me feel? How could I tell her that the Yemeni people loved dancing, but it was only to be done at weddings, with men in one room and women in another, to a very strictly prescribed set of steps? How could I reveal that I'd been so restrained by culture and tradition and a sense of right and wrong that I'd never danced in my life?

The thoughts tumbled through my mind as I watched a woman I'd known for barely seventy-two hours waving me to join her, dancing with a blissful abandon, a spontaneous expression of joy, of being alive.

I took a few tentative steps. And then I shut my eyes. I felt the music, forgot about everyone else, and let my body go. A strange sensation came over me.

I felt free.

◇◇◇◇◇

The following day, everyone departed, promising to keep in touch; but I had one more day to spend in Jordan. World Relief had been so happy that I would be at the conference as their representative that Nate Harper had invited me to take an extra day to explore the country. I could choose any activity that I wanted, and Nate would join me.

I chose to go to the river Jordan, the site where the Bible tells us that Jesus was baptized. On the east bank of the river sat Al-Maghtas, the Arabic word for "immersion," which was also known as Bethany, possibly derived from the Hebrew words *beth-ananiah,* or "house of the poor." On a cerebral level I understood that the ancient Jews, Christians, and Muslims had all been here, but the weight of that shared history was beyond my imagination.

I walked along paths winding through the desert, shrubs and wildflowers intermingled with the rocks and parched earth. A few acacia trees lined a stream, the Wadi Kharrar, that led from Jabal Mar-Elias (Elijah's Hill) down to the baptism ponds close to the river. This was the site where the Jews crossed the river Jordan and entered the Promised Land. It was also the location of the Prophet Elijah's ascension into heaven, as well as the ancient Church of St. John the Baptist.

During the Six-Day War of 1967, the location was heavily mined, but after the Israel-Jordan peace treaty of 1994, the Jordanian royal family took it upon themselves to clear the area and restore it as a pilgrimage site. I was moved by the gesture, by how an Islamic country could help heal old wounds and preserve sacred history for Jews and Christians.

On one side of the water sat Jordan, on the other side Israel. The Jordanian side seemed as if it was little changed from antiquity. The Israeli side nearly blinded me with its whiteness, its polished modernity. I had heard people say that one of the problems with the Arab world was that it too often focused on the past while Israel looked to the future.

I sat on the hard ground for a long time watching the waters of the Jordan flow past me. If I could swim, I could have entered Israel. There were no checkpoints. No armed guards. No disputes over whose was whose. A long time before this, I'd read about a hotel in Europe that straddled an international border. If you stayed in a room on one side of the hotel you were in the Netherlands; if you stayed on the other side you were in Belgium. You could easily be in one or both countries. I thought of Morocco and Algeria; of Egypt and Saudi Arabia. Borders, these artificial constructs, were the cause of so much turmoil.

If only I could swim, I wouldn't need anyone to come and part the waters. I could make the short distance on my own.

Nate came up to me and told me that we needed to start making our way to the airport. "You don't want to miss your flight," he said, presuming too much.

"You're right," I told him. "Just a few minutes more." I used my good hand to push myself up from where I'd been leaning, my palm dented and lined from rocks, a relief map of ancient history.

Just before we boarded the plane, Nate presented me with a watch, a gesture of gratitude for all the work I'd been doing. It was one of the most beautiful things I'd ever owned. I watched as the second hand twitched forward, almost hesitant, as if it wanted to reverse directions at every tick. I understood that impulse.

◇◇◇

CHAPTER 13

A MAN OF MY WORD

An aerial view of Aden, Yemen's biggest city in the south, and its main port

Getting off the plane was a reality check. A Houthi approached me, asked to see my ticket, and questioned why I had been in Jordan. I said I had been at a conference, and he let me pass, no further interrogations.

The road home wasn't clogged with the usual traffic. Instead of cars, I saw pickup trucks with machine guns mounted in the beds. Houthi militiamen stood next to them, scanning near and far. Along the side of the road, on sidewalks, and spilling out of cafés, men with raised rifles clustered. A few camouflaged military vehicles—armored personnel carriers—fought for space in the dusty streets. Houthi men in ragged clothes walked along with their *jambiya*, their traditional daggers, hanging from their belts. Others carried rocket launchers on their shoulders. Every now and then, someone would raise his knife in the air and shout. The rest of the mob would respond, knives and rifles rising and falling like pistons.

All along the road signs hung from buildings: "God is great! Death to America! Death to Israel! Damn the Jews! Victory to Islam!"

My throat closed on itself, my chest desperate for air. *This is what an asthma attack must feel like,* I thought to myself, my head getting light. While the Houthi fighters were on the same religious sectarian side as I was, I had no doubt that if they found out about my interfaith work or thought I was an Israeli spy, they would kill me—if I was lucky.

I got home and the main salon looked like a warehouse. Food sat in neat rows of boxes and bags, tufts of greens sprouting from some of them. My mother looked like a farmer among rows of produce, inspecting boxes with a face creased by concentration and worry.

"Why all this?" I asked her after we exchanged greetings.

"We have to be prepared," she said, scowling at a bag of onions. She held one up, and the papery outer layer parachuted to the floor. "In case the war comes. We will still have something to eat."

"Do you really think—"

"We don't have time to think," she said sharply, paring the end of my question. "We have to act. No one can predict what the Houthis will do."

My legs felt like they were about to give out. I tried to excuse it on the plane ride, on my exhaustion from the conference.

"Maybe it would be a good idea to stay home tomorrow. A few days. See what goes on," she said.

We all did. The Houthi weren't a trained and disciplined army; they were a ragtag bunch of militiamen from the mountains, made even more frightening by their unpredictability. Like President Hadi, we all felt as if we were under house arrest. We ate our meals seasoned with tension and tried to adjust to our new reality. I worked from home as much as possible, as did my father. With no government in place, there was no funding going to military institutions, which meant that there was no salary for the staff at the hospital. Eventually he stopped going to his clinic as well. Few people were coming in; fewer still were able to pay. Maybe those Syrians had it right. Maybe Yemen wasn't a good place for refugees, or citizens.

Before I'd left for Jordan, the Houthis had announced that they'd formed a transitional government. A five-man presidential council would be in charge. The UN Security Council condemned their coup and urged in the strongest terms possible that the Houthis participate in a power-sharing agreement brokered by the GCC. The rebels had refused.

Now the Houthi banners were everywhere: "God is great! Death to America! Death to Israel! Damn the Jews! Victory to Islam!" They covered the faces of buildings, defaced the lovely ancient walls of the Old City. The sounds of car horns and calls to prayer were replaced with the Houthi battle cry and artillery fire.

The tension in the house was at a breaking point. My father was sleeping all the time; when he wasn't, he was agitated. My mother worried about his health. She worried that any disturbance would be detrimental. She wouldn't even clean while he was at home.

At dinner one night in mid-February, she had mentioned that she'd heard of certain individuals who'd gone missing under mysterious circumstances. Had they fled on their own or had they been detained by the insurgents? And why had they disappeared? They'd done far less than I had in my interfaith and peace-building efforts. I had to do something. I couldn't live with putting my family in jeopardy.

When I told her I had to get out, that I was putting the family at risk, she understood. I didn't need to say more. For a few days I stayed at a hotel in Sana'a. I worked a bit remotely, and tracked the latest developments in Yemen through bloggers and Facebook friends. I did whatever I could to keep my mind occupied.

I got in touch with Megan and she went to work on my behalf trying to find jobs for me outside of Yemen—anything temporary, anything within the scope of my previous experience. When the fighting in Yemen died down, I'd feel better about returning. Not surprisingly, no one was looking to hire someone who would only be available for an indeterminate amount of time.

I woke up the morning of February 22 and scanned the online headlines. Al Jazeera was reporting that Hadi had managed to escape house arrest. He'd traveled to Aden and reversed his position. He was the legitimate leader of the country, he said. He'd only resigned under pressure to appease the Houthis and avoid bloodshed. He was going to establish Aden as the new capital, build a provisional government, and resume leadership.

I turned on the radio. It confirmed the reports. Aden would be the new capital; the government and police force would join Hadi in the south. I knew it: Aden was the answer! As my mother stockpiled groceries, I collected job opportunities. I interviewed with Oxfam, the long-standing NGO that worked to alleviate poverty and injustice throughout the world. I also interviewed with Save the Children. Fortunately, through my work at World Relief, I was a known quantity. Yemen wasn't a particularly desirable or welcoming place for foreigners to work, and the fact that I spoke English was an added bonus. I received offers from both organizations, and chose Oxfam. They had an office in Aden and I could start as soon as I was able. I tendered my resignation at World Relief, and Nate apologized again that he hadn't been able to accommodate my request. He understood that with the conditions in Sana'a being what they were, I would be leaving as soon as possible.

With all the pieces in place, I spoke with my father and mother after Friday prayer. I told them I had a better offer at a new organization, and that, of course, Sana'a wasn't safe for me since the Houthis were starting to target anyone who worked at NGOs. My mother was pleased; I'd be away from the unrest, and close to her family. My father was displeased; he told me I couldn't go. I hadn't considered his opposition. I had no backup plan. I stood there feeling as helpless as he did. With the Houthi takeover, he could no longer support the family. He couldn't fulfill his obligations. I could pick up and leave at a moment's notice;

but he could not. What he didn't know, what my mother didn't know, was that if I didn't leave, I might compromise us all.

As my mouth swung open and shut, my mother went to work. She told my father that her brother had found me a suitable apartment. She said that I'd have a very respectable job, and I'd bring honor to the family. Finally, he relented. Thankfully I hadn't told my mother that as far as advancing my career was concerned, my position at Oxfam was two steps back. My new title would be Logistics Officer. Presently I was running the show, the country's representative; soon I'd be a glorified administrative assistant. But what did that matter? I'd be alive.

On the last night at my parents' house, I packed a few of my clothes. This was only temporary, I told myself and my siblings. I'd be back. *Don't worry about me, take care of yourselves. I'll see you soon.*

I'm a man of my word.

◇◇◇◇◇

I checked my phone one last time before stashing it away. It was 2:00 P.M. on March 15, and the aircraft was sitting on the runway. As we waited to take off, I heard a clatter of steps and a rustle of voices. The flight attendants bustled to the hatch, and Houthi rebels boarded. They walked down the aisle, demanding identification cards, asking about the nature of our business in Aden. With Hadi now in Aden, the city was considered enemy ground, and anyone traveling there was under suspicion. I handed over my ID card, a film of moisture where my thumb and forefinger had gripped it. I said I was reporting for a new job. They moved along; I breathed.

As soon as I set foot in Aden, I looked for the blue berets of the police. But instead I saw two men in plaid shirts and munitions vests, carrying Kalashnikov rifles as they eyed the departing passengers. Trucks were draped in the black flag of Al Qaeda in the Arabian Peninsula (AQAP). Fighters milled about. I tried to blend into the crowd, but I was painfully aware that my lighter skin marked me as a northerner in a southern stronghold.

As my uncle Kamal pulled away from Aden International Airport, I pressed my head against the back of the seat. Everything the media had reported was a lie. This was little better than Sana'a, but now I was the interloper, the odd man out.

We wound past a block of apartments. More black standards, white letters spelling out various slogans, pocked the sun-soaked stone slabs. This, the south, was their territory. I'd escaped the jaws of the Houthis only to wind up in the belly of the AQAP beast. Hadi, a southerner, may have been in his element. I was not.

When the Youth Revolution began in January 2011, the real political predators were the Houthis, Saleh, and the Gulf Council states. AQAP was a minor, if lethal, player. With perhaps only as many as three hundred members, it focused its efforts on violence against westerners. It enjoyed local support among the tribes and certain government officials, but it was nothing more than a minor irritant, a mosquito buzzing around. Little did we know, that mosquito would turn out to be carrying malaria, dengue, and West Nile. AQAP used grassroots recruiting to enormous effect. It moved across the south and aligned with other local Sunni groups. There was now a formidable army ready to fight against the Houthi/Saleh (Shia) alliance.

I spent the rest of that day with my uncle Kamal and my cousin Yasin in my uncle's apartment. They were fairly strict in their beliefs, so the men dined alone, without my aunt Dinah and my cousins Dalia and Lulu. I wondered if Dinah knew that her name was so prominent in the Torah. Definitely not, I decided. I filled Kamal and Yasin in on my new job, letting them know that my work was a step down for me in terms of salary and responsibility. I was cautious when talking about money. The disparity between my father's family and my mother's was still a sensitive subject, and I was wary of being viewed as a family banker.

After a pleasant meal, Kamal and Yasin drove me to my new place, which was right near the city's central bank. Duty discharged, they left. Whatever excitement I felt at living on my own for the first time in my life was more than somewhat dulled by the circumstances. I sat on the couch and stared at the wall opposite me. I didn't dare pull back the white curtains from the windows, so the filtered light rendered everything in a gauzy, unfocused aspect. I assumed that I was the only person in the building from the north. The people we'd passed in the hallway and on the four flights of stairs up to my apartment had thick accents, easily distinguishable from my own. All that now separated me from them were thin bits of wallboard.

On March 16, the morning sun woke me up for my first day at my new job. The Oxfam office was a fifteen-minute drive away. The Sudanese man who headed the outfit was out of town on holiday, so I met another logistics officer, an accountant, three drivers, and the cleaning woman. The drivers were especially friendly, and called me "Mr. Mohammed" out of respect. As the logistics officer, I was in charge of them, but they didn't have to be as friendly and deferential as they were. Without the man in charge of the office present, the atmosphere was informal. There didn't seem to be much to do, so I looked over a few files, read the list of standard operating procedures to better understand how requests for goods would be handled, and spent a few hours on the laptop they'd given me trying to familiarize myself with the upcoming projects on health, sanitation, and education throughout Africa.

At the end of the day, one of the drivers, a man named Aidroos, drove me the full fifteen minutes home to my apartment, even though he wasn't supposed to. No one had mentioned that I was from Sana'a or a Zaidi, and I breathed a little easier. Maybe I'd been overreacting. Aden was a crucial port city of nearly nine hundred thousand people from different parts of the world. No one was looking to get me. The city seemed fully functional, despite the militants in the streets.

The following day, the same schedule repeated itself. But after work, Aidroos invited me out to a meal. I agreed to go. As a Yemeni man, I'd never learned to cook, and living on my own had left me hungry. When we entered the restaurant and sat down, Aidroos noticed my eyes wandering. Men with black hats, white robes, and bandoliers were eating and laughing.

"Don't worry," he said. "Things will calm down. Al Qaeda will only attack you if you attack them. You have nothing to fear." I swallowed my anxiety with my food and washed them both down with tea. Perhaps he was right. Perhaps we could all get along. After all, these men seemed like regular people; just another political group going about its business. But still, there was no reason to risk it. I planned to keep my head down, go to work, and go home—that's it.

On the third day of this, I was already tiring of my routine. But as soon as I worried that my new life would grow monotonous, I found a fresh opportunity to jump out of my skin. After a busy day at the office, I settled into my bed, eager to read the news, but was jolted to attention by a knock on the door. At first I sat still, hoping I could pretend I wasn't home. But then I realized the lights were on and my music was playing. So much for that. I crept to the door and cracked it open. There, before me, stood a short, balding man holding a plate of food; threat neutralized. He introduced himself as my new neighbor and offered me juice and *zalābiya,* fried dough, like my mom would make special for me. I thanked him, said good night, and closed the door, too anxious to do anything else. As I lay in bed, staring into the darkness, I realized I hadn't even invited him in for tea. *Ana hemar,* I thought. *How shameful.* As I drifted off to sleep I promised myself that next time, next time I would invite him in.

◇◇◇

CHAPTER 14

CLEAR AND PRESENT DANGER

The international community takes notice as conditions deteriorate

T he morning of March 19 brought startling news: Saleh loyalists, allied with the Houthis against Hadi, had stormed the Aden International Airport. The fighting started early in the morning when Saleh's special police force attacked pro-Hadi forces. Commercial planes were sprayed with gunfire, and at least two shells were dropped, killing three. In the end, though, the Houthis and Saleh loyalists took the base.

I felt sick. The fighting was miles from where I lived, but I couldn't help but think of the people who'd been killed and injured. Three dead—was this the beginning or the end? I heard a warplane overhead, and I knew that we weren't done with the grieving and the dying.

And for what? Was it just about north or south leadership, or were there bigger forces at place? If the Iranians were intervening on behalf of the Houthis, it was most likely at the behest of former president Saleh. Was this all for Saleh, or was this a fight between Saudi Arabia and Iran? And what interests did Russia, the United States, and China have in the outcome?

Was this a military battle, or a war against civilians? Sana'a was of strategic importance. What would happen to my parents and siblings if the fighting intensified there? Almost two million people lived in the area. One stray bomb or shell could wipe out entire families.

And for what?

◇◇◇◇◇◇

I contacted my program manager at Oxfam to find out what the situation was like at the office. He'd been away on holiday the entirety of my three-day tenure, but I figured that I should take him up on his previous offer to let him know if he could be of any assistance.

"Things are okay here. The Houthis will be coming, but it's nothing to worry about," he said with a move-along-nothing-to-see-here attitude. "They'll take the city in twenty-four hours. Things will be calm again."

I wasn't certain if he was even back in Aden. How could he assess the situation clearly? But I didn't want to press him too much and make a bad impression, so I hung up without asking him any follow-up. I'd been at Oxfam so briefly and taken the job under such hurried circumstances, I had no idea how long the man had even been in Yemen, for that matter. For all I knew, he had just come here from his home country of Sudan. Given what I knew about Sudan and its up-heavals and struggles, the man's nonchalance was hard-earned and a necessary survival tool, but I wanted a better on-the-ground view of the situation.

So I called Aidroos, the driver who'd shown me around.

"Mr. Mohammed, I'm very sorry, but I will not be able to come to get you to the office. I cannot leave my house. I'm in Al-Ma'ala; there is fighting here."

I thanked him and hesitated before wishing him well. I didn't want him to think that I was frightened on his behalf.

Calls to the other two drivers produced the same result. They each lived in the Al-Ma'ala neighborhood. They wanted to stay with family, to make certain that they were safe. I thanked them, grateful for confirmation of some of the media reports. Clashes had erupted throughout the city.

As soon as I hung up, my cell phone rang. It was my father.

My father never called.

"Can you come to Sana'a?" he said. No time for formalities.

"What do you mean?"

"Can you come home? We want you to be safe."

His tone was even, calm. This was the first time he wasn't angry with me in . . . years. I felt my mouth go dry. Things must be really, really bad. But I couldn't go home; not enough time had passed. I had a target on my back, and I couldn't compromise my mother, my sisters, my father . . .

"I'm fine," I said. Trying my best to sound like an Al Samawi. "There's no need for me to come home. Things are well here. I don't know what you're hearing, but please don't upset yourself by believing it. If I need anything, I can call Uncle Kamal."

There was a lengthy pause, and then he said, "Okay," sounding satisfied.

A few minutes later, my mother called, her words quick and clipped. "What is going on there?" she asked. "Are you okay? I've been trying to reach Kamal. He won't answer the phone. Is he in danger?"

I reassured her, just as I had my father. "Everything is okay. I am okay. There's no need to worry."

"Are you eating?" she asked.

"I'm trying," I answered, truthfully.

"Go to the market. They will have prepared foods there. Go before the places get shut down. Bring back as much with you as you can."

I promised her I would. I was twenty-eight and didn't like being fussed over like a child. But she was right. There was a reason she worried about my ability to care for myself, even under the best of circumstances.

I walked out of my building, straight to the market. I thought I would find it bustling, business as usual, Yemeni style; but instead I found a locked and gated entrance. I ran my hand along the metal and read its oxidized surface as if it were braille.

This is not good.

I turned away from the door and saw a few men quick-stepping their way home, robes luffing like a ship's sails. I shrugged my empty backpack onto my good shoulder; I never thought I'd complain that it was too light. I had a small bottle of milk at home, a packet of cookies, and a box of cornflakes. That would have to do. I walked home as quickly as I could, conscious of how much friction my right foot produced, of the dust devils that swirled in my wake. I kept my eyes trained in front of me, away from the deepening shadows of the late afternoon. *I have a mustache,* I thought. *I have to take care of myself.*

Having made it home without incident, I called a woman I knew who worked in Oxfam's Sana'a office.

"Hi, Rehab, how are you?"

"Everything here is crazy. I hear it's bad there, with the Houthis coming. I've been told that Oxfam is trying to come up with a plan to get its people out of Aden. They've already done that here."

"What do you mean?"

"All the international staff has been evacuated."

"All of them?" I asked, wondering why I hadn't heard about this from my own office.

"Yes. Country representatives, too. I'm in Sana'a. Many of the others are with me. We're trying to do what we can, but it's hard from here. How can we get you out?"

Rehab was on the verge of tears. I didn't want to make things worse for her. "Please don't worry. I'm fine here. I'm not frightened. It's a big city. I have nothing important that they might want."

I wanted to believe the words I was saying, but I didn't want Rehab to. I needed her to send help. I understood why Oxfam would evacuate foreign workers. These people had come to the country voluntarily, to help us. But what about us, the Yemenis? What could be done for someone like Rehab, for someone like Aidroos, for someone like me, a Yemeni, a peace activist with ties to Jews? What could or would Oxfam do?

A faint boom echoed from the distance. The muffled thuds of artillery shells followed. They were growing faster, and louder. They were moving this way.

I dialed my uncle's number, hoping that I could speak to him and that he'd have some guidance. My phone beeped ... and beeped ... and beeped, but the only response was the crunch and crackle of a city on fire. My phone slipped out of my hand. I crouched down to pick it up; I needed someone to speak to me, to give me advice. I called Ahmed.

"I don't know what to do."

"Yes you do," he said, dispensing with his usual humor. "Stay where you are and stay calm."

"I'm freaking out," I went on, grateful that I had someone with whom I could be honest.

"That's natural," he said. "That's okay. Freak out a bit and then get calm again."

I told him what I'd learned from Rehab and from the drivers here in Aden.

"One of them sounded so worried, Ahmed. I feel bad for him. He has a family."

"I think you should call him again, check on him. That will help take your mind somewhere else."

"I will. I should. Maybe."

"Do you have anyone you can go to? Being alone is making things worse. You can't cook. You have very little food. No one to talk to."

"I'm talking to you."

"You know what I mean. I know how you can be. Too much of being alone will make you crazy."

I was about to protest, but he cut me off.

"I know you don't like to ask for help, but it's okay. You're not being weak; you're being practical. Anyone would need help at this time."

When Ahmed and I hung up I felt better, but that didn't mean I listened. Instead of finding help, I sat down on the couch and watched the news. I turned the volume up as high as it would go, to drown out the sounds of the shelling and to be certain I caught every word, every detail. I sat there blinking, as if the sound waves were crashing against my face. I wished, not for the first time, that I could drive. Outside, cars streamed past. I scanned them hoping to see a taxi, but none appeared. I paced around the apartment, thought of the cornflakes but decided against them. I knew that if I started eating, I wouldn't be able to stop.

Again, I phoned my uncle; again, no response. This time, I texted him. "Uncle, I'm a little bit afraid. I haven't heard from you. Are you well? Please respond." By the time I sent it, I wished I could press unsend. I sounded too needy. Maybe I should text him again?

My mother called me one last time. She asked again about her brother. She told me she had friends she could call.

"Yes," I said, trying to comfort her. "I have a friend here also. If I need to, I will call."

The shadows lengthened, and as night fell, I heard shouts of "*Allahu akbar!*" reverberate off the building, sending shrapnel of worry through my spine. I looked out the window. Al Qaeda fighters.

"Come out of your homes and join the jihad!" they called, shooting their guns into the air. An explosion punctuated the night, and a few seconds later, the power went out.

Unlike in Sana'a, where rolling blackouts were commonplace, the electrical grid in Aden was legendary. The fact that it had been breached pushed my fear to another level. This wasn't an average skirmish. On the Internet, the discussion focused on Iran and Saudi Arabia. Rumors swirled that the Houthis up north had gotten a major injection of supplies from Iran, their fellow Shia nation, and that Saudi Arabia, its archrival, was funneling major military support to its fellow Sunnis, AQAP. Was this true? Both countries seemed equally intent on having "their" people conquer Aden, a strategic location that controlled the seaport and the airport. Was this how Yemen would use the millions of dollars in military equipment that the American government had given the Yemeni government back in 2012?

I grabbed my laptop, my phone, and a blanket and pillow and hunkered down in the bathroom. I lay against the tub, my weight against the porcelain. Soon it was no cooler than pottery from a kiln. No power meant no air-conditioning, and the temperature in my bunker was beginning to climb. I was dehydrated. Whatever managed to leak out of me dried immediately, leaving a thin crust of salt on my skin.

The light of my phone cast an eerie glow. I checked Facebook:

Aden is under attack.

Pray for Aden.

Houthis have run wild.

Through bleary eyes, I read the newsfeeds. Headlines called this a war between Sunni and Shia. But how could that be? Before the war, for as long as I could remember, there was no difference between Sunni and Shia. A Muslim was a Muslim.

Stiff and sore, I tried to rise to my feet, but my head swam from thirst and hunger. Leaning across the doorway, I waited for my vision to clear. If I could make it as far as the couch, I'd be better off. A single gooseneck lamp stood in the living room, powerless. It reminded me of a giant question mark.

◇◇◇◇◇◇

I slept through the morning of the twentieth, the city surprisingly still. When I checked the news on my phone, I understood why. There'd been a brace of terrorist attacks in Sana'a. Two pairs of suicide bombers had attacked the al-Badr and al-Hashoosh mosques during Friday midday prayers, and the death toll had climbed to 142, with more than 350 wounded. This was the deadliest terrorist attack in Yemen's history. Islamic State of Iraq and the Levant (ISIL), an offshoot of Al

Qaeda, eventually claimed responsibility. They targeted Shia/Houthi worshippers, hoping to make a statement against Iran's involvement in backing the northerners.

I immediately phoned home. I didn't know anyone who worshipped at those mosques, but I needed to hear that my family was okay. The destruction was incomprehensible. My mother picked up and assured me that everyone was well, but the tremor in her voice told a different story.

"We are glad that you made the decision you did." She paused for a few beats and I could hear her breathe. "I think your father better understands why you were in such a hurry to get to Aden."

We didn't say anything more on the subject, but there was an unspoken understanding between my mother and me. Somehow, she'd intuited the situation in a way that my father could not. We each promised the other to be well, to be safe, to be cautious—and I pressed the end button.

◇◇◇◇◇◇

On Saturday, March 21, the United States evacuated its remaining troops and special forces from Yemen. Between the Houthis' and Al Qaeda's growing presence in and around Aden, the threat was too great.

The State Department released a statement in support of President Hadi. "We call upon the Houthis, former President Ali Abdallah Saleh, and their allies to stop their violent incitement that threatens President Hadi, Yemeni government officials, and innocent civilians."

Simultaneously, Hadi, who'd been absent since arriving in Aden, made his first appearance. He, too, demanded that the Houthis pull their forces out of Sana'a, return their weapons, and abandon their project in Aden. "We shall deliver the country to safety and raise Yemen's flag on Mount Marran in Saadeh instead of the Iranian flag." This was the first public accusation that Iran was actively colluding with the Houthis.

Emboldened, Team Hadi pushed their advantage. The Saudis launched airstrikes against Sana'a (now a Houthi stronghold), and Al Qaeda fighters were reported to have taken revenge against any Shia living in Aden. In reaction, the Houthis put out their own declaration calling for "mobilization" against Hadi and any of his Sunni supporters.

Taking advantage of the temporary power supply, I clicked for updates. An image appeared on my laptop. Unkempt and tangled hair. A shaggy shrub of brows. Then a thin ribbon of red from the cheekbone down to the lips, and the white bone of the chin. A slice through a piece of meat. I X'ed out of the window and wrote my own status update: "Al Qaeda exacts punishment on Shia from the north. Violence intensifies as key stronghold hangs in the balance."

The time for pretense was over. No more reassuring others. No more trying to make my father proud. No more compensating for my disability by trying to be more or better than. It was time for just the truth. I needed help.

I spent the rest of the day sending messages to anyone I knew. I began with my friends and colleagues in Yemen. The message was simple: *I don't have much food. I don't have a way to move from place to place. I need somewhere to go so that I can be safe. Can you help me at all?* No one could offer any assistance. You can't save a drowning man if you're drowning yourself. I expanded my net, messaging anyone I'd ever met across the Middle East. Most people didn't reply; a couple offered to pray for me.

By the time evening fell, my phone was down to 6 percent. I grabbed my cable and plugged in my phone and my laptop. I couldn't let myself fall asleep. I couldn't risk the power blinking out. Without connectivity, I would be absolutely alone. True, I had a landline, but who knew how long the phone lines would hold. I felt that if my batteries died, I would die along with them.

I retreated to the bathroom, where I walked tight circles around myself. When the anxiety grew too overwhelming, I hurried out to the living room, over to the window. I crawled over to my laptop and crouched to open another window, caught between an impulse to see everything and to shut it all out.

A ping pulled me out of my head. Tina, the woman I'd met at the MJC conference in 2013, had responded to my request for help. She wrote that she wanted to do whatever she could. She was going to reach out to everyone she knew. She'd put everything in her life on hold.

I didn't know what to say. She was on a tight deadline for her book, and on top of that, she was going to be moving soon.

Then she asked if I remembered an American by the name of Daniel Pincus.

Yes, I replied. *I met him in Sarajevo. He is the man who stood on his head.*

Contact him, she said. *I believe he'll be able to help you.*

CHAPTER 15

◇◇◇

CALL TO PRAYER

A photo my uncle took of an explosion in Aden

I spent the following day writing and rewriting a message until the letters lost their meaning. Right before midnight, I pressed send.

March 22, 2015

Hello Daniel,

I hope everything is great in your side!

I hope you still remember me. I was speaking to Tina—and we thought it will be a good idea if I ask you if you can help me out. If you watch the news lately, you may have heard about what's happening in Yemen lately. For that I am writing the following request. If you know someone who could help please let me know.

I hoped. And I prayed. And ten minutes later, I received a message. It was from Daniel.

He asked if we could move from Facebook to Skype, and when he picked up, I heard music in the background, people talking and laughing. It was seven hours earlier in New York.

"Is this a bad time?" I asked, hoping against hope that it wasn't.

"No such thing," he said. "I'm just at a wedding. How can I help?"

We talked in spurts, my connection freezing up every minute or so. Daniel said he'd do what he could to help, and before we signed off, he asked me to send him my résumé. I promised I would, and thanked him for his time. Then I shut down my laptop for the night and retreated to the bathroom to collapse on the floor and fall asleep.

Monday morning, March 23, I woke up with a mission: revise and update my résumé. It was a strange exercise at a time like this, but I didn't care. Finally, I had something to *do*. For three days, I'd been receiving snatches of advice and well-wishes, but this was my first concrete action. Daniel had given me a task to accomplish, which meant I had something to focus on besides the uncertainty of waiting.

While I worked into the afternoon trying to think of as many "active verbs" as possible, Daniel was waking up in his prewar loft in Manhattan, ready to start his week. His apartment, covered in tarps and a thick layer of dust, was under renovation. He fought through the layers of plastic to find his backpack, and then was off to his office. A biomedical engineer, he worked at a consulting firm—a far cry from the Muslim Jewish Conference. He arrived at his office—bare, save for a single loose photograph of his family—and took out his laptop. Sitting in his ergonomic chair, he read up on the situation in Yemen.

The Houthis, a group of Shia rebel fighters from the north, had taken over the capital of Sana'a. They sided with the former president, Saleh, and were receiving support from Iran—a fellow Shia nation. Meanwhile, Al Qaeda, Sunni fighters from the south, had moved into Aden. They supported the recently deposed president Hadi, a fellow Sunni, and were possibly receiving backing from Saudi Arabia—a Sunni nation, which was also the regional archenemy of Iran. The ground fighting was concentrated in Aden, a strategic location, as whoever controlled the city would control the seaport and the airport.

It sounded bad, but while all this was happening, Daniel knew that Iran was negotiating the nuclear deal with the P5+1, the five permanent members of the UN Security Council: China, France, Russia, the United States, and the United Kingdom, with the addition of Germany. The proposed agreement called for Iran to reduce its stockpile of uranium and limit its nuclear-related activities for ten-plus years, and in exchange, countries around the world promised to lift their economic sanctions on Iran. If all went according to plan, this would be a huge boost for Iran, and it would threaten to tip the Saudi/Iranian balance of power in Iran's favor. Surely Iran wouldn't compromise the Joint Comprehensive Plan of Action negotiations to get into a pissing match with Saudi Arabia over Yemen.

The cost/benefit seemed clear. In Daniel's estimation, the fighting in Yemen would die down, but just in case it didn't, he started to look for a country that might let me in. He sent my résumé to a series of friends: an Egyptian human rights activist, a friend running an NGO in Uganda/Rwanda, an Egyptian American interfaith activist, and the head of the Africa Institute at the American Jewish Committee.

Then he sent me a message: You're not alone.

◇◇◇◇◇◇

Nearly 5,600 miles away from New York, Megan Hallahan and Natasha Westheimer were meeting at a bar. They weren't discussing the U.S. presidential election, or new art exhibitions. They were discussing me.

Within five minutes of opening Megan's email, Natasha responded: "Have you contacted the State Department?"

Natasha, who'd spent the summer of 2013 interning at the Global Programming division of the State Department, believed in the system. The U.S. government was set up for this; some programs even issued grants to activists in urgent need of legal counsel or relocation.

No, Megan replied when she woke up. She hadn't. Did Natasha want to pursue the lead?

The two women decided to meet for a drink that evening. Which is how at 6 P.M. on Monday, March 23, the two ladies were sitting together in the Florentin section of Tel Aviv. As they sipped their cocktails, both admitted that they knew next to nothing about Yemen. I was the only Yemeni they'd ever met. The first step, then, would be research.

◇◇◇◇◇

Ten time zones away from Tel Aviv, Justin Hefter was getting off a plane in San Francisco. He'd just returned from a weekend skiing with friends in Utah and was in desperate need of sleep; but even more urgently, he needed some new investors for Bandura Games, the company he'd started fresh out of college. The start-up world was a killer, and it was time to bear down or give up.

After putting in a solid eight hours at his computer, Justin crawled into bed. He normally stayed up until the early hours of the morning, but the weekend had left him wrecked. He'd completely forgotten about the email he'd sent Megan early that morning until he felt around his nightstand and pulled off the book he'd been reading, *In the Garden of Beasts* by Erik Larson, the story of Germany in 1933 and the men in power who did absolutely nothing to change the fate of millions of people. It would have been easy to dismiss this as coincidence, but Justin was too accustomed to finding connections, patterns. Was he in a position to help change someone's fate? Was he going to sit by and do nothing? He dozed off, but when he woke up the next morning, the questions had hardened. He tried to focus on fund-raising goals, but throughout the day his mind was somewhere else.

Raised in an observant Jewish family in Highland Park, Illinois, Justin grew up hearing stories of his parents' activism. In the 1980s, they helped a Jewish family escape religious persecution in the USSR. His mother marched on Washington in support of the Soviet Jewry movement; his father helped a Bangladeshi Muslim immigrate to Canada. They pushed Justin into philanthropy and community service. As preparation for his bar mitzvah, he exchanged letters with a seventy-something-year-old Muslim man from Croatia who revealed that during World War II, his family had helped save a Jewish family. In fact, he was listed as one of the thirty-four Righteous Gentiles in the synagogue in Zagreb. If his family had been discovered, they would have been executed. The selflessness, the activism was mind-boggling. But perhaps if there had been more people like this, Justin's paternal grandmother wouldn't have lost seventy-six relatives in the Holocaust.

Tikkun olam, he thought. *Repair the world.*

It was 5:37 A.M. on Wednesday, March 25, when a new Facebook message pinged onto my phone. It was Justin Hefter. "Hey, I heard about your situation. Send me an email on how I can help. Do you need an invitation out of the country? A job? A place to stay?" He asked me what religion I was, if I had a dual citizenship. I ignored the former and answered the latter: "No. I'm just Yemeni."

And with that, Justin scrolled through his contacts and dashed off an email to a former professor of his at Stanford who'd once worked as a naval submarine commander, and later served as an assistant to the secretary of the navy. He asked whether it was possible to evacuate a Yemeni onto one of the U.S. Navy's aircraft carriers in the Gulf of Aden. Minutes later, he received a call. It was from his professor.

"Justin," a deep voice said. "You need to change your passwords immediately. Someone is trying to use your email account to ascertain the location of U.S. warships."

Oops. Justin backtracked. After his hasty explanation of the situation, the professor let out a long sigh.

"Justin, how well do you know this guy?" he asked.

"Not well," Justin said.

"So how do you know he is who he says he is?"

"I don't," Justin said.

"And how can you trust that the messages are coming from him? I mean, even if he is who he's claiming to be, isn't it possible that someone might have hacked his account and is trying to get sensitive information?"

Justin hadn't thought of that.

"I think, rather than trying to seek a military solution, you should try to seek a diplomatic one. Get in touch with the officials at embassies that are still open in Yemen. It may take some time, but the diplomatic corps have more experience dealing with issues like this. Why use a hammer when a scalpel might be the better tool?"

And with that, they hung up.

◇◇◇◇◇

Unable to fall back asleep, I stood and stretched my cramped muscles. There was a quiet in the air; the sound of a city still asleep. Only a few isolated pops disturbed the illusion of peace. I was glued to Facebook. By the afternoon, I found posts reporting that Al Qaeda had issued an ultimatum:

"Anyone who is Shia or from the north has 24 hours to leave Aden or we will deal with them." The streets were filled with the smell of burning wood. I wanted to leave, but couldn't. There was a checkpoint right at the foot of my building. If I got caught by Al Qaeda, I'd be identified as an enemy right away. As a northern Yemeni, I had lighter skin, distinctive facial features, and an equally distinctive accent/dialect. Not to mention that my surname, as listed on my government-issued ID, was a renowned Shia name. I stood out by my appearance, my voice, and my name.

But even if I did manage to slip by, what then? Aden is on a volcanic peninsula and the only two roads to the mainland passed right around the airport on the isthmus. The problem was, the Houthi militia and allied army had already seized Aden International Airport, and just that morning they had secured the air base near Lahij, where up until the previous Saturday U.S. and European troops were training local Yemenis to fight against Al Qaeda.

Unconfirmed reports plastered my Twitter feed: President Hadi had left the country, fleeing on a helicopter to Saudi Arabia, or a boat to Djibouti. Houthis had announced a $100,000 bounty for his arrest. Al Qaeda had opened up military storehouses, handing out guns and ammunition to its supporters, some of whom were involved in the Popular Committee. People were looting Hadi's compound, men running through the streets holding toilet seats and gates and windows, anything they might be able to sell later. Saudi Arabia had moved armored forces to the border.

A message from Daniel crossed my screen. His initial assessment of the war had been wrong, he typed. It didn't look like the Houthis were backing down, and it seemed like the recently crowned Saudi King Salman and his twenty-nine-year-old minister of defense wanted an opportunity to display their strength to Iran. And they were strong— the United States had recently sold Saudi Arabia $60 billion in military equipment. Yemen, a country that controlled the southern entrance to the Red Sea and Suez Canal, was about to become the theater for their devastating and ruthless show of force.

"Are you okay?" Daniel typed. "Do you have food? Could you list your assets?"

I thought of my mother and her concern for my diet; it was the simple questions that showed the depth of one's humanity. I looked at the nearly empty shelves. Canned tuna, potato chips, chocolates, cookies, milk, juice, fifteen liters of bottled water, IBM laptop, Android, land-line phone, 3G voice/data service, electricity (intermittent), wallet, six U.S. hundred-dollar bills, a few thousand rials ($100 USD equivalent), and my Yemeni identification card. Not among my assets—my passport. In my rush to escape Sana'a, I'd left it in my apartment. Leaving the country had never been part of the plan.

His reply came short and sweet: "Hang in there. I'll see what I can do."

Daniel logged off Facebook; he had a busy evening. While I tried to sleep, he headed to the basement of New York City's Temple Emanu-El for the American Jewish Committee's ACCESS interfaith model Passover seder. An advocacy group founded all the way back in 1906, the American Jewish Committee worked to preserve the civil liberties of Jews in the United States, and to advocate for human rights for all people in America and elsewhere. ACCESS, a newer program, was the young professionals' subdivision.

After forty minutes on the subway, Daniel joined a group of twenty-and thirty-year-olds from America, Italy, Japan, Africa, Korea, Switzerland, and Germany who'd gathered to discuss the story and themes of Passover and how they were relevant to young people around the world. Sometime during the telling of the Exodus, Daniel mentioned my situation to a friend of his, Alexis Frankel, the staff director of the national ACCESS program. Alexis shook her head, processing. Of course she knew me. She happened to have attended the same 2013 Muslim Jewish Conference as I did, and remembered me well. She promised Daniel she would see what she could do to help.

I woke up in the middle of the night to footsteps and voices outside my door.

"We should go there. It's just opposite the bank. Directly across the street from it."

"What can we get there that we can't get here?"

"I heard he has a lot of gold."

"Who has gold?"

"The old man I'm telling you about."

"And you believe this?"

"Yes. Why not? His people are from Sana'a. Very wealthy. Televisions. Computers. Jewelry. Watches."

"And if he's there?"

"We take him."

"Hostage? Ransom?"

"We'll have enough. We kill him."

I sat frozen in place as their voices faded down the stairwell.

Who were these people? Were they my neighbors? Did killing a northerner mean nothing to them? I thought of the old man they were discussing. Would he be able to fight back?

What would they do if they found me?

I thought again of Al Qaeda's ultimatum, the death threats I'd received. Voices brought the danger to life in a way that words on a screen could not. This wasn't like hearing the dialogue of a TV show drifting down the hall from another apartment. This was real.

I took deep breaths and told myself I just had to make it through the night. Analysts had predicted that by morning the Houthis would control the entire city. The north would take back power. What they hadn't predicted was that Saudi Arabia, along with a coalition of Arab nations, would begin airstrikes in Aden. The tide was about to turn.

◇◇◇

CHAPTER 16

THE JUSTICE LEAGUE

My rations in my apartment in Aden

Thursday, March 26, arrived with a text message from Justin. He'd sent it at 5:19 P.M. his time, 3:19 A.M. mine:

Hey Mohammed, I have a friend from the UN who might be able to help, but what is it exactly that you need? Why can't you fly

to Egypt and stay with someone for a short while just to be safe? Do
you need an official invitation? Let me know more details about what
will be helpful.

I didn't have the answers; my thoughts raced along with the news
crawl on my screen. Saudi Arabia was bombing key locations in Sana'a;
the kingdom had 150,000 soldiers ready for a ground offensive. Egypt,
Pakistan, Jordan, and Sudan were also preparing to send troops.

A new post appeared on my feed.

DANIEL PINCUS: Anyone have any idea how to quickly get a Yemeni
citizen out of Aden, Yemen?

Comments started to trickle down the page. There were a series of
well-wishes and positive thoughts, and one guy even offered to buy my
ticket to the United States should I ever get out of the country. The offer
was generous—and absurd. Even in the best of times, Yemenis seldom
got visas to enter the United States.

I messaged Daniel to see if he had any updates. He told me he was
looking into flights, but he didn't know if he'd be able to find a country
willing to issue a visa or to let me in without a passport. His goal, he
said, was to find a person or a company in another country—probably
Africa—to sponsor a visa. His logic: *If you can't push yourself out, we
need to find someone to pull you in*. I said I might not need a visa
for Jordan or Egypt, and Daniel said he'd also look into Ethiopia. But
would anyone let me fly without a passport? I kicked myself and wondered if this oversight would cost me my life.

After several more minutes, Daniel decided he'd go ahead and buy
me a commercial flight out of Aden. "Let's hope that someone at the
Egypt Air counter has a heart and will let you on without a passport,"
he said over Skype. But as he clicked the "purchase" button, the flight
was canceled. Frantically, he tried another travel site. But after scroll-
ing through site after site, it seemed that *all* flights from Yemen to
Egypt had been canceled, and the few countries that had allowed

Yemenis to enter without applying in advance for a visa had changed their policies.

Over the next two hours or so, Daniel and I exchanged messages off and on. I told him I had a contact at an NGO in Yemen, and she said that all international staff were being airlifted out. Daniel was enthused and urged me to get on their flight, but I wasn't sure how that would work; I wasn't "international staff."

He suggested posting on the website Movements.org, where activists and people who want to help activists can connect. I told him I'd already posted, back on March 18. I didn't mention that I'd only received four responses, none of which had led to much, though there was one young woman, Irina Tsukerman, who seemed very intent on helping.

Instead I messaged: "A friend of mine advised me to leave my apartment, even if I already paid the rent. She said I should take the loss and move somewhere safer. Maybe closer to my uncle." There was a pause, then a new message arrived.

"Who is your friend?"

I told him about Irina, whom he—surprisingly—already knew through AJC. Then I mentioned Megan.

"Huh," he typed, thinking out loud. "Could you put us all in touch?"

With a new task at hand, I sat down at my laptop to compose an email.

Dear Daniel, Dear Megan, Dear Irina,

I hope my email finds you well!

I am sending this email so we all can coordinate to help me to leave Yemen ASAP safely.

Megan knows my situation from the beginning. She is the one who's trying to help me from the start, she is from Yala Young Leaders and she knows me well. Megan has connection with ASHOKA.

Daniel is from MJC. Daniel is the most kind person I have ever met and he is the one who advised me to do coordination between us. Daniel is trying to communicate with different INGOs about my situation.

Irina, she is so kind with me and trying to help even she never met me and she only knows me after I put a request on movements.org and she has connections in the UN.

Quick updates about today:

I have enough food for a week I believe.

I have money but not much after renting the apartment.

The airport is closed in Aden and Sana'a but there is a news I received that a flight will take all the international workers in Aden to Jordan or Egypt.

All the roads outside Aden are closed.

Gun shooting and explosion was heard all the day every couple of hours.

The situation in Sana'a today is worse because of the Saudi airstrikes.

Aden become a city of looting.

Qaida or the popular committees is searching for Houthis, I am afraid because of my surname.

My Family name is popular as Zaidi.

Please keep communicating to each other and share what you tried to do or what are you planning to do, share your networks or any information.

Thank you all.

Mohammed

After receiving the message, Megan emailed back: "Good idea to coordinate together on one thread. I'm looping in Nimrod, Nizar, Rexy, Justin, Tiffany, Nadine, and Hamze who have all been trying to help . . ."

And just like that, my own personal Justice League came together, a loose coalition of very different personalities: Daniel, the can-do engineer. Natasha, the empathetic environmentalist. Megan, the operational taskmaster. Irina, the connector. Justin, the dogged optimist . . . And there were others I didn't even know about. Now we all had a central thread where people could come together to brainstorm and pool our resources.

Megan went through her Rolodex to find useful contacts, though she was unable to officially leverage her position at YaLa Young Leaders, since this wasn't an official YaLa initiative; and Irina sent emails to her contacts at the UN.

Justin, following his professor's advice, suggested that they look into embassies, and named Saudi Arabia, Qatar, and Russia as possibilities. I replied that Russia was the only one that might still be open; all the others had closed. So he turned to LinkedIn for leads. He identified Safer Yemen as a target, and found that the Head of Risk Analysis was a third-degree connection. He messaged their shared third-degree contact, who put him in touch with her second-degree contact, who put him in touch with the person he'd been trying to reach from the start. Each response fell into place within two hours. *This works,* he thought. *This kind of ladder system gets to people. No one is saying no here.*

Meanwhile, Daniel went to dinner with his friend Toby Locke, a human rights activist known for pushing the boundaries. Daniel explained my situation, and Toby said he would help. This was in fact the exact sort of work that he did. By the end of the evening, he promised he'd follow up for more information and mobilize his network of aides and officials in D.C.

I sat at my laptop, reading updates and replying, letting the soft *clack-clack* of the keyboard lull me into a state of placidity. Suddenly, a cry of *"Allahu akbar!"* broke through the white noise of the afternoon. "The war is here! The Houthis have come to fight us!" I edged toward the window that overlooked the main avenue that passed by my building and nudged the curtain aside with a thumb. On the horizon, plumes of smoke looked like cotton candy above the low skyline. It was almost beautiful.

Houthis.

Army loyalists.

AQAP.

ISIL.

The Popular Committee.

Up and down the streets, dozens and dozens of people ran, limbs flailing. The southerners fired on Houthi rebels with small arms; the invaders launched rocket-propelled grenades and mortars.

I posted a running commentary to Facebook:

Houthis in Aden

Explosions Now

Aden Airport is Closed

Looting in Aden

War is Ugly

I uploaded video of street scenes outside my window, men running for cover to a soundtrack of distant sounds of gunfire and artillery rounds being fired. The Saudi air force had bombed the airport in Sana'a. I wasn't certain if my family wanted to leave the city, but if it came to that, they wouldn't be able to book a flight. Also, if the Saudis were capable of dropping bombs in Sana'a, what was to keep them from doing the same in Aden?

By nightfall my eyes were bleary from texting and typing. I needed rest. I needed water.

I wished that the rheumy liquid that came out of the faucets was potable. Rationing the few bottles of water that remained was a torture—dehydration worsened my screen-weary eyes. I reminded myself that I wasn't alone in this situation. Millions of Yemenis in Aden, Sana'a, and elsewhere were in equally dire straits—many in worse shape. I hadn't wanted to keep track of the death toll. The images I saw of the destruction were enough. Numbers would only numb.

Before retreating to the bathroom to sleep, I checked my devices once again to make sure the batteries were at a safe level, flashing consistently, like the monitors I used to watch at the hospital while my father worked on his patients. Something caught my eye: a picture of President Hadi arriving at the airport in Riyadh, Saudi Arabia's capital city, being greeted by Saudi prince Mohammed bin Salman Al Saud. If anyone had refused to believe the speculation before, it was now clear. The battle lines were drawn:

—The Houthis, pro-Saleh loyalists, and the members of Iran's Revolutionary Guard

—Al Qaeda, Hadi, the Popular Committees, and the Southern Movement, all of whom would be aided with air and naval support from Saudi Arabia, Qatar, the United Arab Emirates, Bahrain, Egypt, Jordan, Kuwait, Morocco, and Sudan

Exhausted, I left the world with one final post: *This isn't Sodom and Gomorrah. This isn't a post-apocalyptic thriller. This is my home.*

CHAPTER 17

◇◇◇

THE ONES WHO SAID YES

Daniel's Facebook profile picture

Friday, March 27, 7:00 A.M., and Aden was already boiling. Overnight, Megan had sent me an email and cc'ed the team:

I'm writing to anyone I know at the UN or with links to the Indian Government. But let us know if you hear of any other embassies still open or about to close down. Is it true that all the Egyptians have already been evacuated? Also are you anywhere near the Catholic Church?

India? That was a new idea. Justin immediately began a new search. One window followed another, and soon he was clicking through sixteen tabs of news reports. He emailed his mother: "I think the India thing might be the last hope for Mohammed. He is talking now as if he is giving up evacuating and just trying to stay and be safe."

Fully aware of her son's dogged pursuit of answers, Justin's mother reached out to a contact at the Indian embassy in the United States, as well as an important activist named William Bleaker, a man with a long record of international activism, who happened to have a particularly close relationship with the higher-ups in the Indian government. Bleaker connected with Justin and told him that the Indian embassy was indeed still open, and that they were going to be evacuating thousands of their own citizens from Yemen. Perhaps they'd be able to include Justin's friend on one of the ships?

Justin sent me a recap, and after I finished reading, I scrambled to my feet. My head started to spin from the drop in blood pressure. I needed food and water. My eyes adjusted to the sun beating through the thin curtains as I pushed myself into the kitchen. I'd already depleted my rations by half, and I didn't know how much longer they had to last me. I savored the sweetness of a single sugar cookie and the saltiness of a couple of potato chips. They both dried out my mouth, and while I hated to wash out the taste of the food, I needed water. My eyelids scratched my eyes as I unscrewed the top from a bottle. Then I put the cap on and forced myself back into the living area. I couldn't afford to eat and drink anything more. I would have to wait at least a few hours before having a meal of canned tuna.

If I was going to survive, I was going to need more water and food, but to get them at black-market rates, I would need more money. And without a job or any incoming rials, I didn't know how that would happen.

Just then, I found a message from Daniel, who, like his namesake in the Bible, seemed able to read dreams. "Do you need any money?" he had asked, offering to send a wire transfer. "Yes," I replied. "Yes, I do." I couldn't worry about my honor at a time like this.

Western Union was still technically open, but they wouldn't have funds until Saturday at the earliest. If the situation was too dangerous, it would take even longer. But the bigger problem was that in order to claim the funds, I would need my passport.

I called home, and my younger brother, Saif, picked up the phone. I was glad it wasn't my mother; I didn't want to add any additional stress to her life. Saif had always been levelheaded, and since he was younger than I was, he treated me with a certain amount of respect. Not like Hussain. There would be no "How could you have left without your passport?" No interrogation or recriminations.

After a brief greeting and exchange of news—the family was well, the neighborhood relatively calm, the battles distant—I asked him to go to my floor of the house to retrieve my passport. He agreed, no questions asked. I was grateful. Better to not have my family worry about where I might be going. He promised to update me on progress, and we said goodbye. Five minutes later, my phone buzzed.

"Mohammed, I'm sorry. I couldn't get in your apartment. The door is locked."

"Of course," I said, not sure where to direct my exasperation.

"I'm sorry. I tried to get it open."

"No, Saif, I'm not upset with you, just the situation. I wouldn't ask you for this if it wasn't serious. You need to get in there any way you can. Take the door off the hinges. Knock it down. *I need that passport.*"

"I will try. I'm trying to be quiet. Father needs it to be restful."

I shut my eyes and bobbed my head, a nod he couldn't see.

Fortunately, Saif was easily able to break into my apartment, which was something I decided to worry about later. The next hurdle was higher. How was he going to get the passport to me? We had no courier services, mail was irregularly delivered at the best of times, and flights were not an option. Who would be willing to drive more than eight hours into a war zone? I wouldn't ask him to come himself, but did he know anyone desperate for money?

My brother asked around and learned that attitudes in the north were shifting. Some of our friends in Sana'a, people originally from the south, were getting nervous. Reports were circulating that northerners in Aden were being rounded up and killed or imprisoned. They feared that their neighbors in Sana'a would retaliate with house-to-house searches and reprisals. Many of these people decided to flee Sana'a and return to Aden, despite the fact that it was going up in flames. One of Saif's friends was part of this migration, and so my brother asked if he'd be willing to carry a small package with him to Aden and give it to me once he arrived in the city. He offered him 3,000 rials, about $12, 1 percent of the average salary. The man took the package. I just needed to wait.

Speaking with my brother disarmed me. I missed my family; I wished my father would talk to me again; I wished I could see my mother. Decades before, she'd grown up on these very streets of Aden, scrabbling for food, haggling and bartering with market vendors, finding scraps of material to use for clothes. Fashioning meals and outfits from what others had discarded. Her family was very poor, and though my mother wasn't the oldest of her siblings, she was a fighter, and she took responsibility for their well-being. When I was young, I heard her stories as if they were school lessons from some dim past that had no real bearing on my life.

Yes, Mother, I know, times were tough. May I please have another helping of chicken ogda? *And why is this flatbread so well done? I don't like it this way. I'm going to my room now. I need to finish the next level on* The Legend of Zelda.

If only she could have joined me now. It was 79 degrees outside and sunny. The clear blue sky was a cruel contrast to the streets darkened by clouds of dust and debris. Trying to lift my spirits, Daniel messaged: *It's a war zone, but at least it's a nice day!*

I cast around for something to say back. Several days earlier, I'd seen someone selling guns outside my building. I grew up around guns—Yemen is second only to the United States in gun ownership—and I wasn't unused to people walking around with rifles slung across their chests and swords stuck inside their pants. That said, I'd never had a gun of my own, so I sent Daniel a Facebook message:

MOHAMMED AL SAMAWI: Do I need to buy a gun or something?

Daniel received my message in the middle of a morning work meeting. Thoughts toppled over each other. *Would owning a gun protect Mohammed or make him a target?* Daniel had no idea.

DANIEL PINCUS: I don't think you'll be able to defend yourself. You may be best off without it.
MOHAMMED AL SAMAWI: True.
DANIEL PINCUS: Pretend you're a mute. Don't talk to anyone.

The advice wasn't the most practical—even if I refused to speak, I was still identifiable as a northerner by my skin tone and facial features—but I was relieved that Daniel was still engaged. Acknowledging his own limitations, he replied that he was going to enlist a security expert.

◇◇◇◇◇

While I waited for an update, Daniel called his friend Eric, who'd been in the U.S. army and fought the Taliban in Afghanistan. He asked Eric whether I should buy a gun, and Eric, who was still active duty, said he couldn't help, but that his friend Cole, who was out of the service, might be able to. On Friday afternoon Eastern Standard Time, Daniel received a call from Cole, retired U.S. military. He began a line of rapid-fire questions to determine the situation:

Who is Mohammed? What is his last name? Where was he born? Where did he spend his life? Is he Sunni or Shia? Is he Zaidi? What city is he in? What neighborhood? Is there electricity and phone service? Does he have a computer, cell phone, landline? Is he inside? What shade is his skin? Does he have a beard? What's his food/water supply? Is he alone? Does he have a car?

Daniel told Cole to hold on.

DANIEL PINCUS: Are you Zaidi Shia?

Why was Daniel asking this? Was there a right answer? Would he block me if I said the wrong thing? How could I make it clear to him, an American, that all the different groups and sects and lines of lineage were as tangled as the mess of power lines outside my window? How could I make him understand when so much of this made no sense to me? And perhaps, most perplexing of all, how was it that I was untangling this knot of identity with a *Jew*?

Shia. Houthi. Shia Iran.

Sunni Saudis. Wahhabi.

When I was growing up, we were all Muslims. Distinctions beyond that didn't seem to exist. A Muslim was a Muslim. Was I just naïve?

I stared at the message, at the tiny icon of a tall, lanky man standing on his head. This was the man to whom I'd entrusted my life. But how to answer this question? I felt torn. I didn't want to be rude. Daniel was working to help me, which meant I needed to be polite, not defensive. But if I could, I would have shouted back, *What does it matter?*

I was a man. I happened to be Muslim. I was a peace activist. I was more than a sect of Islam that my family followed. I was more than an assembly line of labels—none of which had led to anything good. But now, in Aden, these things did matter: they were the difference between life and death.

DANIEL PINCUS: Are you still there?

Tentatively, I replied:

MOHAMMED AL SAMAWI: My family is Zaidi yes.

I didn't know if this answer was "right" or "wrong." I felt the dead weight of my right hand on my lap. I waited, debating for many minutes if I should clarify. The seconds stretched out, torturing me as if I were waiting for Iftar during Ramadan.

DANIEL PINCUS: Ok. I don't care what religion you are. The military experts were asking me your identity to see where you would find security.

I could breathe again. Daniel didn't care about my religion or my family's ethnicity. But who were these military experts, and did they care? Governments looked at labels defined by check boxes.

◇◇◇◇◇◇

After getting his answer, Daniel circled back to Cole. "Zaidi," he said. "And, oh yeah, he's disabled." Without missing a beat, Cole replied, "I have an airline outfit in Nairobi that can have a plane on the ground in Aden in twenty-four hours for $50,000."

Daniel was stunned into silence. He thought Cole was calling to offer advice on whether to buy a gun or not. Instead, he was offering an answer to an entirely different question. While I was pacing around a sixty-square-foot rectangle, Daniel was considering a fundamental moral dilemma. He was prepared to spend $2,000 to help a guy he barely knew—but $50,000?

He sat at his desk with his head in his hands. His colleagues looked over their computer screens and wondered what was going on. They heard talk of "filtration," a common biotech industry term, which was really no cause for alarm. Little did they know he was actually discussing exfiltration.

But Daniel didn't respond to the sidelong looks. He was spinning through the ramifications: was it legal to wire $50,000 to Kenya to hire a plane to fly into a failed state with no permission to enter the airspace or land at an airport that was under siege and take a person with no passport to a country to which he had no visa? What was his liability if the plane was shot down by the Saudis, the Houthis, Al Qaeda, or some kid with an RPG? What happened if the crew was killed or held hostage? What if the Kenyans stole the money? What if Mohammed was killed getting to the airport? Could he even get to the airport? *Did Daniel need a lawyer?*

The pause in the conversation was palpable and awkward. Cole assumed that Daniel was willing to save his friend's life at any expense. If he wasn't prepared to pay the price for a mission like this, why would he have called Eric?

"What are you thinking about?" Cole asked.

"I have no idea how to think about this," Daniel replied.

Cole let the silence sink in before he continued: "Well, maybe you've never dealt with a situation like this before, but I have. So let me tell you the situation your friend is in, and maybe that will help you make a decision. Yemen collapsed and the president fled the country. Yemen may be today where Syria was five years ago: the civil war will get a whole lot worse before it gets any better. The U.S. has evacuated its consular and counterterrorism operations. They were inadequate to stop what seems inevitable: an all-out war. The Saudis bombed the runway at the Sana'a airport and it'll take two weeks to rebuild if they start now, and they're not starting anytime soon. Aden's airport runway is intact, but there's no air traffic control. The airport is under siege and will probably be destroyed soon. Saudis are setting up a no-fly zone and naval blockade, and they're not letting any Yemenis out of the country—they want a clear, decisive end to the Shia revolt. Your friend is alive and not injured. He's in a secure location, for now. He's not hiding in a field, running in the streets, or held hostage—yet. He has a laptop, cell phone, and landline. There's electricity, phone service, and data service. But the Saudis may be monitoring all communications and the infrastructure may be destroyed soon. His disability means he can't run, climb, or crawl. He has a few hundred dollars, a week's worth of food and water, and won't likely be able to get more. You have a live offer to rescue him and a very fast-changing situation. And if any one of these parameters changes, you've probably lost the window to save his life."

The phone line went quiet, and Cole realized that Daniel wasn't ready to pull the trigger. Patience nearly spent, he asked, "This is your friend, right?"

Cole had spent his career risking his own life to save the lives of his fellow citizens, most of whom he'd never met. To a guy like Cole, this was simple: what's money compared to a human life? But to Daniel, this was anything but. His thoughts swam in circles. Millions of civilians were in this situation. Fifty thousand dollars could go a long way to help so many people, not just one man. Sure, if this were his parents, he'd spend the money. If this were his brother? Of course. Even if this were a decently close friend, he was certain he'd give the go-ahead. But on the spectrum of people he knew, from family to friends to casual acquaintances, I was barely on the scale. But he didn't want to explain all that to Cole.

"Yes," Daniel muttered.

For the first time in his life, Daniel was forced to face himself on a deep, fundamental level: was he a man who said yes or a man who hesitated when given the chance to save someone's life? It was a question he'd never asked himself, because it had never been relevant—and now that it was, he might not want to know the answer.

The clock on his desk tick-tick-ticked, and Daniel heard his colleagues, in neat button-downs and slacks, tapping away at their computers. After a few seconds that felt like an eternity, Cole broke the static: "You never know if or when you're going to find yourself in this situation. But if you ever did, you'd be really glad to know that there was someone on the other side with the ability and the will to do what it takes to get you out."

This got Daniel to stop thinking with his head and start thinking with his gut.

Before World War I, Daniel's maternal grandparents had escaped from the pogroms in the Russian Empire. In 1938, right at the start of World War II, his father's parents escaped the Holocaust in Nazi Germany. Some of his family died in the Lodz Ghetto; his father still had the letters that had chronicled the eroding situation. Had he been born in Europe only two generations before, he would have been in my shoes, hoping that there was someone on the other side with the ability and the will to do what it takes to get him out. Daniel said to himself, *If this isn't what $50,000 is for, then I don't know what it's for.* He made a decision: he was in.

"How many people can you fit on that flight?" he replied, thinking that maybe others could benefit from the mission—and split the bill.

The answer came back like a bullet: "You only asked for one."

Daniel called me to ask if I could get to the airport. I replied without hesitation, "No way. I'm a handicapped man with no car trying to get to an airport five miles away. Al Qaeda is right outside and there are checkpoints all along the route with fighters looking for people like me. And, by the way, you're trying to fly an airplane into an airport that's being bombed as we speak. This plan can't work!"

With that, Daniel went back to Cole and told him I couldn't get to the airport. Cole said it didn't matter anyway. The Saudis had declared Yemen a no-fly zone and the Kenyans wouldn't fly in. Unmoved, he said, "I'll call you back in five minutes."

The plan disappeared along with the electricity, but even though we were back to where we started, both Daniel and I were satisfied. He was the guy who said yes.

That evening, the fighting picked up. Khormaksar. That's what they were targeting: a neighborhood that was maybe a ten-minute drive from my apartment. I checked Arab Press: at least 54 dead and 187 wounded in Aden. I continued clicking through Yemen News, Al Jazeera. All the same. Each time I came across the numbers I felt as if someone was pinching my trachea, cutting off blood and oxygen to my brain, making it more difficult to think clearly.

The sun set to a cacophony of explosions and gunfire. The lights flickered again and then stayed out. I heard the piercing whistle of rocket-propelled grenades, followed by a deep thudding sound somewhere in the near distance. I had no desire to go to the window to follow the arc of the fireballs; I didn't want to watch the smoke rise in serpentine spirals. All that would do was bring to mind images of severed limbs, twisted corpses lying in the dust, blood leaking out, across the ground, into the dirt of this darkened continent.

Instead, I went back to my nest in the bathroom. I raised my left arm to lift my blanket, and the smell from my body pricked my nose. I tried to remember the last time I'd bathed. Bottled drinking water was too precious a commodity to waste on vanity.

My most vital resource was dwindling with my phone battery, depleting second by second.

Hope.

Every sign pointed to the situation growing worse. The likelihood of my escape diminished by the moment. The Houthis hadn't advanced this far to suddenly turn tail and retreat. The Saudi-led coalition had no need to give in. Large forces were at play. Individual lives didn't matter.

As I sat leaning against the bathtub, the acrid smell of smoke and the sounds of war penetrated the flimsy shell of my apartment building. The windows rattled. I lay down to try to sleep, to rest my overactive mind. I looked up at the bare ceiling, a faint cloud in the darkness illuminated by my laptop. My eyes dropped to the shower head and the pipe that it hung from. Not for the first time, I wondered how heavy a burden it could bear, if it could sustain the weight of a sheet and a human body.

Which was stronger, a taut strip of metal or a loose thread of four strangers? Which would be able to hold?

CHAPTER 18

◇◇◇

GOOD NEWS AND
BAD NEWS

Speaking with Natasha on Facebook

S aturday, March 28, began with a message from Daniel. Cole had
found a Greek fishing company with a boat in the port of Aden,
and they needed to get it out. When they were ready to go, they'd
come pick me up and take me to Djibouti. *Did God finally remember me?*
My phone vibrated. It was my mother.

"*Habibi*, Mohammed. Are you okay?" Her voice strained with tension.

"Hello, Mother. I'm glad to hear from you. I'm doing well."

"Is that so?"

"Yes."

"Then the rumors I hear are not true?"

My mind raced for a reply. I didn't want to worry her more than I already had. "What is it that you're hearing—?"

"You dog," she cut me off. "You know what I mean. Why, Mohammed? Why? You couldn't sit still, could you? You couldn't let things be."

This was a familiar refrain. Only this time I had to agree with her.

"I'm sorry to worry you. You know that was not my intention."

"Not your intention? What did you think would happen? What did you think would come of all your craziness? Mohammed, I don't—"

A sob strangled her words.

The dust stung my eyes, scratched its way down my throat, into my belly. "I'm fine. I'm fine," I managed at last.

She followed up with a question about my uncle Kamal, her brother, the man who'd found this apartment for me. I considered my words. When he'd finally returned my calls it was to say that his house was too crowded, and it would be too improper for me to be there with his unmarried daughters. That it was *haram*, forbidden. She didn't need to know that, didn't need to have one more item on a list to keep from my father.

"*Allah yusallmak!*" she said with a sigh, and I replied in kind. Allah would have to protect us both. I hoped that I had not offended Him too much, that He would have mercy on me. That He would forgive me for all the ways in which I'd failed Him. I also wished that my mother would forgive me for all the ways in which I'd failed her.

◇◇◇◇◇◇

Throughout the day, the heavy shelling in Khormaksar continued.

My friend Nimrod from YaLa Young Leaders posted a message on Facebook: "Does anyone have any connections to the Indian government? I have a friend in Yemen whose life is in danger. I would like any connections or ideas." Justin and Megan quickly reposted it, and then Justin continued to investigate on his own.

Justin had already followed up with his mother's friend William

Bleaker, asking about Kerala, a state on India's southwestern coast. Bleaker, in turn, contacted a friend of his from Kerala, who promised to help me if I could get to India. This was a thin thread, but Bleaker offered some hard-won wisdom: "Stick with it. Sometimes each person refers you to another place, and then another person, until you strike gold." We hadn't found a productive vein as yet, but the mine was growing wider and wider.

The likeliest and most immediate solution, it seemed, was the Greeks. So around 2 P.M. I contacted Daniel to ask for an update. He wrote back quickly:

DANIEL PINCUS: 1) we're waiting to hear about the boat. You will need to meet them. Can you make it to the port? They could pick you up, but need to know where to get you.

2) It seems we can get you to Uganda and you may be able to get a visa upon arrival there. I have a friend with a company there and I spoke with her. We'll see about a place for you to stay there.

3) I will look into flights to Kampala from Djibouti.

In essence, there was no concrete news, but Daniel was optimistic! In anticipation of the evacuation by Greek fishing boat, he posted a message on Facebook:

DANIEL PINCUS: We need a visa to Djibouti. Can anyone help?

Then around 8:00 A.M. EST he went to Western Union in Manhattan and tried to wire me $5,000. The limit, they said, was $1,000 per day, so he sent that instead. He messaged me that there were funds waiting for me at the bank, but I still didn't have my passport, which meant I couldn't receive money from the United States. I desperately needed cash to buy more food and water.

I grabbed my phone and called Ahmed, who worked at the Kuwaiti-Yemeni bank in Sana'a. I told him my friend wanted to send me some money through Western Union, but I didn't know if any banks were open. He told me there was a Kuwaiti-Yemeni bank in Aden, that it should be open, and that there was a Western Union inside.

It was a little after 3:00 P.M. in Yemen, and the sun was at its strongest; perfect. I pocketed my remaining rials and hurried out the door. No one wanted to be outside in 90-degree weather. Even battle-hardened fighters needed to retreat to the shade, to the abandoned marketplace, to chew qat and eat lunch. Sure enough, the streets were empty, save for a couple of stray cars and the checkpoints, guarded by pairs of soldiers, hiding from the sun under makeshift umbrellas they'd put together from empty cardboard boxes. The air shimmered with heat, and I quickly ducked off the main road into the nearest alleyway.

After ten minutes, I arrived at the Kuwaiti-Yemeni bank, but Ahmed was mistaken. The bank was closed. I grabbed my phone and searched for "Western Union" + "Aden." I called number after number, but no one picked up. Everything was closed. I was sweating and thirsty, which meant that when I returned home I would need water. This whole trip had been a bad idea.

I took a different route back to the apartment, just in case anyone was tailing me, and in the distant haze a crowd of kids took shape. *Just a mirage,* I thought. But as I got closer, the image materialized. A very small store was still open, and there was a man inside selling vegetables. I hurried to him and bought water, milk, and chocolate—Galaxy bars with nuts. What would have normally cost 4,000–5,000 rials now cost 10,000, the equivalent of $50—a steep markup. My wallet was nearly empty, but I would have water for another several days.

◇◇◇◇◇◇

On Sunday, March 29, Daniel's optimism paid off. There was a Greek fishing boat nearly ready to go—they just needed to know where I was, which was a very good question. I had no idea. I was new in town, and there were no street names or numbers. Typically, directions in Yemen were some variation of "Go past the mosque with the blue minaret and turn right at the café." But since the bombing campaign began, I couldn't even describe my location by using landmarks. Nonetheless, I tried. "I'm by the Pizza Hut near Sera Hall."

Daniel, at a loss, asked me what kind of cell phone I had. An Android. He told me to open Google Maps.

"What's Google Maps?" I asked.

He walked me through, step by step: "Click on the picture of the map. Select satellite view. Zoom all the way in. Drop a pin on your building. Take a screenshot. Zoom out, screenshot. Zoom out, screenshot. And that's where you are."

I did as he instructed and saw my building shrinking with each image. It looked so insignificant, so unimportant as the map pulled farther and farther away. I emailed him the images.

DANIEL PINCUS: Got them. Which floor?
MOHAMMED AL SAMAWI: The 4th, black door
DANIEL PINCUS: Nice door

Later in the day, Daniel was at the Museum of Modern Art when his cell phone buzzed: it was Cole. "I have good news and bad news," he said. "The Greeks are ready to go, but they want $700,000."

When Daniel repeated the news to me, my first thought was, *Is God testing me?* If $50,000 felt like a stretch, $700,000 felt like lunacy. But the Saudi coalition had set up a naval blockade and ordered that no Yemenis leave the country. The Greeks knew the risk of smuggling out a northern Zaidi, and they needed to make it worth their while. Further, the fishermen probably didn't imagine that an American was arranging a rescue for just a regular Yemeni (like me). It was much more likely that the person in question was important, and if some Americans wanted him out so badly, they probably had the money to pay.

Daniel and I agreed that this was impossible. I didn't even have $700; and anyway, it was clear that the Greeks didn't care about my life, they just wanted the money. Even if we robbed a bank and gave them half the cash up front, they likely would have pocketed the money, thrown me overboard, thus eliminating their risk, and sacrificed the second half of the payment. Or they could have taken me on board and held me for ransom, asking for even more money. The fishermen could have done a lot of things, but I didn't believe they'd risk their own lives just to save mine—and I couldn't even blame them. Daniel called Cole to deliver my decision: it was a no-go with the Greeks. Cole understood. He said, "I'll call you back."

Defeated, I was about to collapse on the floor when my phone lit up.

"How's it going, my handsome friend," said a high-pitched, dramatically feminine voice. "I miss you so much!"

A layer of tension lifted. "Hello, Ahmed, it is so good to hear your voice." This was one of his games. Ever since we were teens, Ahmed loved to call my home and impersonate a female, scandalizing my mother whenever she picked up. *Who is this forward girl who dares to call my son!*

We talked about what was going on, how things were in Aden and Sana'a. By the time we hung up, guilt, loneliness, and homesickness spiced my dinner of cookies and water. It all came together in a nice slurry of regret. I should have been a better friend, I should have been a better son, I should have been a better activist . . .

Better late than never, I thought, and sent Daniel a message saying, "In case something happens, I want you to know that you did all you can to help me. I can't imagine someone would do the same for me. Thank you, Daniel. God bless you and I hope to have the chance to thank you in person."

Daniel sent an update to the rest of the group. There would be no Greek fishing boat; keep working your other angles. Justin caught the ball, and told the team he was working on India. "I was able to get a message through to the Indian embassy in Washington," he emailed. "I believe a boat is coming in 3–4 days and so will continue to keep everyone posted on whether we can get Mohammed on that ship." India was sending a boat with a fifteen-hundred-person capacity; the problem was, there were some forty-five hundred Indians still left in Yemen.

In Tel Aviv, Natasha's phone buzzed against her hip. Blue and red lights pulsed around her, illuminating the three women who stood on the stage, electronic beats underpinning their Middle Eastern melodies. She'd been waiting for this concert for months; A-Wa, a trio of Yemeni Israeli sisters, was one of her favorite bands. But instead of jumping up and down to the beat, she was jumping to respond to Justin's message. Lost in the juxtaposition of the two realities, she realized she was listening to the music of Yemenite Jews who had left Yemen for Israel in fear of persecution, while assisting a Yemeni Muslim who grew up hating Jews before teaching religious tolerance and putting his own life in danger. This was the rhythm of the Middle East.

◇◇◇

CHAPTER 19

A NEW HOPE

Across Aden, young men such as these—an engineer, a doctor, an unemployed youth, and a university student—have joined the Southern Movement

By the morning of Monday, March 30, the likelihood of ever meeting Daniel in person had flatlined. Overnight, the Popular Committee had announced a curfew. Civilians were only permitted to be outside their homes from seven in the morning until seven at night. Few people were crazy enough to go outside in the dark anyway, but the message was clear: Aden wasn't safe. A curfew meant that more "soldiers" would be on the streets, more checkpoints would be scattered about.

I sat in my underwear, listening. I heard artillery in the north and to the east. Explosions pounded the earth, as if two giants were plodding toward each other from Khormaksar and the coast. Dishes and other crockery rattled in the kitchen cabinets; the metal sink buzzed with vibration. I took my spot in the bathroom, back pressed against the shower stall. By the afternoon, I gave up.

MOHAMMED: That's it, I can't move today. Big explosion and gunfire now near my place heavy shelling.

DANIEL: I just woke up to read this. Are you still there?

MOHAMMED: Yes. The fighting is too near me. I am now in the bathroom, I consider it as the safe room in the apartment.

DANIEL: Ok. I am going to get you out. Have not given up.

MOHAMMED: The heavy shelling is everywhere. I am ok though. Air strikes now.

Within hours, Daniel messaged me again. Cole had called back with one last option: a helicopter from Djibouti for $80,000. At this point, placing a dollar value on a rescue mission to save a human life was becoming an absurd exercise for Daniel. If he was prepared to spend $50,000 on a plane, but $700,000 for a boat was too much, where did $80,000 factor? Given the givens, it was an easy call. He was prepared to spend the money on a chopper; what was another $30,000? Going without Starbucks for twenty years? "When things are quiet again, see if there's a way you can get to the roof," he wrote. There was no point in initiating an air rescue if I couldn't get to the landing zone.

The rest of the team was on board, and Justin was already three steps ahead. What if the helicopter landed on the roof during an electricity and Internet blackout? Was there a contingency plan? How would I know when to get to the roof? What if somebody knocked on my door to rescue me, but I didn't know if I should open it, because I didn't know if it was a good guy or a bad guy? We needed to come up with a code for people on the ground to use to communicate. Operation Dragon Blood?

As I sat hunched over on the bathroom floor in my underwear, my fingers stuck to the keys. Who did these people think I was? A commando from *Black Hawk Down*? Incredulous, I pushed myself off the ground and pulled on some pants. Edging along the wall, I made it to the front door. I pressed my ear against the paint; nothing. Easing it open, I slid into the hallway, which was thick with the smell of cooked onions and dust. Breathing heavily, I made my way up a narrow staircase to the roof access door. This was the most I'd moved since the day before, and I wasn't sure I had enough water or calories to justify the effort. Bent double, I gathered myself, grabbed the knob, and turned. Nothing. I wiped my slick hands on my pants and tried again.

Nothing.

Locked.

With a sigh of relief, I headed back to my apartment.

"No go," I messaged Daniel, taking a small sip of my remaining water, slumping back to the floor.

"Look," Daniel responded. "You're running out of food and water. You can't get out by car because of the checkpoints, by plane because the airport is bombed, or by boat because of the naval blockade. The only way you'll survive is if the war magically ends or if you get on a helicopter."

The words cut through my resolve as easily as a *jambiya* through a hard-boiled egg. *Don't tell me not to give up and then list all the reasons I should do just that.* I looked out the window. Smoke and dust rose in curdled clouds against bright patches where fires burned. Contrails from fighter planes and bombers frosted the sky. An explosion rattled the glass windows, and few blocks northwest, a mushroom cloud rose over Khormaksar.

There was no way a helicopter could fly in without getting shot down. I told Daniel it was impossible.

He asked me to hold on.

Minutes later he contacted me again. He'd asked Cole if he believed that the unit could fly in, and Cole had said, "The helicopter won't get shot down."

But no reassurance was enough. Even if the helicopter itself didn't get shot down, everyone would think I was a high-value target, and while I was waiting to board, *I'd* get shot, or bombed, or captured. Unconvinced, I told Daniel I'd rather hide in my apartment than the alternative. He should save his money.

Cole conceded that a helicopter was among the noisiest and most conspicuous ways to get out of a place and, hell, some people survived wars. Maybe I'd be one of them. Daniel urged me not to give up hope, but it seemed we'd run out of options, so that was easier said than done.

Hours passed. The power went out, but the sun was strong enough to compensate. Exhausted as I was, and coming down from a series of adrenaline highs, my vision turned hazy, and the thump of shells started sounding more like the bass beat coming from a passing car. I drifted in and out of awareness until my phone buzzed again.

Saif. The friend he'd given my passport to in Sana'a had arrived in Aden, but he wouldn't come into my area of the city because it was too dangerous, so he gave the package to his driver. The driver, originally from Aden, could easily get around the checkpoints, but since he'd spent significant time living in Sana'a, he was still friendly with people from the north, like me. My brother gave me his number, and when I called, we agreed to meet up in the morning.

This was something to look forward to. A passport meant that should a Western Union open, I could finally pick up the money Daniel had transferred to me. Which meant that I might not die of dehydration. I might still die of a bullet, an explosion, decapitation, or suffocation, but at least I'd be able to eliminate one threat from the list.

◇◇◇◇◇◇

In the gray-green of the bathroom, minutes oozed into hours. Time wasn't relevant; hunger was persistent. At some point, Justin checked in with me. He had a new lead. His contact, William Bleaker, had reached out to some people he knew in the Indian Ministry of External Affairs (MEA). They told him that if we could get a U.S. senator to send an official letter of support on my behalf, they *might* be able to include me in their evacuation from Yemen to Djibouti. "Try Senator Mark Kirk," Bleaker had told Justin. "The Indian government says that the key to all of this is Senator Mark Kirk." Apparently, someone in India really liked the U.S. senator from Illinois.

Justin did a double take. Mark Kirk? He represented Justin's home district, Highland Park. His parents were friends with him. Years back, in the summer of 2006, Justin had actually interned for the then congressman during his congressional campaign, helping to organize campaign rallies, delivering signs, knocking on doors . . . Nine years later, these personal connections could be the exact thing he needed to convince Senator Kirk to reach out to the Indian government on my behalf.

CHAPTER 20

◇◇◇

NETWORK OF NETWORKS

Dar Saad (death zone) saw some of the fiercest fighting, as indicated by the remains of a tank and the destruction of the streets and buildings

The aerial attacks began early on Tuesday, March 31, and by 11:00 A.M., bombs were falling like Tetris pieces. Saif's friend wouldn't be able to bring me my passport today; it was too dangerous. There was no running water and no electricity, which meant my number one priority was saving the battery on my cell phone.

I allocated thirty minutes for phone usage, and then I would force myself to step away from my mobile device. First, I opened WhatsApp. I found a message from Natasha saying that she was trying to engage people in the upper levels of the U.S. State Department to write a letter of support that we could send to the Indian government. She also emailed her contacts at the State Department and requested to be connected with the staff person in charge of sending relief.

Second, I checked Facebook. There was a message from Justin asking me to send him a copy of my passport so that he could forward it to the Indian Ministry of External Affairs. I thanked him for his efforts, but I couldn't. I still didn't have my passport.

I had no idea at the time, but Justin was building a profile on me. As he thought about approaching Senator Kirk, his former professor's warning came back to him: *How well do you know this guy?* He flipped through our interactions. He knew my age, citizenship, religious affiliation—biographical basics. But how did he know I hadn't worked with a terrorist organization? How did he know I wasn't formerly a Houthi, or Al Qaeda? He was pretty sure I was a decent guy, but before approaching a U.S. senator for a monumental favor, he needed to be certain. And not only for himself. He'd need to make a strong case that my humanitarian and interfaith work was enough to potentially get members of the U.S. government involved. This was a sensitive issue. After all, a number of countries were working to get their own citizens out of Yemen. Not to mention that the United States was tied up with Saudi Arabia, to which it had been supplying military aid.

Justin emailed Daniel asking if Daniel had a picture of my passport on file from MJC that he could send to the Indian government. Daniel forwarded a picture of the passport, and reported that he'd wired money to Western Union, but as far as he knew, it hadn't yet been received.

Within thirty minutes, Justin sent a second email, this time to both Daniel and Megan, asking for backup. "As I am getting closer to the tops of the U.S. and Indian government, people are asking me questions about Mohammed that I can't answer because I don't actually know him personally, aside from a few conversations at the GATHER conference . . . Would either of you mind telling me more about his roles in these peace organizations/NGOs and how you know him? Anything more concrete would help me convince some people to keep pushing the message forward that Mohammed should be allowed on this ship from India."

It was only a matter of minutes before Megan, the person on the team who'd known me the longest, personally vouched for me. She forwarded Justin the first email she'd written about my situation, back on March 7.

Hi Justin,

Please find below some things I have written about Mohammed as well as his CV and cover letter attached.

Let me know if you need anything else.

Megan

Dear friends,

I am writing this appeal on behalf of my dear friend, who I have gotten to know since 2012 through my work in the YaLa Academy MENA Leaders for Change training program. Mohammed Al Samawi, a gentle soul from Yemen who is caught in the middle of what is expected to be an all-out civil war within a month. His family has already been ripped apart by the Houthi take-over and his job at World Relief has come to an end as nearly every international organization and diplomatic mission has now closed their doors in Yemen. He is in grave fear for his life and safety because of the situation especially given his activism with YaLa Young Leaders (co-founded by the Peres Center for Peace in Israel and YaLa Palestine) and other peace movements, which are in complete opposition to the official Houthi mantra of "Death to America. Death to Israel. Etc."

Mohammed is a highly intelligent and motivated individual with unshakable dedication to humanitarian and peace work. After overcoming a childhood bout of improperly treated pneumonia, he has already achieved a great deal so far in his short 28 years of life—a Bachelors Degree in Business Administration, English diploma/ TOEFL certification, positions with organizations such as PartnerAid and World Relief as well as voluntary work for Yemen Red Crescent and online activism for Yala, MasterPeace, My Face for Peace, the Muslim-Jewish Conference and more (see CV attached). And even despite his precarious situation, he attended the Gather +962 conference in February organized by Seeds of Peace. In the YaLa Academy training programs, in which he participated until now, he has always been among the top 3 students—reliably completing all online training punctually and excellently and greatly enriching our online discussions and face-to-face workshops with his intelligent and unique perspectives. He has also been active in the YaLa Young Leaders movement's Core Leadership group (composed of the 150 most active members) and in its online campaigns—contributing videos and photos to support the vision and messages of this regional peace.

It was good enough for Justin. Without another thought, he asked his father to help him approach Senator Kirk, and then he got to work building a case that I was someone for whom two major countries should stick out their necks.

Hi _____.

I have a friend from Yemen who has been involved in the Middle East peace community for several years, and whose life is in danger in the current civil war there. He is in hiding, and is down to a few bottles of water remaining as supplies. He has been unable to receive the money that his friends from the US and Israel are sending, and I am extremely concerned as the situation there grows more violent.

I'm reaching out because a group of us trying to help have been in touch with the Indian government that is currently sending rescue ships and planes to Yemen to evacuate 4,000 Indian citizens. We have asked if they could add my friend Mohammed to the list of evacuees and they asked that a US congressman make the request to the Indian embassy. We would appreciate any help that you might be able to provide in regards to getting Mohammed's name on the list of evacuees.

I only recently met Mohammed Al Samawi at the Seeds of Peace conference in Jordan, but I was extremely moved by his story and his commitment to Peace and to helping make Yemen a better place. Even though he was out of the country just last month, he returned, hoping that he could make a difference. Now his life is in danger. His views on peace and his online peace activism through YaLa Young Leaders, a Peres Center for Peace initiative, and his involvement in the Jewish Muslim Conference make him a target of many extremist groups there. It is imperative that we help do what we can to get him out! Mohammed is 28 years old, a Muslim Yemeni citizen who believes in peace, and his CV and passport are attached for more info. I am also attaching a powerful letter from Megan Hallahan, who helps run YaLa Young Leaders, and has seen Mohammed's passion for peace first hand for several years.

We don't need Mohammed to join the evacuation all the way to India, but just on the short trip from Yemen to Djibouti. It is our understanding that the boats are taking Indian citizens from Yemen to Djibouti and flying them to India. We only need safe passage to Djibouti, and from there we already have a Human Rights Organization sponsoring his Visa in Djibouti and who can help him find safety once there.

Please let me know if you can help!

Justin told Megan he was about to send a letter to a very influential U.S. senator who might be able to petition the Indian government on my behalf.

MEGAN: Great Justin! Should I be trying other senators? Mine for CA or others I may be able to get in contact with? If yes, do you have any draft letter I work off of?

JUSTIN: Senators can definitely help, and if they do it together, that would be even more powerful, and probably make them feel more secure about their request.

With that, Justin shared the draft of his letter so that Megan could use it as a template for her own outreach efforts. She then shared it with the rest of the group and encouraged everyone to adapt it for their own diplomatic efforts to U.S. senators and government officials.

At this point, each member of the team went in his or her own direction. Megan reached out to Senator Dianne Feinstein, her representative in California; Natasha got to work on her home state of Georgia; and Daniel covered New York. The responses would be quick, but disheartening. Evacuations out of Yemen were few and far between. Countries across the world were weighing the dangers of evacuating their people, and every nation—from China to Pakistan, India, Russia, and Somalia— was being forced to abandon some of its own citizens on the docks and landing pads. There were simply too many people to safely take out.

The United States was about to issue its own statement: "There are no plans for a U.S. government–sponsored evacuation of U.S. citizens at this time. We encourage U.S. citizens to monitor the news and seek available departure options from Yemen, via air, land, or sea." The State Department had urged Americans to leave Yemen back in February, and now, at the end of March, Yemeni Americans had no hope of the United States stepping in. Which circled back to the current predicament: if citizens of other countries were having a difficult time leaving Yemen, no one, but no one, was evacuating Yemenis.

How could four people without any political capital tip the scales?

◇◇◇◇◇

While the team was in high gear, I was circling the perimeter of my apartment. Then time stopped. The loudest blast I'd ever heard knocked me into the wall, vibrations working their way from my feet to my hair. For a minute, I couldn't hear anything at all. Then, a ringing, and a rumble, and the soft sift of plaster plinking against the sink.

I felt my way along the wall to the window, the surface growing warmer with every step. A gash gaped from the building next door, beams piercing piles of scattered stonework. Flames licked the outside of my wall, but, *alhamdulillah*, thank God, the wind was still. I reached out to Daniel, Justin, Megan, and Natasha and told them I needed help, ASAP.

Megan reported that she'd been in touch with a friend of hers who worked for the UN Department of Peacekeeping Operations. According to her source, the UN national staff were being moved to the Gold Mohur Hotel, formerly the Sheraton Aden. From there, they were going to try to get on a boat to Mahrah, an area at the Yemen-Oman border. She wrote that if I could get to the hotel, she could get my name onto the list of people who were authorized to stay there. At the very least, I would have water, electricity, and shelter, and maybe I'd be lucky enough to join the UN evacuation. I couldn't imagine a hotel staying open in the middle of a war zone, but it was all I had to go on. So I found the number online and gave the hotel a call.

"*Salaam alaikum*," I said. "Are you open?"

"No," a man replied. "There's a war here."

"But the UN said you are open!" I said quickly, catching him before he hung up.

"Oh!" the man said. "Are you with the UN?"

I paused. "Yes."

"For you, we are open," he said.

Right after I hung up, I posed the question to the team: should I stay in my apartment or relocate to the Gold Mohur Hotel? Daniel asked Cole, and Cole emailed Daniel right back with two pieces of advice, which Daniel proceeded to forward to me:

I would stay away from Western Hotels. If the Houthi are looking for Westerners, that would be a place they would go to. A recent example is the hotel in Libya a few months back. I understand the power and safe room, but I would be weary of utilizing the hotel for a safe site.

Now, that being said, a group of people to talk to would be good for your friend on the mental side of things. A group could also be better at making a good exit plan, securing vehicles, and identifying safe routes.

I know I'm not giving you a definitive answer as I do not see one.

The risks were clear, but was staying in my apartment even an alternative? The buildings on my street were disappearing by the hour, leaving holes in the skyline, like missing teeth. I didn't know how much longer I had left.

◇◇◇◇◇◇

That night, like many other nights, I stayed up working into the early hours of the morning. I emailed Alexis Frankel from the Muslim Jewish Conference. Alexis, who lived in Queens, New York, worked on the staff of the American Jewish Committee and had connections both inside and outside her organization. I asked if she knew anyone who might be able to support my case with the Indian government. Alexis referred me to an Indian Jew she knew from AJC, a man named Nissim Reuben, who was the assistant director of AJC's Asia Pacific Institute.

Meanwhile, just a borough away, Daniel was at Carnegie Hall watching the legendary Itzhak Perlman play klezmer music. It wasn't Daniel's music of choice, but he'd been given a free ticket, and he thought the concert might be a good opportunity to run into people from the advocacy community and to ask for their assistance. With his mind somewhere between Aden and India, he realized that Perlman had started to play a hora. If that weren't odd enough, in a moment of spontaneous abandon, the audience jumped up, joined hands, and danced down the aisles. *This doesn't happen every night,* thought Daniel, and out of the corner of his eye he saw the president of the American Jewish Committee, Stanley Bergman, doing the grapevine.

Desperate, Daniel threw his hands in the air and danced through a row of seats.

"Stan," he panted. "I need to get in touch with India. Who do you know?"

Stan said three words: "Call Nissim Reuben."

CHAPTER 21

◇◇◇

LUCK BE A LADY

The port of Aden, before the war

On Wednesday, April 1, there was a break in the aerial campaign. I called Saif's friend's driver about my passport, and he said he could bring it right away. I crept downstairs, and shortly afterward, I saw him pull up on the near side of the building. "Are you Mohammed?" he asked, and when I nodded, he threw me my passport and sped away. With that, I hurried back upstairs.

I thanked God that people I didn't know were willing to take a chance to help me and that one of the major mistakes I'd made had been amended. At first I had tried to dismiss the fact that I didn't have my passport as inconsequential. I had my government identification card, and with both major airports shut down to commercial flights, what did having a passport matter? As the days passed, however, it became clearer that I had to get out of Aden by any means possible, and that the lack of a passport might have doomed everything. With my team investigating many different channels that involved government officials, it had become clear to me that proving beyond a doubt who I was would be very, very important.

With my passport in hand, I arrived at a decision. I would go to the Gold Mohur Hotel, and I would say that I worked for the UN. The only missing piece of the plan: how to get there. I was on the eastern side of the bulb-shaped Aden peninsula. The hotel was on the western side, on the other coast, situated on a jut of land known as the Elephant's Tusk. Google had it at less than nine kilometers away—about five miles.

I wondered how many checkpoints manned by AQAP or the Popular Committee stood between the hotel and me. I didn't have a car, there were no taxis left in Aden, and none of the drivers at Oxfam would answer my phone calls, not even Aidroos. Not for the first time, I wished I could run. But I couldn't rely on my legs, so without any other option, my fingers tapped out the work number for another coworker at Oxfam. I told him that all I needed was a car to drive me five miles.

"Mohammed," he said. "You're our logistics officer! If we needed a car, we would have asked *you* to make the call!"

I explained that none of them were picking up my calls. Sympathetic, he said he'd see what he could do.

I stood at the window hoping and waiting for a car to appear. About thirty minutes later, a black sedan eased down the street past a pile of debris, parking down the street from the building—right across from the nearest checkpoint. I thanked God, and Oxfam, for listening to my request, and I planned my escape route. I couldn't sprint, of course, but I wouldn't let that stop me. This was likely my only chance. If I moved quickly and quietly, I just might sneak past the AQAP fighters.

Stepping gingerly, head down, I hurried back down the stairs. I nudged the main door open, and tried to keep to the shards of shadows. When I was feet away from the black car, bullets from two AK-47s whistled past me. I froze. My good leg shook so badly that I fell to the ground. A pair of AQAP fighters advanced in my direction, shooting over my head, yelling, asking if I was a suicide bomber.

"No! No!" I screamed. "I'm not! I'm not!!"

One came toward me and yanked me to my feet by the collar.

"What are you doing?" he shouted.

"Meeting a friend," I said, speaking as little as possible, faking a southern accent.

"Where are you from?" the other barked.

"Aden."

"No, you're from the north. You're a Houthi."

"I'm not a Houthi!" I cried. "I swear!"

"Show us your ID," the first demanded, waving the barrel of his rifle.

"I don't have my ID. It's upstairs," I said, feeling the edges of my passport in my pants.

"Okay, we'll go upstairs with you, and you'll show it to us."

I prayed my legs would keep moving as I walked between the fighters, who were dressed in black, guns slung across their chests, with long beards and head coverings. The pocked pavement crackled under our feet.

At my door, I fumbled with my keys and held up my bad hand to the light, hoping they would take pity on me. One of the two grunted; the other looked bored. The lock clicked; these were my final seconds. I was shouldering open my door when, suddenly, one of the fighters stopped me with a question that would save my life.

"Is there a woman inside?" he asked.

"Yes," I said, door ajar, no woman within ten yards. "There is."

"Get your ID and come back here. We will wait."

These men—men who killed innocent boys in cold blood—would not be in the same private room as a woman. It was *haram*—just as it was *haram* when I asked my uncle if I could stay with him and my female cousins.

I was shaking as I walked into the room and closed the door behind me. I couldn't feel my hands or my legs, and the world tilted forty-five degrees. These men knew I was from the north. This was just some sick cat-and-mouse game before they slit my throat, or blew me apart with an RPG, like in the videos I'd seen online. I forced my fingers to take out my phone and to tap out what would probably be my last message ever.

Daniel, I got caught by Al Qaeda, what do I do?

One minute passed.
Then another.
No answer.
And then my cell phone died.
This was it. This wasn't some first-person shooter game where I could find an extra life somewhere. This was goodbye. I picked up the landline phone and dialed my parents' number back in Sana'a. Saif picked up, and I started choking on my words, asking for him to give me my mother.
"Mama, Mama, it's Mohammed!" he shouted. "It's Mohammed!"
The patter of my mother's footsteps gave way to her voice. The only thing in the world that I wanted to hear.
"What's happening? Please, what's happening."
"I'm well. Don't worry. I just called to apologize."
"For what?"
"Coming to Aden. Worrying you. Every—"
"Mohammed," she started to shout, "what's happening to you, what's happening to you?"
"I'm so sorry, about everything," I repeated. "I need to go."
"Stay with me," she commanded.
"Mama, no. I don't want you to hear this."
But she kept pushing, as only a mother could do, and I told her everything: about the fighting in the streets, about Al Qaeda outside the door, about the fact that they'd kill me as soon as they got too impatient. She said she'd call my uncle to come and speak with the fighters, but I told her it wasn't worth it; they'd just kill him, too.
I wanted to glue the phone to my hand and take my mother with

me; I wanted to curl up in her arms, to practice strange Russian words together; I wanted—

My self-despair was pierced by the sound of screams.

"Allahu akbar!"

"Allahu akbar!"

I tried to ignore the noise, to keep focusing on the sound of my mother's voice. I had hoped that this would be the last thing I heard before leaving this world. But the chanting kept getting louder and louder, so loud that I told my mother I needed to see what was going on.

"Okay," she said, "but don't hang up. I need to hear everything that's happening."

From the window, I watched as different Al Qaeda fighters dragged a man into the middle of the street. His mouth was agape, his eyes wide. The man had lighter skin and finer features: a northern Shiite, like me. In that instant, I saw the future: they were going to kill him. Local civilians trickled over, one and two at a time, and within minutes a crowd had encircled the fighters, like a cockfight's audience. The Al Qaeda men started kicking the man, then bringing the stocks of their rifles down on his shoulders, head, arms. The man flailed his arms, shouted, his keening wail echoing through my room.

I waited for someone to step in, to stop the violence. Surely all Yemenis—Sunnis and Shiites, north and south—were decent people, and it was just the few extremists causing the war? Surely the crowd could overpower the two fighters?

But the onlookers shouted, "A Houthi fighter has been caught! A Houthi fighter has been caught!"

Even children cheered with abandon. Bile seared my throat. This was my own fate playing out before my eyes.

I turned to look away and saw that the black car was still there, parked between my building and the mass of braying mules. I walked to my door and looked through the peephole.

The hall was empty. The fighters must have joined in.

I grabbed my laptop, cell phone and charger, one T-shirt, a bag of potato chips, and stuffed it all into my backpack. The forgotten landline dangled by its cord, and I stumble-ran down the stairs and into the unrelenting sunlight.

I moved out the door, across the street, the sounds of shouts and cheers dripping down my spine, sweating through my shirt. Without looking back, I jumped into the black car, shut the door, and shouted to the driver, "Go! Go! Go!"

The driver yelled, "Who are you?"

I yelled back, "I'm with Oxfam!"

The driver turned to face me. "What is Oxfam?"

My throat clamped shut on my voice. All I saw was a bushy beard. The driver was not with Oxfam. He was a southerner, probably a conservative Sunni.

Stupefied, I stared.

"Are you a Houthi?" the driver asked.

I shook my head. Daniel's advice to act like a mute rushed back to me. I showed the driver my misshapen right hand.

He regarded it impassively and then looked me in the eye. With a single word, he could have signaled Al Qaeda and I would have been hauled to the center of that circle, tortured, and killed in act two of this tragedy. I waited for him to make a decision, the static sound of emptiness like dried leaves on cement.

"Where do you need to go?" the man said, cutting the thick stale air.

"The Gold Mohur Hotel."

"You have 20,000 rials?"

"Yes." My voice rasped like a struck match.

It was wildly expensive, the equivalent of $93 USD, but we were in a war zone, and petrol was expensive. Whatever this man asked, it wasn't enough. He was risking his life to take me in his car, and Al Qaeda would have given him far more if he'd handed me over to them. I hated the idea that my survival depended on my ability to pay. I was grateful that I could do so, but how many others like me were not so fortunate?

The engine barked to life.

I ducked down in the backseat.

Doubled over, I crossed the city, checkpoint after checkpoint. Every couple of minutes the car would stop, and the driver would open his window and call *As-salaam alaikum*. I'd hold my breath, close my eyes, and try to disappear, in case anyone would ask to search the car and find me in it, resulting in not only my death, but the driver's as well.

But we passed through all the checkpoints without any interference. No one suspected that a man with dark skin and a big beard would be hiding a northern Shiite in the back of his car. This man, this hero, was the true spirit of Islam. He was risking his life to save a complete stranger. He reminded me of the Yemen I knew, just months back, before the beginning of this ugly war. When people helped each other; when understanding was more important than hate.

I caught a glimpse out the window and saw we were approaching an undamaged skyline. It looked like there hadn't been any fighting in this zone. Maybe the Saudis had agreed not to bomb the area around the hotel while the UN was still inside. They wouldn't want to do anything to jeopardize their friendship with the United States.

Not half a mile away stood the Gold Mohur Hotel, a big white building dwarfed only by the granite mountains surrounding it. I was almost to safety; but between the car and the hotel, there was something even more imposing: one final checkpoint. I held my breath as I ducked back down. The car slowed, hesitated for a few moments, and I heard the call of *As-salaam alaikum*. And then we were moving again. By the time I opened my eyes, the hotel gate had passed overhead like a scimitar.

We stopped, and I thrust a wad of bills toward the driver. He met my eyes in the rearview mirror and nodded. I nodded back. *Shukraan. Thank you.* With my left arm, I gathered my things and swung the door open. Then I was out, across the driveway, and through the revolving door.

I shivered. The lobby's cool air whipped against my sweat-soaked shirt. The effect was bracing. I could think clearly again. The cavernous space was infused by light, so different from the confines of my apartment, or the Toyota I'd just been riding in. My footsteps echoed as I crossed the marble floor. To my left, a staircase wound upward in plush red carpet. Behind the reception desk, a man stood slightly stooped attending to a screen. He looked up, and even in that nearly deserted hotel, he turned on—an oasis of charm in a war-torn city.

"Good day, sir. Welcome to the Gold Mohur Hotel. My name is Hani. How may I be of service?"

I was relieved that he presumed I spoke English; no need for a fake southern accent.

"Good day to you as well. My name is Mohammed Al Samawi," I said, and paused, unsure of how best to put things. "I believe you are expecting me."

He regarded me and nodded, once, twice. "I shall see."

He pulled out a folder, a quiet whistle escaping through his nostrils.

"Yes. Here you are," he said, pointing at one of the papers. "And here you are," he said again, smiling and thrusting his hand toward me, palm up to indicate my presence in front of him.

I said a silent prayer of thanks to Megan and her contact at the UN.

"Yes. I am here," I replied. "And I am pleased I am able to be."

The remaining hotel staff members wandered in and clustered around me. They could tell that, like them, I was from Yemen, and we exchanged greetings in Arabic. After that, they told me that the hotel had water and backup generators, and they pressed me for details of life in the other sectors of the city. I filled them in on what I knew of events in and around Khormaksar, the neighborhood to the north of me where the University of Aden, the Sheba Palace, and the Al-Jumirah Hospital stood. The shelling had been the most intense there. The rest I knew from the news. Houthi fighters had again taken portions of the airport. President Hadi was confident that his government could command the ground without foreign intervention; they just had to cut the Houthi supply lines. As I spoke, I heard a chorus of distant explosions.

Out of information and nearly out of breath, I told them I would like to get some rest. I'd used the last drops of the adrenaline that had propelled me across the city. Grateful for the news, they rewarded me with a nice room. Before flopping onto the white, plush queen bed, I plugged my cell phone charger into the wall, and watched the screen come to life. Then I crouched in front of the mini-refrigerator: a lone Snickers was all that was left. Wedging the cold bar in the crook of my bad arm, I tore at the wrapper with my teeth. I swallowed chunks of chocolate and caramel, barely chewing them. It was 4:30 P.M.; my breakfast and lunch.

It took a few minutes for the sugar to have an effect. My vision cleared and I stood at the window gazing out at the Arabian Sea, the curved landmass where Little Aden and the oil refineries sat on another peninsula. On maps, that bit of land always reminded me of a charging bull, a pointed horn, a gaping mouth, legs ready to gallop across the waters and trample the Aden peninsula. I sat on the edge of the bed and wondered which of the factions controlled that bull. My tongue worried a bit of peanut from between my teeth before I ground it down and swallowed it. *The last food I'll eat in a long time,* I thought, before I drifted off.

I woke in a wedge of evening sun. Groggy but hungry, I headed downstairs. The hallways were vacant. I peered through the glass at an empty gym. The idle machines, engines of a different kind of war, stood fixed in place like plastic soldiers. I thought briefly of going inside, to work out my tension, but I didn't think I had the energy to do much but sit.

I followed voices into a common room off the lobby and saw people gathered, talking. I stopped short before joining them. Two of them appeared to be from Asia, four others from Yemen—southern Sunnis by the look of them, their dark skin and angular features as good as name tags. It took a moment before I realized that my own skin tone and features made the same kind of introduction. We stared at each other. I had just escaped AQAP, but who was I with now?

An Asian woman wearing a floppy hat waved me over. Formal introductions ensued, but I wasn't able to keep track of all the names. Two of them were from the Philippines, the rest Yemeni.

"Join us for dinner," one said.

There's food, I thought. I couldn't have been more excited if I were a cartoon character with my eyes bugged out and my tongue lolling out of my mouth.

Even though the hotel was closed, the staff continued to provide a buffet! I grabbed a plate and heaped on portions of rice, two types of *zorbian*—chicken and beef—and flatbreads. After I took my seat, I asked the man to my left about the evacuation plan. He shrugged and told me that he didn't know any of the details except that only UN employees would be flown out.

"I can't stay here," I told him politely. "I'm in a dangerous situation. It's even worse for me than it is for you guys."

He nodded. His eyes were kind but unfocused. "I hear you, but it's not my call. If you send an email to our manager, and she says yes, we'll definitely take you."

He wrote the information on a piece of paper and handed it to me. I looked at it and saw that he'd also given me the emails of the local staff. Grateful, anxious, unable to eat as much as I'd hoped, I returned to my room and immediately messaged Megan:

The UN local staff said they could take me if they have approval! Could you please petition your contact at the UN to include me in the evacuation?

Megan wrote back quickly to let me know that she was on it and would get back to me as soon as possible. I did a little dance around my bed. This could be my chance! But opportunities were disappearing as quickly as freshly baked *bint al-sahn*. Would this one last?

A few moments later my phone lit up with a message from Megan. It was short and direct:

MEGAN: The UN says no.

The UN reported that a hundred employees and eighty foreign diplomats had been flown out already, and they had plans to evacuate another two thousand individuals. There would be no room for refugees. And besides, no one was allowed to take Yemenis out of the country. Even one exception could compromise everything; if AQAP found out that a single northerner was leaving with the local staff, everyone could be killed.

I was stunned. Megan, Justin, and Daniel were as well. I thought back to how I'd felt just ten minutes before. It was as if I'd finally finished the race. But I hadn't. Someone kept moving the finish line farther and farther away, and no one would tell me how much longer I needed to run, or even what direction I needed to go in. Frustrated and frightened, I sank into the bed. How many times could this go on? I sent a message—

MOHAMMED: Daniel, I need to speak with you urgently. Can we speak?

Daniel called. He found a new solution to the problem. He said that he had a friend at the UN whom he would email regarding the situation. He wouldn't take no for an answer.

That was something, I told myself. And the congressional push with Senator Kirk was something. But was any of it going to go anywhere? There still hadn't been a formal request to have me included in the evacuation. The senator seemed like a promising lead, but as far as we knew, his aides were still the ones making the calls, not him.

I stared out the oceanfront window at the endless expanse of blue. I saw planes dropping boxes, probably filled with weapons and ammunition. I heard bombing. I read a text from a contact still in Aden: the apartment building I'd been living in up until the day before had just been blown up. I felt the concussive effects of the news as all the what-ifs of the last hours tumbled through my mind. Saif getting into my apartment. The driver delivering my passport when he had. If he'd been a few minutes later, if he'd stopped somewhere along the route, I might have been out on the street instead of that other northerner. That could have been me. What if the driver of the black car had decided no money was worth the risk he was taking? What if he was with the

Popular Committee? And what if I'd decided that the risk was too great and that I would stay in that apartment?

I remembered reading an article once about the subject of accidents and choice. Some people believed that there was no such thing as an accident—that all the choices we made each and every day led us to be in a particular place at a particular time. In other words, we always chose our fate, instant by instant. It was almost too much to contemplate, to believe that every moment was so weighted with consequence. Were there such things as luck, fate, destiny, God's plan? Why was I continuing to benefit? What about my neighbors in that building? What about the man who'd brought me juice and *zalābiya*? I'd never paid back his kindness, and now he was likely among the rising number of victims.

Shortly after midnight, Daniel forwarded me a draft of an email he'd written for the woman at UN headquarters who was in charge of the UN's evacuation of local staff:

I am writing to you with an urgent request to help save the life of Mohammed Al Samawi, a Yemeni citizen and human rights activist by evacuating him with the UN staff from Yemen. Thank you for your prompt attention to this request.

Mohammed Al Samawi, born Sana'a, Yemen 30/11/1986 (age 28), is currently in the Gold Mohur Hotel, Aden, Yemen (+96XXX1166XXX), Room 204. The area immediately around the hotel is under attack.

He is specifically targeted because:

1) He is from northern Yemen, and those from the North are unwelcome in the south of Yemen.

2) His surname suggests that he is a Shia, and the Shia are being targeted by Al Qaeda who are fighting for control of Aden.

3) His work, promoting human rights, interfaith, and intergroup dialogue, have made him a target by all sides. He has worked with OxFam, World Relief Deutschland, Partner Aid International, Althraya Development and Investment, My Face For Peace, Muslim Jewish

Conference, Master Peace (Sudan), Yala Young Leaders, Seeds of Peace, A Safe World For Women.

There are no viable commercial routes for him to leave Aden. The Saudi-led Arab coalition has blockaded the seaport and airspace, the Houthi and Al Qaeda militias have set up checkpoints throughout the city. He cannot leave on his own and once found will almost certainly be killed immediately.

There are UN staff at the hotel who say they will be evacuated imminently. We humbly request that he be evacuated with the UN staff. The staff have indicated that they cannot do so without the explicit request of the people on this email. That is why you are receiving this request.

Once out of Yemen, we can find any number of places for him to go. He already has work opportunities with Spark Microgrants in Uganda and Rwanda.

I am a US citizen, a consultant of The Quantic Group. I serve on the Board of Governors of American Jewish Committee, Jacob Blaustein Institute for the Advancement of Human Rights.

Thank you again.

Daniel Pincus

Unable to type quickly enough, I messaged Daniel: "No Dani! These are strict Muslims on the local staff. They're different than the people in UN headquarters. You shouldn't mention anything about Jews."

"Okay," he typed. "Let me correct it."

"It's a danger to mention anything of my activities to the local staff."

Pause.

"Okay."

And in that one little pause, I understood exactly what had happened.

"Did you already send the letter?" I asked.

"Yes," he said. "I feel terrible. My friend at the UN told me to copy the local staff on the request and to send it right away because it was urgent. Did I put you in danger?"

Yes! I thought. *This was a big mistake.* The local staff were all southern Sunnis, and I had no idea of their political leanings—but I'd never explained this to Daniel. He didn't know that by exposing my interfaith activities he'd doomed my chances of anyone at the UN taking me with them. And that, even worse, they might first turn me over to the militants down the driveway. This might be game over. But after all Daniel had done for me, there was no reason to say this; there was no reason to make him feel bad. So instead I wrote back that things were okay, that I would play it cool with the UN, and that I just might have to leave the hotel earlier than planned. That night, I tossed in bed.

I grabbed my laptop and looked at the *Hindustan Times* to see if there were any developments on the India front. My heart dropped. A ship had already come and gone. Was the evacuation over? I immediately messaged Justin.

MOHAMMED: Justin do you think we are late, or are we speaking about another ship?

JUSTIN: That was the first 400 people evacuated, but they are sending ships to rescue 4,000. I don't think we are too late.

MOHAMMED: Glad to know that.

JUSTIN: I will call the hotline soon to find out more though. I am hoping to get more news regarding my congressman tomorrow.

I put my computer away and counted my breaths, trying to clear my head. But sleep would not come. I picked up my phone and opened WhatsApp. I didn't want to be a nuisance, but I needed human contact.

MOHAMMED: Heavy shelling now. It's so close, the closest ever.

JUSTIN: Stay away from windows, let me know when it's over. I am writing so many letters on your behalf, and I hope to have the US government helping soon!!

MOHAMMED: Justin, thank you, you really gave me a big hope, even if I couldn't be with the Indians in Djibouti it's enough for me that we tried, thank you really.

After a fitful night, I headed to the dining room for breakfast. There were thirty round tables, each draped in a white tablecloth, each outfitted with ten plush red chairs trimmed in gold. The sight was majestic, regal, but, empty of people, it was completely and utterly haunting. Every table was vacant except for one, which was filled with the UN local staff. I walked over to them, and as soon as I sat down, they all got up and moved to a different table. They spoke to me cursorily, letting me know they'd respond to my email.

I hurried up to my room and sent Daniel a frantic Facebook message: "Daniel, I don't think the UN plan will work. I believe we shouldn't focus on the UN anymore."

He agreed.

Within hours, I found out that the UN local staff had been evacuated.

I was down to one option.

India.

◇◇◇◇◇◇

The night of April 1, while I was asleep, all efforts focused on the congressional push. Megan contacted a friend of hers named Joel Braunold, an activist who happened to be at the same GATHER conference as we were in Jordan. Joel was the executive director of the Alliance for Middle East Peace, a collection of interfaith organizations that included YaLa Young Leaders. In fact, Joel was the person who invited Megan to the GATHER conference to begin with, and Megan was the person who then invited me.

Megan shared my story with Joel, and asked if there was anything he could do. Joel was hopeful; he regularly worked with the U.S. State Department, as well as USAID and the National Security Council. When the two finished speaking, Joel emailed his friend Toby Locke, who was involved with Movements.org: "I have an urgent situation for you. It's about a young man named Mohammed Al Samawi."

Toby Locke read the message and realized that Joel was referring to the very same person that his friend Daniel Pincus had told him about just days before over dinner. Without wasting any time, Toby wrote up an email and sent it to his contacts in the U.S. government: aides in the offices of Senator Marco Rubio and Senator Kirk.

Senator Kirk's aide, Gretchan, responded quickly. "Toby, thanks for reaching out. Is there any way you can provide more info on Mohammed, or has Movements.org done any type of vetting?"

Toby replied to her email by referring her to Joel and Daniel. Joel connected Gretchan with Megan Hallahan, and Daniel replied directly:

> I can personally attest to this young man's sterling character and the danger that he is in by virtue of the good work that he does in Yemen that made him a specific target among the present and active militant groups battling to take control of the city of Aden where he is. I sit on the Board of Governors of the American Jewish Committee, acting board director of Muslim Jewish Conference, Jacob Blaustein Institute for the Advancement of Human Rights, President of the Board of American Friends of Beit Hatfutsot. I have been an active member of civil society promoting interfaith relations and Mohammed Al Samawi is a tremendous asset to this cause.

About four hours later, Gretchan followed up with Daniel. She asked Daniel if AJC and Jacob Blaustein were formally behind this case. She needed to identify as much support as possible, and the names of the AJC and the Jacob Blaustein Institute carried a significant amount of weight.

Within two minutes, Daniel replied, "Yes, they are . . . Please understand the urgency of this case. The Indian evacuation is happening imminently. AQ has set up checkpoints throughout the city looking for Shiites to kill them. Sorry for the crazy email. I feel like I have someone's life in my hands."

◇◇◇◇◇◇

At the same time, in San Francisco, Justin was placing his own call to Washington. He introduced himself to Senator Kirk's aide, and after he finished speaking, Gretchan let out a laugh. She'd just heard the same story from a man named Daniel Pincus and a woman named Megan Hallahan. Not to mention, she'd also received word that the offices of Senator Feinstein and Senator Rubio had all received similar emails about this case.

Justin tried to hide his surprise—he had no idea that the others had also been reaching out to Senator Kirk. As he thanked Gretchan for her time, he emphasized that they were only seeking transportation to Djibouti, not India, and that Senator Kirk's support was crucial to the Indian Ministry of External Affairs.

Justin hung up and immediately emailed the group: "Can anyone who's tried to reach a member of US Congress please message me! We'll have a better shot at this if we can coordinate and get multiple Senators to make a request. This is a huge risk for a Senator, and so having some support would be amazing!"

Daniel responded: "Yes, we're currently actively in touch with Mark Kirk's office. We need to organize ourselves. It's a great effort, but we're all over the place."

For the first time, Justin, Megan, Daniel, and Natasha connected on Skype, along with Joel Braunold and Irina Tsukerman. The call lasted over forty minutes. Before, they'd acted as a loose coalition, coming together over email and WhatsApp; now they discussed coordinating a strategic plan of attack. Over the course of this call, a bunch of individuals coalesced into a team.

First, Joel laid out twenty members of Congress who might be amenable to our mission, and in particular, who their key aides were and how best to approach them. He enumerated who we would need to talk to, and what levers we would have to pull. For instance, the Indian Ministry of External Affairs had a relationship with Seeds of Peace. Seeds of Peace was based in Maine, so we needed to contact the congressman in Maine. We should also try Aaron David Miller, an American Middle East analyst who used to work in the State Department. He had also formerly served as the president of Seeds of Peace, and my affiliation with the organization might resonate with him.

Megan grabbed a pen and found a corner of paper. She didn't know Aaron David Miller personally, but her boss at YaLa Young Leaders did. For the first time since this evacuation began, Megan appealed to her boss. She convinced him to write a letter to Miller asking if he could help get my name on India's evacuation list. Within the next twenty-four hours, Megan's boss would send Mr. Miller an email, which he would forward to Tony Blinken, the Deputy Secretary of State, who would flag it as important and forward it to his chief of staff to handle.

Second, with so much incoming information, the team needed a system of organization. Justin volunteered to make a Google Docs spreadsheet assigning people to tasks. Justin would focus on Senator Kirk and calls to India; Dan would focus on the American Jewish Committee's connections to Senator Kirk and Nissim's connections to India; Natasha would focus on her contacts at GATHER and select programs within the State Department; Megan would focus on the State Department through her YaLa contacts; Irina would try Senator Ted Cruz's office; and Joel would play behind-the-scenes adviser. There was a rainbow of tabs: "India," "Senators," "Congressmen," and "Other Efforts" (including Russia, CARE, the UN . . .).

As Justin crawled into bed that night, he remembered William Bleaker's most recent string of advice:

Keep pressing and calling as often as necessary.

It doesn't matter what other people think—that's the key to success.

If necessary, fly to Senator Kirk's office and stay there until you get the answer you want.

Think big.

Act as if a man's life hangs in the balance, because it does.

◇◇◇

CHAPTER 22

THE WAITING GAME

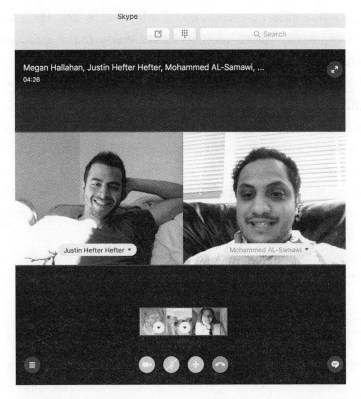

The team—Justin, Daniel, Megan, Natasha—touching base on Skype

I ate lunch in the dining room, alone, listening to bombs and rockets. The war was raging back and forth. The Houthis were pushing south. Their allies had taken control of the center of the city, the aptly named Crater neighborhood, as well as the presidential palace.

Houthi mortar shells were falling on the port, driving out Al Qaeda operatives. But the Sunni coalition's retreat was tentative. Even if the Houthis took the port and the airport, the Saudis still controlled the seas and air with a naval blockade and a no-fly zone. They also had another ace in their pocket. The Saudis had amassed troops on Yemen's northern border, and they were ready to send soldiers into Houthi-controlled Sana'a at any point. Advance and retreat. How different their aims were from ours.

For Justin, Megan, Natasha, and Daniel, Thursday, April 2, began with a lull. The day before, they'd set their plans into motion, and now they had to wait for something to happen. There were many promises of action, but diplomacy was a slow-moving train, and time kept chugging along. The evacuation could happen any day now—or not at all—and to complicate matters, the whole world was about to head out of town or turn off their phones. It was Easter weekend. Congress was closing at 1:00 P.M. EST the following day. Furthermore, it was a holiday in India that weekend, and Passover was on Friday night. The window of possibility was closing with every tick of the clock, and patience was a dwindling resource.

Despite encouragement from Gretchan at Senator Kirk's office, the senator still hadn't submitted a formal request to put my name on the evacuation list. The U.S. State Department's Yemen Desk was still unaware of the Indian evacuation; and the Indian embassy in Delhi told Justin that they still were unable to confirm that there would even be an evacuation out of Aden. We were racing against the clock, and the U.S. government was moving slower than we were. The team decided that they couldn't keep pestering U.S. officials with the same requests, but they also couldn't sit on their hands and rely on indirect diplomacy. They came up with a supplementary plan: they would find points of contact on the Indian side with whom they could communicate directly about getting my name on an evacuation list.

Justin found an emergency hotline for Indians stuck in Yemen, and he called the number twice. Both times he spoke with men who

introduced themselves as Mr. Komal, though both were clearly different people. The second man told Justin that the Minister of State was
in Djibouti overseeing the evacuation and resettlement efforts, so we
might want to get in touch with his office and work the Djibouti side.
Natasha volunteered to find his contact information, and in doing so,
she became the group's liaison to Djibouti.

Daniel followed up with Nissim Reuben at the American Jewish
Committee. Per Stanley Bergman's recommendation, Daniel had called
Nissim, who organized high-level diplomatic relationships with India
and who'd already proven to be an invaluable resource. Without wast-
ing a minute, Nissim had sent an email to an officer in the West Asia
and North Africa (WANA) Division at the Indian Ministry of External
Affairs in New Delhi, and requested that the officer follow up with his
Sana'a-based colleague, a man by the name of Mr. Dilbag Singh.

Then Nissim connected Daniel directly with the Indian embassy
in Washington, D.C. Daniel placed his first call to the First Secretary
(Congressional Liaison), and asked if India would consider including
me in their evacuation. The response was an unequivocal *no*. There
were thousands of Indians in the country, he said, and the boat that
was coming would only be taking hundreds. They couldn't evacuate
a Yemeni before they'd gotten all of their own people out first. Before
the officer could hang up, Daniel followed up by saying, "All we're asking is if your boat is there, you've gotten all of your own people out,
and there's room on the boat, and our guy is right there on the port,
would you even consider putting him on the boat?" After a beat, he
said, "Maybe."

While Daniel was working the Indian embassy in D.C., Natasha
remembered that there had been an Indian delegation of peace activists at the GATHER conference in Jordan. She contacted one of the
representatives from the group, who gave her the telephone number
of a senior official at the Indian Ministry of External Affairs in New
Delhi, a man named Sayd.

Megan called the number that Natasha gave her, and Sayd provided two phone numbers for people who worked in the Indian embassy in Sana'a. One of those numbers was for a man named Mr. Dilbag Singh, the Head Orientation Officer. Megan sent those numbers to the team.

Daniel, juggling five different threads at once, didn't catch the email. So when Justin picked up Megan's thread and made the call to Mr. Singh, he was completely unaware that Nissim Reuben at AJC was concurrently petitioning the very same man.

The call between Justin and Mr. Singh was warm and encouraging, and Mr. Singh promised that he would help get me on a boat to Djibouti within the next forty-eight hours. When they finished speaking, Justin passed along the good news and told me to call Mr. Singh as soon as possible. All I needed to do was mention Justin's name and Seeds of Peace.

That night, I called Mr. Singh. The tone was nothing like what Justin had described. Mr. Singh told me he couldn't guarantee anything, and that he had many of his own citizens to worry about. Nonetheless, he said, I should send him a letter so he could think about it.

When I got off the phone, I emailed the group.

"He wants me to first send an email to him and he said he will think about it. Can I have his email and what should I tell him in the email? He said they are leaving sometime this week, and I will hear from him before they do."

The team got on a Skype call to help me draft a letter to Mr. Singh. If we were going to make a personal appeal, we wanted to make it as convincing as possible.

I started to tell my story, but somewhere between the descriptions of the death threats and the accusations that I was a Mossad spy, a bomb exploded at the end of the hotel driveway. I told the team I had to go, and they told me to stay safe—which was obviously the plan.

After I disconnected, Daniel drafted my story into a formal letter to Mr. Singh, and he sent it directly to Nissim Reuben to pass along to the Indian embassies in D.C. and Sana'a, and to Gretchan at Senator Kirk's office. Then he reached out to Congressman Ami Bera of California, former assemblyman Tom Perriello of Virginia, and former congressman Jim Kolbe of Arizona, asking if they would lend their support with the Indian embassy in the United States.

Megan, similarly, was busy reaching out to Representatives Mark DeSaulnier and Lois Capps of California. Both said their offices would be in touch with Kirk's. She also got in touch with Senators Feinstein, Barbara Boxer, Deb Fischer, and Gary Peters, as well as a string of congressional representatives.

Justin, meanwhile, contacted the Seeds of Peace office in Maine, and then followed up with Senator Kirk's office. Soon after, he messaged the group: "The Indian Embassy in D.C. is taking this very seriously with the requests incoming from Senator Kirk and AJC. They're going through their diplomatic channels directly to New Delhi, which is supposed to be communicating with Mr. Singh in Yemen."

While missiles flew through the skies above me, emails, texts, and phone calls zipped through the heavens, bouncing off satellites and returning home, somehow finding their marks. The chain of communication seemed to be working. It sounded as if the team's efforts in D.C. were being communicated to the Indian Ministry of External Affairs, then in turn passed along to the Indian embassy in Yemen.

DANIEL: Who wants to fly to Djibouti with me to greet Mohammed?
NATASHA: 100% yes.
MEGAN: I'm in.
JUSTIN: We still need to make sure that the full connection of DC-> Delhi-> Yemen is made. But if we pull this off—*hell yes.*

◇◇◇◇◇◇

The next time I heard from Daniel was at 11:00 P.M. local time. He sent me a message saying that he had been able to connect me with someone who could get me a visa once I arrived in Djibouti. Days earlier, a friend of his named Deborah Abisror, the former director of the European Union of Jewish Students, had seen his Facebook post asking for a contact in Djibouti and replied, "When I was living in Paris, I knew a guy from Sierra Leone who I think has a friend in Djibouti." Daniel took hold of that slender thread and asked her to make the connection.

Within days, Daniel received a call from a man named Yusuff, a Sierra Leonean who was living in Paris. After Daniel briefly explained the complex situation, Yusuff agreed to help with the visa. He said, "Send me a copy of his passport, the name of the boat, the day and time of arrival. I'll take care of it."

With the visa handled, all I needed was a country to include me in its evacuation to Djibouti, a boat, a port, and someone to drive me there. Despite all the headway, it was still a very, very long shot, and the bombs were getting very, very close. Before I went to sleep, I got one last message.

DANIEL: I am very confident that India will let you on the boat. We are going to have a big celebration for you when you get out.

I tried to stay optimistic, but as soon as I gave myself permission to breathe, my thoughts went straight to my mother, my father, my sisters, Nuha and Lial, my little brother, Saif . . . I'd been so focused on myself that I'd barely given them thought. Were they safe? Did they have enough food? Did they need more money? I had no idea if the center of the war would stay in Aden, or if the Houthis and Al Qaeda would use the people of Sana'a as a bargaining chip. My mother said the fighting was far away, but I had no idea if her even-tempered reports reflected the real conditions on the ground, or if she was cleaning them up to try to protect me.

I couldn't imagine leaving them without a proper goodbye. And yet, if everything went well, that's exactly what I would do. And if any number of things didn't go well, well . . . My confidence began to drop, like mercury in a thermometer. I knew that the team was trying to keep my spirits afloat, but I was a very leaky vessel drifting on a relentless tide of conflicting emotions.

In the comfort of a bed that wasn't the bathroom floor, I tossed and turned. One doubt led to another. It was just the Sunni hotel staff and me. They now knew that I wasn't really with the UN, that I'd lied to their faces, and that I was from the north. Further, without the protection of the UN, the hotel was particularly vulnerable—like a large white sitting duck. The Saudis were now free to blow the building to the ground, and there were already militants at the end of the driveway. It was either death by airstrike, or capture and torture. There was no way out.

I considered jumping off the roof, or hanging myself, but the thought of my mother, of my sister Nuha, stopped me. They'd always loved me so tenderly, supported me even when they didn't fully understand me. How would they be able to go on if they knew that I had given up all hope? What consequences would my choice have on their lives? To be killed was one thing; to take my own life a very different thing. And if I truly believed the things that I'd been trying to spread, about understanding and peace, then how could I pollute that message with an act of despair? How could I give up?

I prepared for the inevitable, and called Daniel, Justin, Megan, and Natasha to thank each of them personally. "You did more than I could have asked," I said over and over. "Live the rest of your life. Don't feel guilty."

After Daniel got off the phone, he turned to his houseguest, a slight eleven-year-old boy with a mop of jet black hair. Daniel told the boy, "I have a friend in a bad situation. He's in a war zone. He's all by himself. He's very scared, and he's probably going to die very soon. Could you play for him the last piece of music he'll ever hear in this life?"

Joey Alexander took a seat at Daniel's piano, and began.

CHAPTER 23

◇◇◇

FANTASIA

A seventeenth-century fresco of the Exodus crossing of the Red Sea

When I woke up, I had a message from Megan saying that she'd just spoken with Gretchan at Senator Kirk's office. She promised she would do her best to get the senator to approve a letter of support that we could send to India on his behalf. All we needed to do was draft one for him. Less than a minute later, Justin responded to Megan offering his help.

Intellectually, I understood that this was a moment of triumph, but my heart was thumping to the beat of the encroaching *boom, boom, boom*. I opened Facebook for the latest on-the-ground updates. Within the previous twenty-four hours, the tide of the war had shifted. The Saudi-led coalition was now mounting a counterattack against the Houthis, and in response, the Houthis were withdrawing. Amid heavy bombing, they were retreating from the presidential palace, as well as the Crater neighborhood, falling back to Khormaksar. But this wasn't the end. The Houthis, still in control of Sana'a, refused to give in, and they promised retaliatory measures.

Fighting a knot of dread in my stomach, I checked my Facebook messages. There I found a file from Daniel: "Mohammed, here's a piece of music Joey played just for you."

I double clicked, and a picture of a young boy with glasses and a tuft of black hair appeared on the screen. Joey Alexander, a self-taught jazz pianist from Bali, stared back at me. I knew nothing about jazz, but Daniel had been posting about Joey on Facebook when he wasn't busy posting about me. Over the last week, I pieced together two things. First, Daniel had somehow become friends with Joey and his family, and second, I'd be missing out if I didn't buy Joey's debut album. I still didn't understand what Daniel did professionally, but he had some pretty crazy hobbies.

I pressed play, and the music began. The opening notes danced lightly, like birds on the breeze, and then they flew into a soaring refrain. The music cut through the emotional static, the richness of feeling expressed things I couldn't say in words. Beauty still existed. A better world was achievable. Meaning was still possible.

"It's 'Over the Rainbow,'" Daniel typed.

This meant nothing to me, but the name sounded as hopeful as the song itself.

"I am crying," I told Daniel. "I don't know if this is the right reaction."

It wasn't the typical Yemeni thing to share, but I was long past trying to be the typical Yemeni. Daniel told me it was okay, that he'd already cried several times that day. I didn't want to know if they were tears of joy, frustration, or despair.

Daniel urged me to share the music with the other people still left at the hotel. "What you need right now is a friend on the ground," he said. "Create a team."

I agreed, and down the stairs I went.

◇◇◇◇◇◇

I held up my phone as the four men listened to the last strains of "Over the Rainbow," my eyes dripping like the faucet in my bathroom. The hotel workers regarded me with thinly veiled disgust. A man wasn't supposed to cry. And over a song?

"What is wrong with you?" Hani asked me. This was the first time we'd interacted since he'd checked me into the hotel, and since then, everything had changed. Hani was no longer a polite desk clerk, but then again, I was no longer a UN worker. He cocked an eyebrow. "Are you a woman, you cry so easily?" The other three chuckled.

"No," I said, "I'm not. I'm tired and—" I stopped. "It is a long story."

Hani's coworkers lost interest and walked away, laughing and nudging one another. Hani remained. I took Daniel's advice to heart; I needed a friend. Quickly, before he could join the others, I explained who I was and why I was at his hotel. I kept it short and to the point, but made certain that he understood the kind of danger I faced.

When I finished speaking, he raised his hand.

"Follow me."

He took me to a narrow staircase, and we descended. The smell of dirt and moist concrete prickled my nose. *Is he going to kill me?* I wondered, with a kind of morbid curiosity. I ran my hand along the rough surface of the wall and found the light switch. The overhead fluorescents sputtered to life. I trod carefully, not wanting to slip on the filmy concrete. The basement was a large rectangle made of cement blocks and mortar that was portioned off into smaller segments by plasterboard walls. There was no real place to sit down, but at least I couldn't hear the battle sounds. I checked my phone but I couldn't get a signal. There was something acrid, ammonia-like in the air. I followed the smell around the corner; a desiccated cat corpse lay sprawled on the floor. It must have been there for months. No one had any incentive to remove it.

"Don't worry," Hani said from the entryway. "If anyone comes, I will hide you down here."

I felt my way along the walls back to the stairs, considering my options. Would it be better to be crushed by rubble or to go out in a flame of explosion? Would I wind up entombed down here, a man-child buried with a cat like the pharaohs of old, clutching the things he valued most in this world—a phone and a laptop—and hoping they'd be of some value in the one to come?

When we got back to the lobby, Hani patted me on the back. "They won't get you. I don't like them. I don't like what they do."

"Thank you," I said.

"I'd expect the same of you if circumstances called for it. We shouldn't be fighting each other." He took up the same tone he'd had when we first met, a professionalism and pride of position that was welcome at that moment.

I nodded, trying not to think about the dead cat.

He turned to walk away, and then he added, "Thank you for sharing your music."

◇◇◇◇◇◇

While I was getting a second wind, the team was moving ahead with their two-pronged plan of attack. The first part of the plan—getting support from Washington, D.C.—was well under way, as Justin and Megan were drafting their letter for Senator Kirk. The second part—getting support directly from the Indian government—was still indeterminate.

Eager to push forward, Justin decided to call Mr. Singh at the Indian embassy in Sana'a. The team agreed that this was a good idea, and Daniel wrote up a nine-point plan of attack.

1. First thank him for his time and efforts to help people of India, Bangladesh, etc.
2. Confirm that he received all the information that he requires.
3. Mohammed only requires safe passage to Djibouti and has no intent to enter India as a refugee or asylum seeker.
4. Mohammed has no luggage other than a small backpack with essentials.
5. Mohammed requires the location (which port in Aden), time.
6. Mohammed will arrange ground transportation to the port in Aden.

7. Can he commit to including Mohammed Al Samawi on the ship.
8. Make the case that Mohammed's life is at risk.
   - Northerner in the south
   - Zaidi who would be falsely identified as a Houthi by Al Qaeda
   - His intergroup peace building activities have been threatening to extremists
   - He's alone in Aden, his apartment was bombed and he's hiding in the Gold Mohur hotel but will run out of money in two days and with no place to stay, he'll have no place to hide from Al Qaeda and militants who would kill him for his accent, dialect and surname.
9. We want to personally convey the gratitude of the Americans who appreciate your efforts to save Mohammed.

Justin asked Daniel to join him on the call, and within the hour, Justin sent a recap of the conversation and outlined the situation in a three-step action plan:

Hi Team,

Brief Update:

Daniel and I called Mr. Singh at the Indian Embassy in Sana'a. He is aware of Mohammed's needs to be on a ship from Aden to Djibouti. There is a ship coming, but he does not know when. He was rushed, so I was not able to find out whether he had received word from the Indian Embassy or Congress. He told me he thinks the ship is coming in two days in the evening but has no definitive information.

I do not know that having more people contact him directly will help, although it will definitely help us if we can go through back channels, and make sure that the Indian Embassy in DC followed up with the Indian Embassy in Yemen.

I think we need 3 things today:

1. Names and cell phone of other people in Mainland India to contact. It will be the weekend in the US, and the Indian Embassy here will probably be closed, so we need cell phones of people to contact in India who are working on the Yemen case and who will be on call and able to provide us with more information [names redacted].

2. A document to send to the abovementioned people from US Congressmen, that supports Mohammed's cause. In the event that the ship is coming and they say that there is not room, we need to have something to show.

3. A backup plan for the next few days while we wait.

Things are happening and being decided on just hours before they happen. Only a few hours ago India received permission from Saudi Arabia to fly planes into Sana'a and so they are organizing that mission now. They do not know what is happening more than a short period of time in advance, and so it will be our job to stay diligent and stay up to date with contacts.

Here are some good twitter accounts to follow from India for updates . . .

I wanted to speak to Mr. Singh myself, but per Justin's email, I deferred to the team. No need to have too many people hammering the same nail. And anyway, I had other things to do. Natasha had managed to get me some financial assistance from the State Department, and Daniel wired more money for me to retrieve via Western Union. If I could get the money, I would have approximately $4,000 in total. That would be enough to secure a ride to the ports, pay off whoever I needed, and have something left over to live on in Djibouti. The only problem was, I had no way to get to a Western Union.

◇◇◇◇◇◇

By evening, Justin and Megan finished drafting their letter for Senator Kirk, and they sent it off to Gretchan. Would Senator Kirk sign the letter? Would the Indian government grant final approval? No information was forthcoming. One minute passed, then another, until

I stopped counting. I tried to do some stretches, to busy myself with physical activity. Just when I couldn't take it anymore, an email from Megan arrived in my inbox:

WE GOT THE LETTER FROM SEN. KIRK!!!!!!!!!!

I punched the air and let out a shout.

Senator Kirk was sending the letter to the Indian embassy in Yemen, as well as the U.S. State Department. And Daniel was forwarding it to Nissim, who would send it along to the Indian embassy in the United States.

I was reduced to a series of exclamation marks and smiley faces. I didn't have words to express my gratitude. But the news kept getting better: within hours, several other key U.S. officials had signed on to the petition. Daniel sent around a message confirming that the diplomatic push had paid off. People I'd never even heard of had gone to bat for me.

DANIEL PINCUS: We have so many people working here for you. It's been escalated to the highest levels of the US State Department, Indian Ministry of Foreign Affairs, Indian Embassy in DC, a US Senator . . . I don't know what else we could have done. I'm very confident this will be successful.

Good things come in threes, and the hat trick was an email exchange between Megan and the U.S. Deputy Secretary of State Tony Blinken's chief of staff. She informed Megan that Aaron David Miller had recently been in touch with Secretary Blinken, and that the Secretary had reached out to the Indians regarding the evacuation. She recommended that we stay in close touch with Mr. Singh at the Indian embassy in Sana'a. And then she asked Megan to confirm that I'd be able to get a visa upon arriving in Djibouti; there was no point fighting to get me on a boat to Djibouti if I was only going to be turned away on the other side.

Megan expressed her extreme gratitude, and explained that they had actually gotten in touch with Mr. Singh the day before, and that though he'd promised to get me on a boat, when I called, he was less forthcoming and asked for an email summarizing my situation (Megan attached this email to her response). She said that her colleagues followed up again that very day, but Mr. Singh seemed overwhelmed, which she understood, as he was busy coordinating a series of high-wire evacuations. Regarding the visa, Megan confirmed that Daniel Pincus, who worked with AJC, had spoken with someone, who'd spoken with someone, who'd agreed to sponsor my visa to Djibouti. Further, should there be any complications, I had a friend from YaLa Young Leaders who lived in Sudan who would drop everything if need be and come to Djibouti to arrange things.

I couldn't believe it. Everything seemed to be falling into place. But I told myself to exercise caution. I was still waiting for confirmation that my name was on the list of the people to be evacuated. And I still needed the exact location of the ship and its departure time.

We were so close.

It was the first night of Passover, and just before sitting down at the only Passover seder she'd ever been invited to, Megan was on the phone again with Deputy Secretary of State Blinken's chief of staff. The evacuation would happen on Sunday.

For the first time in a week, my four friends tried to ignore their phones and laptops as they began their Passover seders. They wished me good night, and told me that they'd pray for me. And I, a Zaidi Shia Muslim, said something I never thought I'd say: Happy Passover.

With any luck, I would be crossing the Red Sea in the coming days.

CHAPTER 24

◇◇◇

GO, GO, GO

The local fishing boats that ferried people to the
Indian naval ship

By late morning on Saturday, April 4, the bombs pummeled the
ground outside the hotel like the thundering hooves of a thousand Egyptian horses. In a panic, I picked up the phone and
called Daniel.

"What's going on? Are things okay?"

Why did Daniel sound half asleep? *Ana hemar.* It was 10:00 A.M. my time, which meant that it was 3:00 A.M. his time. The reason he sounded half asleep was because he *was* half asleep.

"I'm so sorry, Dani. I know it's late. It's early. I shouldn't have called, but the bombing and the shelling—"

"It's fine. I haven't been to sleep. Hang in there. In just a few hours, this will all be done. Think of the story we'll tell our kids someday."

"Someday . . . That sounds good to me. I didn't think there would be a someday."

I wandered through the hotel, stalking the empty halls. I checked my phone and hit refresh—nothing. Refresh—nothing. Refresh— Finally, a few hours later, I received a message from the Indian embassy in Yemen: they would be sending a car to retrieve me the following day. This could only mean one thing! Senator Kirk's letter must have made it to the Indian Ministry of External Affairs, and they must have passed the letter on to the Indian embassy in Yemen, and they must have approved the request! This could only mean that I was on the list! I could hardly believe it. The team had pulled it off.

I opened Facebook and messaged the team with the good news.

DANIEL PINCUS: So now you can go to the pool ☺.

MOHAMMED AL SAMAWI: I didn't think about that before. Good idea. 👍
I will ask if it's open.

MOHAMMED AL SAMAWI: The staff advised me not to enter the pool.
It hasn't been clean for a while.

DANIEL PINCUS: It looks clean from Googlemaps ☺. Just wait for a
bit. Start thinking of your plan after you get to Djibouti.

After I get to Djibouti . . . The words danced in front of me to the melody of whistling projectiles and trembling glassware. I hadn't thought about life after Yemen. Where would I go? How would I live? Would I be able to bring my family? Could I convince my father to leave this country?

While I was debating if I should call my mom now or after I arrived safely in Djibouti, Justin was pacing in his apartment, trying to relax after a long Passover seder during which he was too anxious to eat. Unable to sleep, he called Mr. Singh at the Indian embassy.

"Could you confirm that you received Senator Kirk's letter and Mohammed is on the evacuation list?"

Silence.

"Is there a problem?" Justin tried again.

"No," Mr. Singh said.

"Great," Justin began, when Mr. Singh cut him off—

No, he said again, they had not gotten Senator Kirk's letter. And not only that, but the evacuation plans had changed—the evacuation ship was no longer coming to the port because the fighting in the area had gotten too intense.

Too flabbergasted to say anything more, Justin promised he'd call back once an hour every hour until there was news, and then he hung up. After all his work cultivating contacts, everything seemed to be over. He quickly connected with Megan and Natasha over Skype, and they agreed to tell me the news—carefully. It was 3:00 A.M. PST when they got off the phone, and in a last-ditch effort, Justin flicked open his Twitter account. Swiping past trending posts on the #bloodmoon and #bieberfever, he searched for #yemenevacuation, and there, in less than 140 characters, was a tweet that changed everything: the evacuation ship had arrived and people were being ferried from the port to the military vessel, which was stationed more than a mile offshore.

Justin called Mr. Singh to confirm the Twitter report, but Mr. Singh could not do this—he could share no knowledge of fishing boats or ferries. Frustrated but determined, Justin contacted the rest of the team. There was a possibility, based on what he'd read on Twitter, that the evacuation was going on *right now*.

Everyone sprang into action. Daniel called the First Secretary at the Indian embassy in D.C. No response. It was Saturday morning at 7:00 A.M. EST. Justin called the Indian embassy in Yemen. No response. Megan reached out to me to ask if I could see any activity from my hotel room. Just a big shape, I said, way out in the sea. Natasha attempted to reach someone at the State Department to see if they could confirm the tweet. Nothing.

No one could verify the report. What if it was inaccurate? What if it was old news and the evacuation was already over? This wasn't a credible source—it was Twitter! The group exchanged a flurry of messages: was it worth encouraging me to leave the safety of the hotel to go into a war zone to wait for a ship that might not ever arrive? Megan made the call: yes, it was.

My Skype blipped. It was Justin.

"You have to get to the port. Now."

I'd never heard him like this before. Frantic.

"Justin," I said, trying to calm him down. "Don't worry. The embassy people told me they'll send a car for me once the evacuation begins."

"They're not coming!" Justin growled. "You need to get to the port *right now*! Speak to anybody you can and find out where the ship is."

"I'll do that. Do you think—"

"You don't have a lot of time. Just go—"

I signed off and hurried to find Hani. We exchanged a quick greeting before I asked him, "If a foreign government is evacuating all of its people, do you know what port they would leave from?"

"Is the evacuation big or small?"

"Big, I think," I said, without conviction. I remembered that the original number was four thousand, *with another round to go*. But which round were we up to?

"If it's a big ship there's only one port it can be," he said, certain. "It's near here. You could walk."

"I can't walk," I reminded him, holding back my exasperation. "If Al Qaeda sees me, they'll kill me."

Hani nodded; he knew the truth of that.

"There is still one UN person here. You could ask him how he is getting out."

I gawped at him like a pricklefish. There was someone else still in the hotel? From the UN? I took down the room number and hurried off, too grateful to ask Hani why he hadn't told me about this person's existence before. Catching my breath, I knocked on a door in a long row of doors leading to empty rooms.

A middle-aged man in a pair of light pants and a Western button-up blinked out at me from a wedge between the door and the frame.

"Why are you still here? Why didn't you leave with the rest of the UN staff?" I began, no introduction.

"I have dual citizenship—Yemen and the UK. I'm leaving with the Indian evacuation. A driver is coming to get me soon."

"Can I go with you?" I asked. No explanation.

"I don't see why not."

"Thank you. Thank you so much."

Before I left for the port, Daniel sent me one final message. "1) You cannot let your phone battery die. 2) Take pictures. You're going to show me those pictures one day."

◇◇◇◇◇

Thirty minutes later, I jumped in the back of a black sedan. I didn't call my mom. I didn't say goodbye. I didn't pay the hotel. I clutched my backpack to my chest and, folded at the waist, rested my head on the back of the front seat, hiding my face from the window. The engine thrummed through the leather, and I repeated the word "boat" over and over again like a mantra.

The spell was broken by a shout. "Where are you going?" It was the man from the UN. "Turn around. Take us to the port!"

"We need more petrol," the driver said, matter-of-fact.

The man from the UN shifted onto his hip and tugged at his back pocket before pulling out his wallet. He clutched a handful of crisp bills and waved them near the driver's ear. I crashed against the door as the driver made a sharp U-turn. I had no idea where the driver was trying to take us, but it couldn't have been for more petrol. The gas stations in Aden had run out days before.

When the car pulled up to the port, hundreds of people crowded the jetty. Shipping containers, vehicles, an area cordoned off by rope, suitcases lined in formation all sat there, but one thing was missing—a boat. The taste of rust and seawater, fuel and sweat stuck in my throat.

I asked a man nearby if he could tell me what was going on. He was older, gap-toothed, and clutching a bright yellow cloth he used to mop his head. "It is too dangerous. They will not bring the ship in. The navy won't risk it. The fighting is very strong right now."

"So they won't be taking anyone?"

"Not here, no. The same with Al Mukalla. The port there has been taken. Al Qaeda isn't going to let them in."

Over the murmur of the crowd a woman's voice demanded attention. I edged in as close as I could and saw a floral scarf and a clipboard. I overheard someone explain that the woman with the list was a private citizen of India, a schoolteacher. When she found out that the Indian navy was canceling its evacuation, she swore she wasn't going to die in Yemen. So she petitioned the Indian embassy and offered the following solution: If the Indian government agreed to let the navy anchor their ship far offshore, out of missile range, she would hire local fishermen to bring the evacuees to the ship; all she required was the list of names of people to be evacuated. The officials agreed to her plan. I squinted, trying to make out the naval ship; I estimated it was a good hour away via a dinghy with an outboard motor.

I messaged my team on WhatsApp, giving them a quick recap of the situation and making an urgent request: *Please make sure I'm on that list.*

I squeezed my way through the crowd and approached the woman.

"I'm on the list," I told her.

She barely looked up.

"You're not on the list."

"How can you know? You haven't even asked my name. You haven't looked to see if I'm there."

"I know you're not. No Yemenis allowed on the boat, so no Yemenis on the list."

I had one opportunity. I clutched my phone in my hand, frantically tapping through my messages to show her the latest emails from the

U.S. senator and the U.S. ambassador to India. I held up the screen, nearly thrusting it in her face. She took the phone out of my hand.

I looked up, expecting to see her reading the messages, but instead, I saw my phone tumbling through the air into the crowd. I was too stunned to say anything. Instead, head down and shoulders hunched, I danced my way through the crowd like the footballer I'd always dreamed of being. I needed that phone. I had to get it before it was stepped on, or kicked farther into the swell of bodies.

I rasped out pleas and apologies as I pushed through legs and arms slick with sweat. I felt as if I were a child again, drowning in that pool, the air squeezed out of me by the press of bodies. What would happen to me if I lost communication with the others? It would be the end of my oxygen supply.

I saw a dark object in the shadows and reached for it. A child's shoe. How awful. What would a child think of all this chaos and confusion? I went to my knees, staggered by the effort, and felt feet on my back, on my legs, on my fingers. I shut my eyes, and when I opened them again, my phone was there, a meter from me, between the sandals of a man with large bony feet. I inched closer, nearly prostrate, and grabbed it.

When I stood up, the sea air smacked me in the face, and a shiver prickled my skin.

I was frantic. I texted Megan, explained what had happened. She told me to get the number of the woman with the list. I ducked and dove back to where she stood, shouting at her that the Indian embassy had asked her to provide me with her number. Not even bothering to look my way, she said, "The embassy has my number."

With my back against a wall of people, I balled up, hoping to embed myself in the crowd. I wouldn't leave unless it was by boat.

Meanwhile, Megan relayed my message to Justin, Daniel, and Natasha, each one glued to his or her computer. It was now 7:45 A.M. in New York. Daniel called the personal cell phone of the First Secretary at the Indian embassy in D.C., and this time, he picked up. Daniel begged the embassy to intervene, to tell the woman at the port to include me in the list of evacuees.

The man apologized through a yawn and said there was nothing he could do, that there might be another boat the following week.

Frustrated, but with no real cause to demand a favor, Daniel repeated his appreciation that the embassy was considering the request, and said goodbye. Before hanging up, the man added an afterthought: intelligence expected that the Houthis would overrun Aden in twenty-four to forty-eight hours, and that it was going to be a bloodbath.

Daniel reported back to the team. The Indian embassy in D.C. would not make any promises.

They were desperate.

Justin called Mr. Singh at the Indian embassy in Sana'a, but he still didn't have confirmation from the Ministry of External Affairs that I was supposed to get on the fishing boats. Justin called the MEA directly, but no one picked up. He tried its Emergency Operations Center, and the U.S. embassy in India, but only the night watchman picked up. Justin begged to be connected with the person in charge, and he was put through to a duty officer who either was new to the job or had a very limited role. Justin started yelling into his receiver, but the only response was, "I am not sure what the next steps would be. I am merely in this role. What I will do is contact the people who are more knowledgeable than me." When Justin asked him who that might be, the duty officer said, "Usually we turn to Washington." Justin hung up the phone, at a loss.

Thinking fast, Natasha realized that if Justin wasn't having any luck with the embassy on the ship's departing side (Yemen), she might be able to get more information on the side of the ship's arrival (Djibouti). She found phone numbers for the Indian embassy in Djibouti, and began to call everyone in the office. For a while, she got passed from one person to another, but eventually someone gave her the phone number of the schoolteacher with the list. Relieved, Natasha called her immediately. The woman hung up on her.

An hour passed. The heat intensified and bodies dripped into one another. I wished I'd brought a bottle of water, but wishes weren't hydrating. I watched as the woman with the list called her last name and then climbed over a fishing boat's gunwales. A crew member released the boat from its mooring, and the last fishing boat to the Indian naval vessel sailed away.

The evacuation was over.

I felt my breath go cold.

Four Indians rushed to the edge of the pier, shouting, yelling for her to come back. But all that remained was the boat's V-shaped wake, a zipper opening up to nowhere. People were hugging themselves, crying. A woman threw herself to the ground; a child wailed. A man stooped down, a phone pressed to his ear. He was speaking English. No one around him had any idea what he was saying, but I did.

"Captain! We're still at the port. Please don't leave without us!"

I hurried over, my desperation matching his. "Was that the captain of the ship?"

"It was," he said.

"May I have that number?"

The words hung between us; even they had nowhere to go.

Finally, he relented. "As long as you don't tell anyone who gave it to you."

I gave him my word, and a moment later I texted the number to Megan along with the caption *the Captain's number*. I hoped that was enough.

Around the port, people clumped in groups or began to scatter as dusk settled and the explosions some miles away drew closer. The Saudis had not yet damaged the port, but no one knew how long they would hold off. I glanced down at my phone; the battery was down to 5 percent. I switched it to airplane mode and waited. There was no Plan B.

Drained and exhausted, I sat down, forgetting to tell the team that I'd turned off my 3G. My WhatsApp status made a painful death march on their screens: *Active 1 minute ago. 2 minutes ago. 45 minutes ago . . .* They had no idea where I was, if my phone was dead, or if I was alive.

And then a miracle happened. In the distance, a handful of little fishing boats appeared, motoring back to shore. Within thirty minutes, they arrived at the port. A crowd rushed forward as one of the men jumped onto the dock. "We are instructed to take all the Yemenis," he said. A wave of bodies crashed onto the ships, but there were more Yemenis on the dock than could fit on the boats, and between my right leg and my hand, I couldn't push my way through. The boats filled up and left, and I remained on the dock with the old, the young, and the unlucky, those too hopeless to cry, crumpled like empty wrappers.

With no word from me, the team didn't know what to do. They volleyed suggestions back and forth. Justin tried to get the Emergency Operations team at the State Department to call the captain of the naval ship, but they refused. Then he tried to get the Indian ambassador to call the captain, but he wouldn't do so either. There was only one option left: someone from the team would have to call the captain of the foreign naval ship directly, on his personal cell phone, and see if he would remain in a war zone—risking the lives of hundreds of Indian nationals—in order to send another fishing boat back to the port, wait two more hours for its return, and board a Yemeni.

Justin suggested that Daniel make the call, and Daniel lobbed the suggestion right back. Justin had already created a relationship with the Indians in Yemen, he reasoned, so it only made sense that he remain the point person. Justin reluctantly accepted, and Megan, Natasha, and Daniel listened in over Skype while he made the most important call of his life.

Justin dialed the number quickly. The call didn't go through. He took a pause to collect himself, and then tried again. This time the line connected. With a heavy Californian accent he began: "Captain! My name is Justin Hefter and I'm calling from the United States! I believe you've been in touch with the Indian government about a Yemeni national named Mohammed Al Samawi. I'm calling to let you know he hasn't made it onto the fishing boats, and he's still on the dock!"

"Okay," the captain said, and hung up.

The team had no idea what this meant. "Okay," we'll come get him? Or "Okay," now bugger off? Daniel quickly relayed the message to Nissim, to see if there was anything he could do. Just thirty minutes before, Nissim had forwarded Senator Kirk's letter to the Deputy Chief of Mission at the Indian embassy in D.C., as well as the First Secretary—the man with whom Daniel had been in touch. Nissim offered to forward Senator Kirk's letter to the U.S. embassy in Delhi as well, but the Deputy Chief of Mission responded that there was no need for that; he was following the case personally.

After speaking with Daniel, Nissim sent a follow-up email saying that a young Jewish leader named Justin Hefter had just spoken with the captain of the INS *Mumbai*, and that the captain said he would allow me to board his ship. He reported that I was currently waiting on the dock to get on one of the fishing boat ferries. He concluded by writing that Daniel Pincus, an active member of AJC, would be very grateful for their efforts.

◇◇◇◇◇◇

While this was happening, I wandered around the port. No food, no water, no electrical outlets. On the one hand, I knew I needed to check in with the team to give them a status update. On the other, I knew I needed to save my battery in case of an emergency. How relative that term had become. I looked at my watch. Forty-five minutes had elapsed. The team must have been going crazy.

There were still clusters of Yemenis waiting, covering the empty dock like patches of stubble. And in a dim pool of light cast by one of the offloading cranes, a man set up shop, selling old phones. I wandered over, a little too eager, and asked if I could buy one. Yes, he said, he'd trade me for my watch.

I hesitated for a second. This was the watch that Nate had presented to me for my good work at World Relief. I treasured it. But I valued my life more. I slipped it off and handed it to the man. In exchange he handed me an old Nokia flip phone. Deal.

Now I had a second phone, but I didn't know how long the battery would last on this one, either. Further, I had no idea who was paying the bill, if it was prepaid, or how to refill the account. Not to mention, I'd completely forgotten how to use T9 texting. But still, I had a lifeline. I opened up my Android and tapped Megan's number into the flip phone. Relearning how to text on nine keys, I carefully typed:

"I'm at the port. Is the boat coming back? People are leaving. Should I stay?"

A foreign, unknown number popped up on Megan's phone. She opened the message; it was me. Quickly she conferred with the rest of the team over Skype. What should I do? The team had no idea. They didn't know if the boat could come back. They didn't know if I should hide, or where I could find shelter or electricity. The only thing they knew was that the big ship was originally scheduled to leave at 6:15 P.M., and the hour was approaching.

Justin dialed the captain's number over and over, but he kept getting the disconnect signal. He alternated between Skype and his cell, in case the captain was blocking his number, and finally the call went through. Panicking, but trying to maintain a tone of professional detachment, Justin asked when the fishing boats were expected to arrive. The captain told him he didn't know what had happened. He'd sent the boats more than an hour ago. Maybe the fishermen had gone home because they were tired or too scared of the violence.

Megan sent a text to my flip phone updating me on the situation. Without another option, the team recommended that I take the risk, stay, and hope that the fishing boat returned. I trusted them. I stayed. My life was on the line.

Just as the sun was starting to drop and it was turning to twilight, a shape appeared in the distance. Was it a wish? A mirage? Or was it a fishing boat, returning one last time? My answer came in the form of a high-pitched trill. The remaining thirty or so Yemenis whooped and clapped. Some linked arms and danced. It was indeed a boat. The last boat. As the fishermen turned sideways and began their docking maneuvers, the cheers turned into screams. Bullets popped through the air, followed by the rumble and screech of tires.

A small group of AQAP operatives scrambled out of a pickup truck, weapons drawn, firing. Spray and pray, spray and pray. This was a scene from *Jahannam,* from hell, the fear surrounding us blacker than tar. A man near me let out an agonized yelp of pain as he clutched his leg. Bodies were running, crashing into each other, folding over. I didn't have time to think. The boat was docked. Empty.

I ran toward the bobbing image so small in the fading light. I had to get there.

I felt the pebbles under my feet as my foot dragged behind me. A bullet snapped past my ear. *Ana hemar,* I cursed myself. *I am a donkey.*

No. I pushed myself.

One foot after another.

Ana thaelab. I am a fox.

I leaped onto the boat and tumbled beneath a low bench. Alert, still, ready. Voices shouted: *We are Sunnis. Sympathizers. Friends of the cause.* In another minute, the gunfire stopped. The Al Qaeda leader accused us of being Houthi fighters coming to unload weapons from the naval ship. He told everyone to line up. He wanted to see identification. I didn't move.

The fighters went through the group, one by one. Checking. They were looking for someone just like me. A Shia. A northerner. A thousand thoughts ran through my mind. My mother rubbing my hand, Nuha smiling warmly, my father telling me how proud he was that I'd donated my allowance to the Muslim Brotherhood, Ahmed's crooked smile. "Over the Rainbow." Emoticons. Prayers. Wishes. Flatbread and chicken thighs.

I stared at the guns and then at the boat.

I shut my eyes and waited.

I waited some more.

Then I opened my eyes. The backs of the AQAP fighters were receding in the darkness, their gun barrels poking up like horns. The twin eyes of their car glowed, tracing an arc along a shipping container's corrugated side. "Death to Israel," "Death to the United States," faded in cracked white paint.

I picked myself up as others joined me on the boat. Hands shaking, I tried to key in a message to Megan, but I couldn't get the letters straight. I pressed send.

"What?" she wrote back.

I took a deep breath and painstakingly pressed the numbers.

"I'm on boat."

CHAPTER 25

◇◇◇

WHAT JUST HAPPENED?

The INS *Mumbai*

Loaded with people, the small fishing boat made its hour-long journey into the sea as Saudi warplanes bombed Aden. The city lit up in flames, the most morbid fireworks display on the planet. I kept my head down and mouth shut. The only northerner on the boat, I didn't need to call attention to myself. For all I knew, they'd push me overboard.

I didn't notice the boat rocking until it stopped, the sound of the water slapping its sides like a light slap to the face. The captain, a reedy

man in khaki pants and a once-white dress shirt as big as a sail, stood
with arms akimbo.

"I will need money," he said flatly. "For fuel."

We all eyed one another thinking the exact same thing. *There's no
petrol in the middle of the sea. And who has any money?*

All of us, tired, elated, emotionally spent, roused ourselves in protest.

How could you do this to us?

Can't you see the young children, the women, the old, the unwell?

What of mercy?

What would Allah think of you?

The man stood there, a sailor impervious to our emotional outburst,
knowing that he had what we wanted.

I reached into my pocket, looking for my last rial. Instead I pulled
out a hundred-dollar bill. Before I could stuff it back in my pants, the
fisherman grabbed it.

He waved the bill in the air.

"See this? You do have money. What will Allah think of you?"

Then he smiled and winked conspiratorially. "You've primed the
pump. The fuel will now flow."

My savings disappeared into his back pocket, and the trip resumed,
the engine belching smoke.

Time disappeared in the darkness, as the waves kept the rhythm of
infinity. In twenty minutes or a year, a spotlight lit the dinghy. Through
the glare, I made out an enormous wall of gray—the side of a five-
hundred-foot guided-missile destroyer. Ropes dropped down, followed
by dark-clad figures, descending like spiders. Men with kneepads,
helmets, and large goggles boarded the fishing boat, weapons held
against their chests.

They maneuvered between us, scanning our faces, checking for
weapons, looking for any sign that we might be militants. One of them
walked to the prow.

"Is Mohammed Al Samawi on this boat?"

I looked around; people craned their heads. I raised my hand.

Everyone turned to look as the big man locked his hands around my wrist and forearm and hoisted me to my feet. He positioned me in front of the rope ladder. I stood and stared upward at the knotted grid. My bad leg throbbed and my gnarled hand refused to loosen. *I am not a donkey,* I told myself. *I am strong. I can do this.* Leading with my left leg, I made it onto the first rung. Blinded by the spotlights, I couldn't tell how far I had to go. It didn't matter. I would get there. With hands pushing from below and pulling from above, I clambered aboard the naval ship.

I stood for a moment, lightheaded and panting, hands on my thighs, bent over, feeling like we'd gone well past injury time, well past over-time, but we'd scored and won.

On the deck, a small group surrounded me. One of the crew approached.

"You are Mohammed Al Samawi?"

"Yes," I said.

"The captain will see you right away." He led me up a flight of stairs, our footsteps ringing on the metal.

In what seemed like a small office, a man about my height walked out from behind a desk. His white uniform dripped with ribbons and brightly colored rectangles. He asked for my identification, and then examined it—and me.

"Are you fine? Is there anything I can do for you?"

There were no words to express the incongruity of the situation.

"No. I mean, I'm fine, but no, there is nothing more you can do for me. You've done everything. You saved my life."

The captain paused. "Follow me," he said. "You should see something."

I trailed him out of the cabin, along a raised narrow walkway. He stopped and nodded at the crowd below us on the deck.

"There are three hundred of my people, another hundred or so of yours."

I looked down. Everyone was gathered together, sharing warmth. Blankets swaddled women and children, and people were hugging and crying with relief.

An awkward silence followed. All I could think to say was "Thank you."

"We'll be under way again in a bit. Djibouti."

He turned and walked out. Another sailor led me away, back down the stairs and onto the deck with the others.

What on earth had just happened?

◇◇◇◇◇

This was the best we were able to come up with. The Indian embassy in D.C. was being petitioned by Justin Hefter, who had personal connections, and by Daniel Pincus, who had a relationship to the Indian embassy in D.C. through the American Jewish Committee. It was also reviewing requests from Senator Mark Kirk, whose decision to help was made in consideration of Justin's efforts and AJC's support via Daniel. The Indian embassy in D.C., in turn, petitioned the Indian Ministry of External Affairs in Delhi, which was also being petitioned by Megan and Natasha's contacts at the U.S. State Department, including Deputy Secretary of State Tony Blinken.

This cocktail of support was potent enough that in just a few days, amid a flurry of communications from the United States, Israel, India, and Yemen, the right people did the right thing at the right time. Did the final approval to allow me on the ship come down from the Indian embassy in D.C., the Indian embassy in Sana'a, or the Ministry of External Affairs in Delhi? I have no idea. Perhaps the Ministry of External Affairs went directly to the Secretary of the Indian Navy to ask the captain of the INS *Mumbai* to include me in the evacuation, bypassing the Indian embassy in Yemen altogether. This would have explained why Mr. Singh at the Indian embassy in Sana'a was unaware of the proceedings. Given the chaos of the situation and urgency of the appeal, it's quite possible. This could also explain how the First Secretary at the Indian embassy in D.C., the man with whom Daniel spoke, was unaware of the quickly evolving situation. Regardless, I imagine it's most likely that a request for my evacuation was approved through the proper chain of command, and that a formal order was subsequently relayed to the captain of the INS *Mumbai*.

But did the request to include me in the evacuation get approved before or after India temporarily called off the operation due to safety concerns? I have no idea. All I know is that everyone had to think quickly and adapt. The schoolteacher who helped organize the evacuation onto private fishing boats asked for the list of people who were to be evacuated. Perhaps my name was on the list, and the schoolteacher wouldn't admit it. Or perhaps the captain knew it would have been dangerous to put my name in writing. It's likely that India was only officially allowed to evacuate its own citizens, no Yemenis. I was one of the exceptions to this arrangement, but only select pockets of the Indian government—and the captain—might have known this. If AQAP were to find out that India had taken me on their ship—or if my name so much as appeared on a list that got in the wrong hands—it would compromise the entire operation. Hundreds of lives would be lost. Which could be why the captain might have left my name off the list. And why, in effect, the schoolteacher could have been correct. Even if she *had* checked the list, my name might not have been on it. *No Yemenis on the list.*

But that didn't mean that the captain was planning to abandon me. What I do know is that after the makeshift evacuation ended, and all the Indian citizens were secured on the naval vessel, he sent the fishing boats back to the dock to pick me up. Perhaps he realized that he had to be clever about it. If he singled me out specifically, he would put my life in jeopardy. If the fishermen thought that I was a person of value, they might hold me for ransom, or take any person who offered the most money and claimed to be me. Either way, a bad outcome. Perhaps the captain reasoned that if he invited *all* the Yemenis onto the fishing boats, he would avoid that issue and ensure my safety. Or, in nautical terms, if he cast a wide net, he would be sure to catch me. What he might not have accounted for? The number of desperate people still waiting at the dock, and my disability.

A little before 6:15 P.M., the captain probably thought that I was on my way to the ship, and that he'd be able to stick to his original departure. But then Justin called and said I was still on the dock . . .

Now the captain had to make another tough call. He was about to be saddled with scores of Yemenis, and I wasn't even among them. If he still wanted to get me out, per his orders, he'd have to wait for the fishing boats to return to the ship, unload the Yemenis, and then have the boats return to the dock one more time—which meant at least another two more hours on the edge of an active war zone with nearly four hundred refugees in tow. It wasn't an easy call, but he made it.

◇◇◇◇◇

I looked around at my countrymen. Under the blanket of night, we all looked the same. Arms, legs, bodies. North, south, Sunni, Shia—none of that mattered. Saltwater scrubbed away our labels, and out here, in the middle of nowhere, we were all simply alive.

I hadn't planned for a future. I was too focused on the immediate goal. The team had tried to get me to think about the long game, but between the Houthis, AQAP, and their sympathizers, the only game that mattered was ducking through checkpoints; there were no extra lives. But now, with twelve hours to stare at the stars, the reality hit me. What would I do once we landed? Was there any way I would be able to bring my family over?

While Aden had been a focal point of much of the fighting, things in Sana'a weren't good either. How long would my family remain safe?

Another hour lapsed before I could reach Natasha to let her know that I was on the military ship and on my way to Djibouti. A while later, she texted to let me know that Daniel had booked me a room at the Sheraton Djibouti on Plateau de Serpent, a short distance from the port. For now, I should rest. This time it was Mohammed, not Moses, crossing the Red Sea on Passover.

⬦⬦⬦

CHAPTER 26

IF YOU CAN'T STAND THE HEAT, GET OUT OF DJIBOUTI

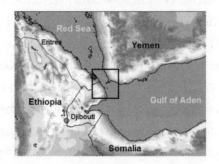

Map of Djibouti, Yemen, and the Red Sea

Djibouti didn't expect to receive around a hundred Yemenis, many without any kind of identification whatsoever, never mind visas. As soon as we docked, a handful of policemen herded us into a small temporary transit center, also known as a police station. The early morning air was already over 90 degrees, and the room became a kiln as men and women tried to unstick from their neighbors. We were being steamed in our own sweat.

There was little electricity and no water. Uncertainty collected and ran down the walls of the room like condensation. At one point, a woman cried out, "We are going to the camps!" A ripple of fear momentarily chilled us all.

No refugee camp is ever a nice place, but a camp in Djibouti was its own kind of hell. One of the hottest and driest places in the world, Djibouti had already felt the impact of four thousand Yemenis escaping the conflict, a thousand of whom had already been routed to the camps. None of us wanted to be added to that number. Overstuffed, undersupplied, and a breeding ground of dengue fever, the camps served as a reminder that getting out of Yemen was just the start of another kind of horror.

Though Djibouti was a small country, about the size of New Jersey, it figured largely in the region. Bordering the Bab el-Mandeb strait, the gateway to the Suez Canal, the tiny country essentially controlled access to the Red Sea and thus international shipping lanes. Djibouti was inundated by U.S. military personnel after 9/11, when the United States decided it needed a military presence in the region. The United States built its largest military base in Africa in Djibouti, Camp Lemonnier, home to four thousand troops and their supplies, including drones. U.S. European allies—Germany, Italy, Spain—erected military installations as well. France put a regiment in Djibouti. Japan, in a move unprecedented since the end of World War II, established an overseas base there, and China initiated construction on a military and naval base. But the benefits of international institutions, the control of a major waterway, and the high-tech infrastructure necessary to build and maintain those things didn't trickle down to the native population. For them, Djibouti was a barren, postapocalyptic landscape: peaks of dunes and rows and rows of refugee tents.

After all I'd been through, I couldn't imagine living in one of them. I knew Daniel had gotten me a temporary visa and a hotel reservation, but how would I prove it? As far as the Djiboutian officials were concerned, I was one of the hundred. I looked at my wrist to check the time and remembered I had traded my watch for my flip phone. I felt a panic coming on, and I counted my breath, remembering how lucky I was, how lucky we all were. This physical discomfort was nothing compared to being caught by Al Qaeda or buried alive under a building.

My fever of anxiety was broken by the sound of someone calling out, "Who is Mohammed Al Samawi?"

I lifted my head and saw a policeman framed in the doorway.

I raised my hand.

"Come with me."

Not for the first time, the rest of the Yemenis stared at me—*Who is this guy?*

I looked around. These were my countrymen, my people. We'd been through so much, survived so much, and for every person here, there were family and friends left behind. Everything seemed random. Why had the Indians agreed to take us out? Why had the Al Qaeda fighters driven off? What would happen to us now? I was lucky enough to have a temporary visa, to avoid the refugee camps. But for the rest of my people? Was this the end of a journey through hell, or the beginning?

At the front desk, I was introduced to a man named Ali, an immigration official. He told me he'd spoken with Yusuff, the man with whom Daniel's friend Deborah had put him in touch. I produced identification verifying that I was in fact who I said I was, and the policeman told me I was free to go. Together, Ali and I went to an office, where they issued me a ten-day visa. Then Ali drove me to the Sheraton hotel, which was nothing like the former Sheraton Aden. People were at the reception desk, laughing, happy.

Through glazed-over eyes, I found my room, and plugged in my phone to make sure the charge got to 100 percent. *My new neurosis,* I thought. Then I collapsed onto a big white bed and immediately surrendered to sleep. I was out for over ten hours, the most sleep I'd had in more than half a month. When I woke up, I took a cold, cold shower, and I shaved thoroughly for the first time in almost thirteen days. I thought of my father, who never let me go a day without shaving. I missed him deeply.

I splashed water on my face, and the shock of water on my skin forced me to focus. I had used up one of my ten allotted days sleeping. Only nine more days before I had to get out of the country, face jail time, or end up in one of the refugee camps. I hadn't gotten out of Aden only to die in Djibouti. I needed a plan, stat.

I began to make a list of all the countries that might let me in until the situation in Yemen improved. Jordan and Algeria were the only countries a Yemeni could legally enter without a visa. But maybe Ethiopia or Malaysia? My good friend Mohamed Abubakr spent a lot of time there. I did some more research and learned that I could get into Egypt without a visa if I was older than sixty or younger than seventeen . . . Not terribly practical. I opened my recharged Android and reconnected with my team: did anyone have any thoughts?

Daniel messaged Justin. What if they got a tourist visa for me in the United States? I could speak at universities and cultural institutions to spread awareness about the situation in Yemen. And in four months when the visa was up, the fighting would be over and I'd be able to return home. Did they think they could rustle up some invitations from established institutions around America? Sure, they decided. Why not!

Soon after, they sent me a message: might I be interested in going on a speaking tour in the United States? *Might I?* Of course! As much as we learned to hate the West, America remained a fantasy, a beacon of democracy and opportunity. Getting a visa to come to the United States was a dream that many, many Yemenis shared, but like most dreams it was fraught with unrealities. Even in times of peace, it was very difficult. Yemen was viewed as a hub of global terror, and the recent outbreak of sectarian violence, and the lack of a stable government, underlined that point.

But if there was a way, if I could tell Americans about what was happening in Yemen, maybe I could help stop the war. Few people knew where Yemen was, and even fewer had ever heard about the current crisis. Coverage was sparse at best. Yemen was just another of those countries out there, a "-Stan" without the benefit of oil. A distant and backward land where everyone killed each other for some reason or another. If I could have the opportunity to talk about Yemen, to bring light to the situation, to make people care, maybe I could make a difference.

The idea was ludicrous, but then I looked around. I was in a pristine hotel room in the middle of Djibouti, a sea away from my war-torn homeland. Ludicrous? Okay. But we'd just done something ludicrous. I told the team they had my blessing to proceed. They got to work on invitations and securing a temporary visa to the United States.

Daniel posted on Facebook: "Does anyone want to invite a Yemeni for a speaking engagement in the U.S.?" Justin and Megan appealed to their contacts: "If anyone would like to host a Yemeni interfaith peace advocate for a speaking event in the United States between mid-April and mid-July, please let me know ASAP. It would be very helpful and very much appreciated." I imagined these posts going out into the air like bubbles—floating for a few seconds and then popping, fleeting distractions.

Daniel reached out to his friend Sandra Grossman, an immigration attorney outside Washington, D.C., who'd also helped arrange Joey Alexander's visa to the United States. Sandra immediately offered to help guide me through the complexities of the U.S. immigration system. First, she explained what was needed in order for me to get a tourist visa for the speaking tour. Under no circumstances could I come to the United States with a tourist visa and an intent to remain there. I was fine with that. I wanted to get back to Yemen, and if the speaking tour could help me pass some time while things settled down, then I greatly appreciated her help in making that so.

Glad to know that someone as capable as her was on the case, and that Daniel and Justin were working on booking events, my focus could remain on what was of most importance to me—family and friends in Yemen.

On my fully charged Android, I dialed my family over and over, but either the call wouldn't go through or no one would pick up. I tried . . . and tried . . . standing up, then sitting down, then standing up again. Unwilling to give up, or to entertain morbid possibilities, I finally made contact. My mother answered. When I said, "Salaam," she gasped, her voice moving up and down the scale, her words colliding with each other. I fell into the sound of her voice, into the melody of our shared emotion. The last time we'd spoken I was holed up in my apartment in Aden; AQAP was right outside the door. She'd had no idea what had happened to me, but she could only expect the worst. Where was I? How did I get out? I began to reconstruct my escape, selectively picking and choosing the narrative. I couldn't tell her I'd been associating with Jews and Christians. She was already dealing with too much.

Her relief sharpened into an acute edge of anxiety. In my mother's mind, I was still her young and defenseless son. How would I survive on my own? At least if I had stayed in Sana'a, I would have been with family. We should have all been together. Even if the Red Cross was flying two planes into Sana'a carrying vital medical supplies, and even if no one could leave their homes because the fighting was growing too intense—even if they only had electricity intermittently, and even if they had to pay four times the cost for bread and rice—we should have stayed together. We were family. We needed to stay together. That was the only way.

I couldn't express just how much I disagreed. This was the hermetic thinking that had forced me to leave, for us to be separated, for this entire war to break out. This us-and-them, circle-the-wagons mentality had brought nothing but destruction. When we hung up, I turned to social media to redirect my anxiety. There I saw pictures of Yemen on fire. Post after post confirmed that the violence had continued to escalate. The Houthis had just advanced into central districts, and some Sunni clerics were calling for a jihad against the Shia invaders—making it even more clear to me that I had gotten out just in time. As casualties mounted the Red Cross issued a warning about the possibility of a catastrophic situation. The Aden that I knew as a child and briefly as an adult was transformed into a scene out of a war film—smoking ruins and rubble-strewn streets in some neighborhoods, others untouched.

Three days passed. Daniel rented an apartment for me, and made sure I had enough to eat and drink, and I tried to occupy myself. It was boiling hot outside, but it was cooler than a bomb blast. I walked through the streets, and instead of Al Qaeda or Houthi fighters, I saw men and women in American and Japanese military uniforms. Yes, I was worried about my future, but at least I had a future, I reminded myself, standing in the sun without fear of a single bomb or bullet. But as the sun set, and rose, and set again, the silver lining began to fray. Five days passed: I Googled local NGOs that might need a logistics officer, or an administrative assistant. Seven days passed: I still didn't have an update on the visa situation.

Nine days after I arrived, on April 14, I received word from my mother that things had gotten worse in Sana'a. Alternating between calm and terror, she told me that overnight the house had come under attack. Gunfire had broken out, and the bullets had shattered several windows. She didn't know if it was a targeted attack or a random act of violence.

Alhamdulillah, everyone was safe.

After ending the call, I scrambled to the Internet for updates. The devastation of the war had literally hit too close to home. I saw horrible, horrible pictures, men who no longer looked like men. *Why?* I thought to myself. *For what are we killing each other?*

I felt a fire somewhere between my stomach and my chest. God had saved *me.* While hundreds of others were dying, I was alive. I stood up, feeling the newly returned strength of my body, and decided to do something I hadn't done in a while—pray.

I went to the bathroom and started doing the *wudu,* cleaning my hands, my face, my feet, and my hair—anything that would touch the ground while bowing down to God. Water splashed from my hands and I realized I was shaking, feeling things I hadn't let myself feel in over thirteen days. As I put water in my mouth, I felt tears wash my face. I walked into the bedroom and stopped in the middle of the carpet. I closed my eyes, remembering God. When I bowed down and touched my face to the ground, I sobbed. The words, words I had been saying since I was six years old, fell away, and were replaced with a new prayer: *Shukraan, shukraan, shukraan,* thank you, thank you, thank you. *Shukraan ya Allah.* Thank you, God. *Ana ahebak.* I love you.

I cried for two minutes, and then I started all over. In Islam, you need to do the moves in order, as they should be. The last time I'd offered *Salah*, I was in my apartment in Aden. I'd promised God that if he saved me, I would be a better person. Now, as I finished speaking to Allah, I was ready to repay the debt.

I was safe. My family was safe. Too many others were not. The idea of traveling to America to tell my story took on a new kind of urgency. If I could put a face to the crisis, if people could actually hear me speak, then maybe someone, somewhere, would intervene. This wasn't just about me anymore. I was safe. This was about the future of Yemen and its people.

I would repay Megan, Daniel, Justin, and Natasha by carrying on their work. They'd specifically told me they wouldn't accept money or compensation of any kind. I would follow in their footsteps. Each one of them had devoted their time and resources to making the world a better place to live. I needed to continue to do the same.

Too many people were being killed in the name of religion. While I was safe in my room, the United Nations cited a figure from the World Bank saying that 59.5 million people were currently displaced as a result of armed conflict. The system was stressed beyond capacity. Too many people suffered in silence without a platform. If people were willing to listen, I would speak for them.

Megan and Natasha continued to check up on me, and Daniel continued to lend support, both financial and emotional. But another week went by, and I was now in the country without paperwork. Daniel and Justin told me they were scheduling as many speaking engagements as they could, but for weeks, nothing changed.

I had nightmares of refugee camps and woke up in cold sweats. I read reports that the camps had scorpions, snakes, and hyenas, and even worse, no Wi-Fi. If I got sent away, I would lose all contact with my family—and my team. Even if I managed to avoid the camps and lived in an apartment in the city, there was a 60 percent unemployment rate, near-constant border skirmishes with Ethiopia, and economic devastation. Overstressed and overtired, I drove myself into a frenzy. Whenever the stress got too blinding, Daniel offered cover with a touch of levity, as scant a resource as shade from the sun.

DANIEL: Look at it this way. You didn't pay anything for the trip from Aden to Djibouti . . .

Daniel was spending a not insignificant amount of money, and Natasha continued her efforts with the State Department, transferring $2,000 so that I could continue to live. By this point, I understood that the money went as easily as it came. This was the ebb and flow of a refugee: funds come in and provide a sense of security, and then they trickle out on necessities and a series of bribes.

At least the speaking requests seemed like they were sticking. Between Daniel, Justin, Tina Steinmetz, and a woman named Tiffany Harris whom I'd met in Jordan, I had official invitations from Stanford University, the International Crisis Group, American Jewish Committee, and Moishe House. With these on the books, I worked with Sandra Grossman to submit my paperwork for a four-month tourist visa to the United States, and I ingratiated myself with local police and officials. I remembered what Daniel had told me while I was in the Gold Mohur Hotel: *What you need right now is a friend on the ground. Create a team.*

When everything was approved, my attorney contacted the U.S. embassy in Djibouti to schedule my interview at the consulate. And then I waited . . . and waited . . . Finally, five weeks after my arrival in Djibouti, I received confirmation that I had an appointment. I'd taken countless exams as a student. I was accustomed to spending long hours studying, memorizing entire passages of the Quran. This time, though, there wasn't anything I could do to prepare.

<><><><>

Monday, May 25, finally arrived. I grabbed my backpack and made my way to the U.S. consulate in Djibouti. I'd faced Houthis and Al Qaeda, but not U.S. government officials. I was terrified. I walked into a small room and saw a crowd of Arabs: Syrians, Somalis, Yemenis . . . I gave the woman at the front desk my name and ID, and she told me to take a seat. I was number 36.

The room was open and I could listen as the consul greeted each person and asked him or her to state his or her name. Every interview began the same way—"Why do you want to come to the United States?"—and after a standard list of questions, every interview ended the same way: "I'm sorry. You're not qualified for a U.S. tourist visa at this time."

Hours went by, and I framed and practiced my responses. Why did I want to go to the United States? I only needed several months of safety until I could return home to Yemen. And if I could hasten that return, all the better. I would go to the United States to tell my story, to inform people about what was going on, to push for political and diplomatic solutions to end the bloodshed, and then I would return to my family. I rehearsed versions of this answer in my head, over and over—until I heard, "Number 36." It was my turn.

I walked over to the consul and sat down, trying not to believe that this interview was futile.

"Please state your name," the man said, more interested in a stain on his shirt than the question he'd just asked.

"Mohammed Al Samawi," I replied, getting ready to launch into my pre-rehearsed speech.

He looked down at his papers. "Who is Daniel Pincus?"

I sat bolt upright in my seat. This was not at all what I'd prepared for. Scrambling for the right answer, I blurted out, "He's my friend."

"Why does he care so much about you?" the man asked, now uncomfortably alert.

"I don't know," I answered honestly.

The consul looked me over. He had every reason to be deeply suspicious. I was a Yemeni applying for a four-month visa to the United States from Djibouti with invitations to speak at leading American academic, policy, and Jewish institutions. It didn't add up. The man thumbed through my folder.

"You have several speaking invitations, including one from AJC," he said. "I'm going to ask you one more question, and I want you to answer me very quickly." He looked at me straight on and said, "What does AJC stand for?"

I blinked. I had no idea. I'd heard Daniel and Justin use these initials, and I knew that Alexis Frankel worked there, but I was so nervous that my mind drew a blank. But I couldn't say that.

"American . . . Jewish . . ." I racked my brain for words that began with "C." *Capital, class, company . . .* I had no idea. I settled on, "Something?"

"You don't know?" he pressed.

I forced a shrug. "I forgot."

The man held my eyes, considering.

"Committee," he said finally. "It's American Jewish Committee. Next time someone asks, don't forget."

I nodded, sitting on my hand, trying to stop it from shaking.

"Congratulations," he finished the interview. "You have a four-month visa to the United States."

I walked out of the U.S. consulate with an enormous smile on my face. It was the first time I had smiled since I could remember.

◇◇◇

CHAPTER 27

THE PROMISED LAND

Flying to the United States!

I'm coming to America, I thought. All I needed was a plane ticket. Which was a problem. After all the visa fees, I only had about $300 left. Ready to pawn my laptop, I received a message from Daniel. Not surprisingly, he had an idea.

Two months before, Daniel had posted a message on Facebook: "Anyone have any idea how to quickly get a Yemeni citizen out of Aden, Yemen?" There had been a string of responses, none too helpful. But one of Daniel's friends from college, a man named Chris Murray, had indeed offered to buy me a plane ticket to the United States if I ever got out.

Now, eight weeks later, Daniel called Chris.

"Chris," Daniel said. "I'm calling to cash in on that plane ticket. You're never going to believe this, but we got Mohammed out of Yemen."

Chris, a lawyer in Houston, looked away from the brief on his computer. "A deal's a deal," he said, laughing. "When and where do you want him to fly?"

"Djibouti to San Francisco. Tomorrow."

Wearing the same clothes I'd had on since I left the war, a smile still plastered on my face, I headed to the airport in Djibouti. I walked through the check-in line, handed the lady behind the desk my passport. She looked me up and down, and then clacked away on her keyboard.

"Sir," she said finally. "Your visa says you'll be residing in New York, but your ticket says you're landing in San Francisco. We need an address for you in San Francisco or you can't fly."

I sent Daniel an urgent message. "They want the address in San Francisco or they will not let me travel." It was 5:15 P.M. my time, 10:15 A.M. Eastern Daylight Time.

Within a minute, he texted me back with an address. I repeated it to the woman, and I was through.

Shukraan ya Allah, thank God.

At 7:00 P.M., I flew in a little commuter plane to Addis Ababa, Ethiopia, where I waited to board an Ethiopian Air Boeing 787, the "Dreamliner." After seven hours in the air, I landed in Frankfurt, Germany. It was 5:00 A.M. local time; I had five hours before boarding my connection to the States.

I sent Daniel a WhatsApp message, telling him I'd arrived.

DANIEL: There is a Lufthansa business class lounge near the next gate.
MOHAMMAD AL SAMAWI: I will ask
MOHAMMAD AL SAMAWI: I am lost actually ☹.

After wandering around the terminal for four hours, I stopped to ask a policeman where to go.

"Show me your other ticket," he said.

"What other ticket?" I said.

"You're going to America," he said. "Where's your other ticket?"

"This is the only ticket I have."

He said, "Come with me."

"Is everything okay?" I asked.

"Just come with me."

He began to walk quickly. I struggled to keep up, and he kept looking over his shoulder, making sure I was still there.

He took me into a small room and patted me down. Then, as I stood waiting, he looked through my backpack. That was all I had in the way of luggage.

"You have a tourist visa to the United States but only a one-way ticket. A tourist visa requires a round-trip ticket. Where's your return flight?"

I had no idea. I hadn't even realized. I'd hardly looked at my ticket except to find my gate. "I need to check," I said. "Someone else bought my ticket."

I sent a message to Daniel asking for my other ticket. It was 3:00 A.M. in New York; he wasn't answering.

I looked back up at the guard. "There is no other ticket."

The guard took my passport and went off to confer with his supervisor, and I sent Daniel a frantic text. A minute went by, then two. As I sat in a tiny plastic chair, thinking, *No, no, no, they couldn't have bought me a one-way ticket if a visa required a round-trip ticket,* I had no idea that this was exactly what they did do. Chris, a frequent traveler, had found a round-trip ticket from Djibouti to San Francisco for 70,000 United miles. But before he clicked purchase, he had a moment of reckoning. *Let's be honest,* Chris thought to himself. *We have no idea if this guy is going back in two months or a year, so why buy him a round-trip ticket? I'd rather use the points on a one-way flight of a lifetime.* Which is how Chris came to buy me a one-way business-class ticket from Djibouti to the United States for 70,000 points.

Oblivious to all of this, I sat alone and counted the tiles on the floor. I had gotten up to 110 when the guard came back.

"You can go," he said.

My head snapped up. I had no idea what had just happened, but it worked for me. I left the room and tried to find my gate. This, it turned out, was the final hurdle in the obstacle course.

It took me another twenty minutes to find where I was supposed to be, and without any time left, I boarded the plane. All I had was my backpack, a laptop from Oxfam, my phone, a charger, a towel that I'd taken from the Sheraton hotel, and the clothes on my back. I was dirty, smelly, exhausted, and flying to America on a one-way business-class ticket purchased by someone else using points. It was a suspicious combination, and I probably shouldn't have gotten through. But I did.

The airplane was two floors, and as we boarded, everyone in front of me walked to the left. I started to follow them, but a flight attendant stopped me and said, "Sir, you're this way."

I ascended to the second floor of the plane, and I saw the most amazing thing: everyone had their own space, with their own screen. I found my chair, on the aisle, and after I sat down, I saw the man next to me reach down to the side of his chair and move the seat back. *What?* I too reached down and fiddled with a piece of plastic, and before I knew it, I was leaning back, and sitting up. Leaning back, and sitting up. Farther and farther I went until I found another trick—I could turn the seat into a bed! I grabbed my phone and took a picture of myself, lying horizontally, on the plane. When I sat back up, everyone was staring. For the first time I noticed: they were all wearing suits.

After we reached altitude, a flight attendant came up to me and asked me what I wanted to order. My heart stopped; did I have to pay for this? I didn't have money. I told her I needed a minute to think, and then I asked the man next to me if he knew how much dinner cost.

"It's free," he said. "Is it your first time in business class?"

"Yes!" I said. "I flew from Yemen to Djibouti to Ethiopia to Germany, and now I'm going to San Francisco!"

"That's nice," he said, smiling politely, anxious to disengage. It was clear he wanted his own space; he'd bought a business-class ticket for a reason.

Sitting in my pod, sipping Germany's finest bottled water out of a plastic cup, I knew I was finally safe. I was on my way to America.

While I was somewhere over the Atlantic Ocean, Daniel, Megan, Justin, and Natasha touched base. They, and a network of countless others, had done it! They'd pushed themselves beyond their own exhaustion and stress limits and gotten me out of Yemen, out of Djibouti, and *into* the United States! So, Natasha asked after a series of cheers, who was going to meet Mohammed at the airport? Megan and Natasha couldn't; they were in Israel. Daniel couldn't; he was in New York. Justin couldn't; he was already booked to speak at a conference. Daniel, about to buy a last-minute plane ticket to San Francisco, thought of an easier solution. A minute later, the following post appeared on Facebook:

DANIEL PINCUS: My Yemeni friend lands in SFO Friday 12:50pm. Anyone want to pick him up?

Jenna Weinberg, a friend of Daniel's who was living in Brooklyn, reposted Daniel's message on the wall of her University of Michigan Facebook group, and Han Zhang—a young man, born in China, with a degree in mathematics and finance from the University of Michigan— wrote back that he'd be happy to do the pickup. Han didn't have a car of his own, so he rented a compact, drove an hour to SFO, and waited for forty-five minutes at the door to the terminal.

After a twelve-and-a-half-hour flight, my plane landed. The flight was so comfortable and stress-free that I wanted to stay in my seat forever; I wished I had twelve and a half more hours to go. But I knew this wasn't an option, and when the flight attendants started tidying up, I grabbed my backpack and took my first steps into America. I followed the signs, and as soon as I felt the kiss of the San Francisco breeze, I saw a big poster that said MOHAMMED AL SAMAWI. Behind which stood a young Chinese man I'd never met.

I hurried up to him. He introduced himself as Han Zhang, and before I could stop myself, I gave him a big hug.

"Thank you!" I cried, trying to rein in my excess of emotion.

"No worries," he said, somewhat taken aback that a ride from the airport could inspire so much enthusiasm. "Where are you coming from?"

"Yemen," I said, giving him a knowing look.

"Wow," he said politely, not at all understanding why I was giving him that look. "What's it like?"

I didn't know where to begin.

We got into the car, and he turned on some music. I recognized the beat; maybe America wouldn't be so different from Yemen after all. After we pulled onto the highway, the traffic patterns revealed another story. This was a completely different world.

Han cleared his throat and, with a sidelong glance and a forced-casual smile, asked, "So, how do you know Jenna?"

I looked at him. "Who's Jenna?"

Han's face fell, and, at a loss for what to say next, I began to tell my story . . .

I counted my steps. Three to get from the door to the wall; two between the toilet and the mirror. My new apartment in Aden was big for one person, but I hadn't planned on living in the bathroom. The gray-green light from the fluorescent bulb scattered off the mirror, blanching the walls, the ceiling, the floor. It had nowhere to go.

Trapped.

My eyes, red-rimmed and shot through with blood, had been hollowed by sleeplessness and stress. They'd retreated, withdrawn from the front lines, as if unwilling to watch Yemen tear itself apart. Rubble-strewn streets; soldiers and citizens shouting and firing weapons; social media emblazoned with the slogans "God is great! Death to America! Death to Israel! Damn the Jews! Victory to Islam!"

I didn't know how much time had gone by, and I had no idea where we were or where we were going, but I recounted everything that had happened, from my apartment in Aden to the Sheraton to the port to Djibouti, and before I knew it, my story ended up right back in this very car.

When I finished, a deep silence spread. Then Han Zhang asked, "Are you hungry?"

"Yes," I said.

"Have you ever eaten American food?"

"No," I said.

"I know just the place." He grinned. Ten minutes later we pulled up to KFC for my first American meal.

◇◇◇◇◇◇

I stayed with Justin in San Francisco. He introduced me to Chinese food and Mexican food, and then he took me to my first speaking engagement ever, at Stanford University. This place looked nothing at all like the University of Sana'a. Men and women sat together, walked together, kissed together. Women wore shorts and sleeveless shirts. *Is this allowed?* I wondered.

Justin took me through a maze of halls, until we got to a room filled with twenty-five people. I stood in front of them, meeting their eyes. This was the first time I'd ever shared my story in public, and as luck would have it, it was to a group of Muslims from the Gulf region (probably Sunnis). How would they respond to a story about how Jews and Christians saved me from a Muslim-on-Muslim conflict perpetrated by their own countries? I had no idea. But there was work to be done. It was my job to make people care.

I began . . .

It begins and ends with a book . . .

I started speaking, trying to ignore the students fidgeting in their seats, and as I went on, the story took on a texture of its own. Stitches were dropped, others were added. People, sounds, emotions. Everything washed over me. My memories were vivid, but asymmetrical, like the intricate weave of a *sajjada*. When I ran out of words, I looked at the clock on the wall. An hour and a half had passed. I'd lost track of myself.

Suddenly I was mortified. How had I been so foolish to think my experience had earned me this much time? I looked around, anxious, apologetic, but everyone was still there—watching me, waiting for more. When everyone realized I had no more to say, a hand shot up.

"I have a question," said a man with a big beard and a head covering. He looked religious, and I was scared he was going to attack me, call me a liar. But instead he turned his eyes to Justin.

"Why did you save him?"

Justin didn't skip a beat. In his Californian drawl, he smiled and said, "We're all human beings. Brothers. Anyone would do this."

When the session was over, the man went up to Justin and gave him a hug.

◇◇◇◇◇

After five days, I flew to New York City to meet Daniel. I moved into his apartment in the West Village and began to figure out who I wanted to become and what I was going to do during my four-month stay in the United States. Whatever it was, I hoped it would make the world a better place.

Still acclimating to my good fortune, I woke up to the bright summer sun and heard loud bursts and yelling in the street. My heart froze. I ran to the next room and asked Daniel if everything was okay. Yes, he told me. It was just the Gay Pride Parade.

Together we walked outside and I saw the streets filled with an explosion of color, music, and mostly naked men. We visited the landmark Stonewall Inn, and a sing-along piano bar. Though I'd known a handful of gay people from my interfaith work, I'd never seen so many people filled with such exuberance at simply being themselves. I felt my mind breaking free from another taboo. Officially there were no gay people in Yemen. What a loss.

Filled with a love of life stronger than anything I'd ever known, I called home. My father picked up the phone and greeted me. He didn't say anything else, but it was enough. He passed the phone to my mother and I felt my heart flop around in my chest, like a fish out of water. Since arriving in America, I'd spoken to her at every opportunity, but I hadn't yet told her that a group of Jews had saved my life. Not certain she could handle more stress, I'd been tiptoeing around the truth. She was already suffering so much from the war. The Saudi airstrikes had moved north to Sana'a, and the hospital had closed down. My father had to stop working, which meant there was no income and dwindling resources; the electricity was only on for an hour or so a day; the phone and cellular connection was unpredictable; and half the time the family was holed up in the basement hiding from bombs. But as bad as the situation was in Sana'a, my mother was more worried about how I was surviving the mean streets of Manhattan.

With every irrational motherly concern, my heart swelled with love. I didn't want to keep anything from her. I took a breath and finally explained the true story of my escape. My mother started to cry and I worried I'd said too much. "Hush," she told me. She didn't care about religion or the fact that Daniel, Justin, Megan, and Natasha didn't believe in the Prophet Muhammad. She cared that I was alive, and that these people had saved me. My mother, who didn't know a single sentence in English, asked to speak with Daniel. I handed him the phone, and she said, "Thank you, thank you, thank you, thank you, thank you."

EPILOGUE

Daniel and me in front of the Statue of Liberty

A fox is bathing in the stream when he sees a school of fish racing frantically through the water. He asks what the trouble is, and they explain that fishermen have cast their nets and are in pursuit. The fox, hearing the panic in their voices, offers to take them to dry land; all they have to do is hop on his back. The fish laugh and refuse the offer. "Fox," they say, "you are wily, but you can't fool us! The water is our home. If we are in danger here, what chance do we have on dry land?"

This parable is attributed to the Jewish scholar Rabbi Akiva, who lived in Caesarea back in the first and second centuries. According to this learned man, the fish are correct. They belong in the water; without it, they'll die. But I offer another interpretation: What if the fox is correct? What if there are instances in which the right choice is to leave your natural habitat? What if the only way to survive is to trust the alleged enemy?

I've been living in the United States for over two years now. This is a land I was taught to hate, filled with people I was taught to condemn. But I've been overwhelmed by friendship, support, and love. When I first arrived, I had no idea how my four-month speaking tour would be received. But one engagement led to another, and soon I found myself traveling to schools, Iftars, and Passover seders in places I never thought I'd visit: Dearborn, Dallas, Boston, Los Angeles, Atlanta, Chicago . . . I tried to use my personal story as a way into bigger, thornier issues about the situation in Yemen, the conflicts across the Middle East, immigration, interfaith activism, and human rights. But even though people seemed to like the story, the war waged on, and I wondered: *Is this enough?*

I didn't have a work visa, so I couldn't work. Instead, I volunteered, translating Arabic into English. I appeared on panels and spoke for cultural institutions. But the war waged on, and I wondered: *Is this enough?*

The second time I was invited to speak in San Francisco, I spoke with both Justin and Daniel. When we finished our presentation, two law school students came up to us and said that we'd inspired them to change the world, and that if we ever came across someone in need of help, we should let them know. It was flowery praise, and I didn't think much of it. But a couple of months later, I sent them a name—my friend from YaLa Online Academy, Mohamed Abubakr.

Before I knew it, the two lawyers put together a grassroots coalition and brought Mohamed to the United States. Now he's here and committed to saving others. With the help of Justin and Megan, he's created his own nonprofit called the African Middle Eastern Leadership Project (AMEL). Through it, he's empowering young people across Africa and the Middle East by giving them the tools to build inclusive, peaceful societies.

But the domino effect didn't stop there. I recently learned that a young man named Dan Smith had attended one of our talks and then similarly took action. Using my experience as a case study, he tried to help an Iranian journalist living in Turkey who was being threatened. With help from Justin and Irina, he reached out to key senators and gathered signatures for a petition. The journalist ultimately received asylum in Israel, so she didn't need refuge in the United States, but to me the engagement was more important than the result.

I may not have had the power to stop the war in Yemen, but with help from my friends, I realized I had the power to make a difference on a grassroots level. I continued to reach out to friends and strangers alike, working on a hearts-and-minds campaign. I spoke with Ahmed, my best friend in Yemen. He'd been so furious that I was working with Jews and Christians. "You're putting your life at risk," he'd scolded me. "Is it worth it?"

Now, knowing what I'd been through, he told me, "Everything you've done is correct."

And he's not alone. Two other friends of mine in Yemen who were equally against what I was doing are now part of YaLa Young Leaders.

This is the power of a story.

◇◇◇◇◇◇

As the four months of my speaking tour neared their end, I feverishly checked the news, hoping I would be able to return home. But the situation continued to deteriorate, and even without the targeted death threats against me, I couldn't go back. Saudi Arabia had blockaded the country, and the airport in Sana'a remained closed to commercial flights. With nowhere to go, and my visa about to expire, I reached back out to Sandra Grossman, the immigration attorney whom Daniel had secured for me.

Given the situation, I asked her if I could apply for political asylum. She agreed to assist me. By August 2015, I had worked with Sandra, my team, and Sandra's paralegal, Paulina Sosa, to complete the needed paperwork. I'd also interviewed with staff at the Department of Homeland Security. Sandra, who was a tireless advocate for me, believed from the first day that I had a strong case. Despite my doubts and fears, the process moved forward.

It took until May 2016 before I was able to get a work permit. By then, I had ended my stay with Daniel. I was so grateful to him, but we both knew that I needed to get on with the next stage of my life. So I moved to Washington, D.C., to effect change in the heart of the nation. I hadn't had a credit history or a job, so securing housing was a huge problem. But once again, Daniel came to the rescue. He helped me find a place in Crystal City, living in the home of a Syrian American woman, signed the lease for me, and continued to support me emotionally and financially. Everything was as good as could be expected for an unemployed refugee. I had survived. That was step one. Step two was repaying the huge debt to so many people who had acted heroically on my behalf.

I started to apply to any job tangentially related to Yemen, and immediately accepted a three-month contract with the International Center for Religion and Diplomacy (ICRD). I was thrilled to be working, particularly in the area that I loved—using religion as a tool to unite and not to divide. I proved to be of value, and after my trial period, my superiors offered me a one-year contract as a coordinator of their Middle East efforts. Now I had less time to focus on my own situation and more time to think about others and how I might be able to help.

My work at ICRD put me in contact with various imams around the MENA region who were outspoken critics of the West, Jews generally, and Christians. Based on my own experience in discovering similarities between Islam, Judaism, and Christianity, I approached them with a plea to give understanding a chance. I tried to convince them that what they believe about Jews and Judaism and what is real are two different things. I sometimes imagined myself as one of those irritating telemarketers who cold-call people.

"Can I interest you in a no-obligation special package of tolerance and understanding?"

The responses I got varied widely, but I kept plugging away, focusing on the successes and not the failures. The cause was too important to give up. Not only did I need to help my country, but I needed to help my mother, my father, my sisters and brothers.

My family are my soul. Though we didn't always understand one another fully, when we needed one another, we were there for one another. Though we disagreed with one another, didn't always accept one another's perspectives, in times of need we provided what we could to improve the situation.

I'm afraid I may lose them.

◇◇◇◇◇◇

On August 31, 2017, the holiday of Eid al-Adha arrived. As I composed these thoughts, I heard my fully stocked refrigerator click on. My laptop was fully charged. My phone had full service. It was evening, and the warm glow of overhead lights illuminated the notes I'd taken. From the street below, I heard the honking of a few cars. Peaceful white noise.

I thought of my family, surrounded by the alternating sounds of silence and blasts. I wished that I could be home with them. I wished we could spend the holiday together. My mother would cook a lamb, which she would divide into three parts—one for us to consume as a family, a second to share with relatives, and a third to give to the poor. This was always my favorite time of the year.

But instead of curling up on the couch with Nuha, I watched as friends and friends of friends post on Facebook, begging for food and medical aid that was being refused. Saudi Arabia stated that it would allow in chartered United Nations and humanitarian organizations' flights, but only on a case-by-case basis. The Yemeni government, caught between the proverbial rock and a hard place, reached out to Russia for aid. A deal was brokered but the Saudis still refused to allow flights in. The Saudis wanted to starve the Houthi rebels into submission, but instead they imperiled the lives of millions of people. By one estimate, twenty million of the more than twenty-seven million people in Yemen were in need of humanitarian aid.

Yemenis, including my family, are caught up in a war that has nothing to do with them. The Saudis and other members of the Arab coalition, AQAP, Iran, the Houthis, the other factions involved . . . these groups have all made deliberate choices to continue the fighting. There are complex international dynamics and agendas at play, and while I understand that there is no easy answer, one thing has become clear. As Peter Salisbury wrote for Chatham House, a.k.a. the Royal Institute of International Affairs, as far back as May 2016, "Yemen's civil war has reached a stalemate in which an outright military victory by any of the many parties to the conflict is highly unlikely. [Because] of the wide variety of local dynamics and grievances, Yemen risks seeing the 'big war' ended only to be consumed by a series of complex 'small wars' that are open to exploitation by national and regional actors." As he also pointed out, all efforts at negotiating a peaceful settlement of the dispute have placed counterterrorism and the safety of other nations ahead of the physical and economic security of the people of Yemen. Not all Yemenis are terrorists. Not all Yemenis deserve to be punished because of the actions of a few.

As I sat in comfort, my countrymen endured two years without electricity. Imagine going one day, two days, without power. Now imagine spending nearly eight hundred days and nights without it. Imagine not having any money. Imagine not having a job. Imagine not knowing where your next meal will come from.

For Eid 2017, millions of Yemenis ate little or nothing. Instead of sitting down to a holiday meal, families huddled together, hoping that they would survive the aerial onslaught. They weren't thinking about lamb and vegetables; they were fearful that each breath might be their last. I know this because I was once in their position. I still lie awake at night, picturing the dimness, smelling the smoke and dust of ruins and retribution. I still flinch at loud sounds. I still feel the tightness in my chest, the emptiness in my belly, the despair in my heart. For me, these are remnants of trauma from a time before. For those still in Yemen, the trauma is real, immediate, and never-ending.

Why do they have to endure this?

Why have they become the sacrifice?

Many people dismiss the fighting in Middle Eastern countries as sectarian violence: conflict between and among ethnic and religious groups. It seems as if no one wants to acknowledge a larger and darker truth. There are countries at fault; there are people to blame; there is a way to stop the violence. Many in the United States decried the Russians backing Syria's regime. Where is the outcry for Yemen?

If the Saudis are truly interested in putting down Houthi militants, a tiny percentage of a small percentage of a minority ethnic group in my country, why are so many others dying, living in terror, starving, and being laid waste by pernicious disease? Why are they willing to sacrifice Yemen?

Can the silence be because, as the *New York Times* recently reported, citing the SIPRI Arms Transfers Database, from 2012 to 2016 the United States and Great Britain between them provided the Saudis with 79.1 percent of the military supplies they imported? The tide may be turning—in June 2017, forty-seven senators voted against a measure to sell more arms to Saudi Arabia—but is that enough? While I understand that Saudi Arabia is of strategic importance in the region for the United States, is it worth sacrificing more than twenty-seven million people?

How can anyone justify this kind of slaughter?

Who has anointed one as Ibrahim and the other Ismail?

Who will turn back the knife?

◇◇◇◇◇◇

In July 2017, representatives of the World Food Program, UNICEF, and the World Health Organization visited Yemen. Water and sanitation facilities there have been crippled by bombings. They issued a statement following that visit: four hundred thousand Yemenis are suspected to be suffering from cholera; three out of every five Yemenis don't know where their next meal will come from; nearly two million children are considered to be malnourished; almost nineteen hundred people have died of cholera since the outbreak began four months earlier.

State-supported health care workers (thirty thousand of them) have gone unpaid for nearly a year. Despite that, many of them do go out in the field or to the hospitals and offices to offer aid. But when the needed supplies aren't allowed in, or they are commandeered by the Houthi rebels—as is the case with much-needed medicines to combat cholera—they can only do so much. We face five thousand more cases of cholera per day. The number of cases may rise well above the present half million.

Disease.

Famine.

As Nicholas Kristof reported in the *New York Times,* every five minutes a child in Yemen dies. As a journalist, he worked tirelessly for months to gain access to the country. One of the factors the Saudis use to make their determination about allowing a chartered flight to land with aid or aid workers is whether or not a journalist is on board. If one is, they refuse to grant that flight permission. They don't want the stories to be told.

Entire families are murdered in airstrikes; parents are committing suicide because they can't provide enough for their children; women are being raped and kidnapped. Children are being left alone by violence and despair. What is to come for a generation of young people who will grow up in a war zone?

This is a dark age in Yemen, and hope flickers with the lights. In the beginning of December 2017, Ali Abdullah Saleh, who had been a partner to the Houthis, announced that he was willing to end his alliance with the rebels, stop the fighting in Sana'a, and begin talks with Saudi Arabia. Yemen waited in anticipation, and the United Nations encouraged both sides "to engage in the peace process." Two days later, the Houthis killed Saleh. All that remained of the country I knew since my birth was gone.

Talk of peace was over, and the Houthis made a televised announcement that everyone needed to pray to thank God for killing Ali Abdullah Saleh. *Baltagi*, thugs, went door to door and demanded that every young man go to the mosque that night. At the end of the *khutbah*, the sermon, they shouted, "Death to America, death to Israel, damn the Jews, victory for Islam!" Everybody had to join in.

If anyone resisted, if anyone was rumored to have supported the opposition, if anyone had a picture of Saleh in their house, they were seen as the enemy. Informants scrutinized social media accounts; Facebook pages became proof of guilt. A friend of mine was taken. If I had been there, I wouldn't have had a chance.

The Houthis continued to solidify power by blocking the social media sites Facebook, Twitter, and WhatsApp. No one could make contact with the outside world. People learned to bypass the censorship by using virtual private networks (VPNs), but these made the Internet speeds—already one of the slowest average download speeds in the world at 0.34 mbps (megabytes per second)—even slower. Between the electricity outages and the power needed for even the smallest downloads, phones and laptops died within hours. My family was lucky enough to buy solar panels, and now they have three to five hours of electricity per day. When they have enough of an Internet connection, and their devices have enough of a charge, they record a voice message and send it to me via WhatsApp. I listen right away, record my own message, and press send. It can take days to get a response.

Recently, I was in an airport in Miami waiting for my flight to Los Angeles when I saw a new recording from my mom. She said, "Hi, Hamoodi, I just want to tell you something, because I know you will hear it on the news and you will worry about us. There are airstrikes now in Sana'a, but we are fine. Don't worry—" And then I heard a *BOOM*, and the recording ended. I started to lose feeling in my fingers. I called everyone in Yemen on WhatsApp, but no one answered; I sent messages to Ahmed asking him to go check on my family, but he didn't reply. After an hour, I received a voice message from Ahmed that he went to see my family and everything was okay and that I shouldn't worry. This is my new normal. I am thankful to God that I live here in America, but what about my family, friends, and other Yemenis?

There is nowhere for people from the north to run. There is no escape. The Popular Committee has taken control of Aden, and even though some of the people may be good, there is a unanimous anti-northern sentiment. If a person from the north is caught in the south, they are sent back to the Houthi-controlled areas.

The fighting shows no signs of stopping. As of January 2018, more than ten thousand civilians have died in the war. More than a million people were thought to have been affected by suspected cases of cholera. And, according to the UN Humanitarian Coordinator in Yemen, more than 8.4 million Yemenis were on the brink of famine.

I know that numbers can numb. It is too much. It is easier to switch channels, turn the page, minimize the window than it is to take action.

But we have to act.

Along with acknowledging our ignorance and embracing the fact that we have to own up to what we don't know, we also need to come to terms with an element of our human nature, our national identities.

Maybe it's time for someone to say what has frequently gone unsaid. It is okay to be self-interested. If the civil war in Yemen seems to be so far away, think of it like this: right now, a generation is growing up as hostages to the Houthis and the Saudis. They don't realize this is the case, but they are. Not only that, but the Houthi rebels have been hoarding relief supplies (including cholera medications) that generous nations and organizations have gotten in despite the no-fly zones. Do young people in need of relief know that this is happening? No. What they see and hear is strictly controlled. When lives are filled with doubt and uncertainty, when you live in unacknowledged ignorance, you resort to believing those in power, those in control. In Yemen, that means extremist clerics. That means Al Qaeda. That means ISIS.

Right now, under our very noses, an army is being recruited and trained by extremists and terrorists. Many in Yemen believe that the world community has turned their backs on them. They believe that no one cares about them or their future. In that void, whom do they turn to? Those who pay them some attention. Those who address their grievances. Those who offer them some prospect of the future other than destruction and violence. This is how terrorists are born and raised. The crisis in Yemen is the beginning of the radicalization of a generation.

An army of hate is being raised across the Middle East. I believe that an army of understanding and action can take on that army and defeat it.

I'm a living example of the power of human connection. I reached out and hands grasped mine. Amid all the images of bombings and bloodshed, disease and destruction, let us please not forget that hands are outstretched. They are asking for no more than basic human dignity and rights, an opportunity to survive. Weapons or water? Munitions or meals? Indifference or intervention?

We all have choices to make.

Action or inaction.

We are all connected. What choices we make will eventually make their way back to us.

I choose hope.

I pray that those in the Middle East and around the world will work together, that we will choose the fundamental principle that underlies the great religions of the world—mercy. I pray that the United States will take action and bring representatives together to sit down at a bargaining table. Just as I had, my people are asking for help. Let them be heard. Let their pleas for help be answered.

Like the fish in the stream, I grew up believing that I was safe in the water; that foxes were evil; that I would die on dry land. But, like so much else, this proved to be false. The people I trusted tried to kill me; the people I distrusted saved my life. But the moral is bigger than me. We are all racing upstream, trying to avoid the nets and hooks that have been laid out for us. I beg you to take a chance and jump onto dry land. It may be uncomfortable, it may be dangerous, or it may help us change the parable.

I should have died three times over, but I didn't. I owe this to all the people named and unnamed who got me to this point. They are the heroes.

As it says in the Quran: Whoever saves a life, it is as if he has saved mankind entirely.

As it says in the Talmud: Whoever saves a life, it is as if he saved an entire world.

We all have our own stories, but if we can start to connect—online and in real life—we can start to see just how similar they are. And then, I pray, we will be able to treat one another as brothers and sisters.

This, right here, is another beginning.

ACKNOWLEDGMENTS

Many cultures have stories about people who have been saved and their attempts to repay the debt. In some small way, I hope these acknowledgments will serve as my first token of gratitude.

Words fail me when I think of the four people who played such a large part in this story. Megan, Justin, Natasha, and Daniel: what you did for me proves the essential goodness of humanity. My destiny is different because of you, and I will try my best to follow your examples. We are forever joined together, and I hope that brings you as much comfort and joy as it does me.

Megan, when I first approached the interfaith community, you opened your arms; and when I first reached out to you for help, you opened your contact book. You were relentless in your efforts on my behalf, and because of you, I found advocates in the highest levels of the State Department, safety in the Gold Mohur Hotel, and two new friends in Justin and Natasha. You don't waste time second-guessing when you can be taking action, and this is something to which I aspire.

Justin, your dogged perseverance knows no bounds. While the rest of the world slept, you wrote petitions to senators, placed calls to government officials across the globe, and held people to their promises. It is because of your vigilance that I made it to the port and onto the Indian naval ship. You believe that no plan is too crazy to try, which is how your craziest plans succeed. I believe they call this *chutzpah*.

Natasha, from the moment I first spoke with you in Jordan, I saw your kindness. When the war broke out in Aden and I was surrounded by people acting out of desperation and fear, this very kindness became a beacon of light. Your help coordinating logistics and getting aid from the State Department cannot be overstated, but even more than that, you helped me survive the emotional complexities of a war zone.

And then there's Dani. You are a man who says "yes." From the moment I reached out, you have stayed by my side. You used every connection you had to get me out of Yemen, but that was only the first hurdle. The life of a refugee is a difficult one: we have no family, no money, no networks, no job, and no home. You gave me everything and asked for nothing. Your selfless generosity and brotherhood have continued to this day, and I only wish to live in a way that will make you proud.

There is a fifth person who is critical to this story, and though she's not mentioned in the pages of this book, she's between every line. That is my literary agent and dear friend, Becky Sweren. There would be no book without you. You've ignored conventions—and the boundaries of office hours—to write my book proposal, revise my manuscript, and take on the dual roles of therapist and life coach. Whatever the job, you perform it to the highest standards. (Did you know that people in Hollywood are still calling the book proposal one of the best they've ever read?) I don't know how agent-author relationships normally work, but your ability to know what to do and how to do it in all phases of my life—personal and professional—is magical. I would be immeasurably different if it weren't for your tenacity, compassion, talent, and intelligence. Humbly, sincerely, and forever, you are my sister. As my mother once said to Daniel, "Thank you. Thank you. Thank you."

I've always been a reader of books, but I never knew how many hardworking people it took to create one. My eternal gratitude to Henry Ferris for championing and acquiring this book; Peter Hubbard for editing my book with acumen and for your guidance; and Nick Amphlett for your keen insights and diligence. Thank you, too, to Sharyn Rosenblum for your boundless energy and support; you are a publicity and media mastermind. Ryan Cury, your marketing is an absolute inspiration, and Natalie Duncan, you've been an unflagging advocate. I am blessed to have this all-star team at William Morrow/HarperCollins, and Liate Stehlik, your leadership and vision have made all this possible.

Thank you, too, to Aevitas Creative Management for supporting this project, and to Chelsey Heller for giving this book an international audience.

Finally, in terms of the publication, a major thank-you to the inimitable Gary Brozek. This is a story with *a lot* of pieces. It's deeply personal, but it also involves four other perspectives, and it flips back and forth across ten time zones. There's a lot to navigate, but you never wavered. I will forever appreciate your patience, thoughtfulness, artistry, and unique ability to capture both the hard and the soft. Thank you, also, for your willingness to roll up your sleeves and become an expert in Yemeni history and religion.

◇◇◇◇◇

This book, and this life that I'm fortunate enough to be living, was only made possible through the humanitarian efforts of two countries and their governments.

To the good people of India: thank you for your limitless good faith and humanitarian aid. I and hundreds of others are here today only because we were included in your daring "Operation Raahat." I can't imagine how many individuals around the globe were involved in that effort, but I will acknowledge those that I can. Thank you to the captain and crew of the INS *Mumbai*. Thank you to the Indian Ministry of Foreign Affairs, including the staffs of the Indian Embassies in Washington, DC, and in Sana'a. You acted when no one else could, or would. I only hope I can reciprocate in some way.

To the wonderful people of the United States: thank you for allowing me to visit this incredible country, and for allowing me to stay when I couldn't return to Yemen. I could not be more grateful. In particular, I'd like to thank members of the U.S. Department of State, including Deputy Secretary Tony Blinken, Laura Rosenberger, and Shaarik Zafar. Senator Kirk and his staff—particularly Gretchan Blum—also have a special place in my heart. The possibilities this country affords are boundless, and I hope to use the opportunity given to me to promote dialogue and understanding from sea to shining sea.

◇◇◇◇◇

My journey to America would not have been possible without significant organizational and personal support from the American Jewish Committee. This incredible organization, led by David Harris, went well beyond its mission to lend its sterling credibility to endorse my cause and encourage others to act for my benefit. I also want to thank Jason Isaacson, Director of Government and International Affairs, who supervised the group's outreach on my behalf.

I would likely still be in Yemen if not for Nissim Reuben and Shira Loewenberg of AJC's Asia Pacific Institute: you both were invaluable in the diplomatic efforts. Similarly, I would like to specially thank Irina Tsukerman and Alexis Frankel (and her mother, C. Kirk Lazell), who helped advance my cause from the beginning and have always been in my corner.

AJC's Jacob Blaustein Institute for the Advancement of Human Rights, and particularly Felice Gaer and Christen Broecker, were also critical to my journey. Thank you for your support and behind-the-scenes efforts.

My visa to the United States was made possible by several renowned academic and human rights groups, and I would like to acknowledge Stanford University, where I had the honor of speaking, as well as the International Crisis Group. A special shout-out to Tiffany Harris, Rebia Khan, and Courtney Lobel, who lobbied on my behalf.

Another institution that is key to my story is YaLa Young Leaders, which created a safe haven for interfaith dialogue and taught me that people are people are people. If it hadn't been for your organization, my eyes and heart might have remained shut.

Similarly, the Muslim Jewish Conference was key to my transformation. The MJC is an inspirational and much-needed organization, and the work it does is critical. Thank you for giving me the space to challenge my assumptions, and for your tireless efforts to engage members of your community to find channels of aid.

Thank you, too, to Seeds of Peace and Gather+962. These organizations encouraged me and gave me the tools to continue reaching across the aisle and connecting with people.

I've similarly been inspired by the Yemen Peace Project, including the work of Executive Director Will Picard and his wife, Dana Moss. Your dedication and support of Yemen makes the world a better place.

I would also like to acknowledge Renaissance Weekend, led by Philip and Linda Lader and their daughters, Mary-Catherine and Whitaker. I am inspired by your commitment to fostering dialogue and building bridges, and it's thanks to the RW extended family that I am where I am today.

◇◇◇◇◇

As for the individuals . . . I could spend the rest of my life expressing my gratitude to all the other people who played a part in this story. However, I've been ordered to keep this book to under fifty pounds, so in brief:

I would like to thank my brothers in Yemen. It is difficult to help others when you cannot even protect yourself. But from the man who drove me to the Gold Mohur Hotel to the workers there who assisted me while I took shelter, you are heroes. You put yourselves at risk to assist a stranger, and I survived because of you.

I would also like to thank Nimrod Ben Ze'ev, Leslie Lewin, and Aaron Richards for doing everything within their power and reaching out to their representatives in the United States Congress and requesting their assistance.

To Joel Braunold, who provided my team with crucial advice, and to David Keyes, for being a key connector.

To Deborah Abisror, former director of the European Union of Jewish Students, and Baki and Ali, who were instrumental in helping me while in Djibouti.

A very special thank-you to Chris Murray, who made good on his promise to buy my plane ticket to the United States.

My immigration attorney, Sandra Grossman, and her assistant, Paulina Sosa, gave me essential and valuable guidance as we navigated through paperwork and critical legal work from the moment I arrived in Djibouti. Your generous support at a critical time is immeasurable. I had dreamed of returning to Yemen, but when the continued fighting made that impossible, you became my friends and allies, guiding me through the various processes and helping me remain safe in the United States. You two are remarkable.

Since I've been in the United States, I've been aided in countless ways by amazing people who have thrown open their arms in ways I never would have imagined possible. Stanley and Marion Bergman, Josh Weston, Joe and Debra Weinberg, Hamza Awawda, Rahma Sghaier, Anne Pence, and Ohood Murqaten have all gone above and beyond. They have reached out to me in ways too numerous to mention here, but for which I am enormously grateful. I'd be remiss if I didn't thank Dr. Michael Sellman as well for his medical assistance and his generosity.

Joey Alexander, you inspired me in one of my darkest hours. Thank you to you, and to your parents, Denny Sila and Fara Leonora, for your friendship and inspiration.

Friends like Josh Nason and Mohammed Ali have made my life as a refugee far easier. Your perspectives and concern have contributed greatly to my well-being.

Jenna Weinberg, thank you to you and your family. Without asking any questions, you welcomed me, provided for me, and made me feel safe. Thank you for your friendship, your willingness to listen, and for showing me how to find the positive side of any situation.

Gisela and Raymond Savdi, you have been like family to me in so many ways. I don't have enough space to fill in all the details.

Hannah and Ruben Iberkleid: knowing that you two have my back and are always available to listen to me regardless of the hour or the circumstances is the true definition of friendship. You have made some of the toughest times easier for me through your presence, patience, and persistence.

Benj Pasek, you wear many, many (very cool) hats, but I thank you first and foremost for being an incredible person. You saw something in me and in this story from the start. From that very first Shabbat dinner we shared, you've been my advocate and mentor. That alone would be more than enough, but then you introduced me to Marc Platt! My deepest appreciation to you, and to Marc, for being better people than you need to be. You both make the world a more peaceful and beautiful place, and you've helped me dream a dream I didn't think was possible.

Mohamed Abubakr, you give me hope for a brighter future. When we first met, I asked you where you were from, and you told me you were "a citizen of the world." At the time, I had no idea what you meant, but now, after years of friendship, I understand. You are a global activist in the truest sense. You've already accomplished so much, and I can't wait to see what you do in the coming years. I know it will be big.

In closing, I offer my sincerest thanks to all the communities and families that have supported me, particularly the Hallahans, Hefters, Westheimers, and Pincuses. Your children are who they are because of your histories, your values, and the way you live your lives. Thank you for supporting their efforts, and for supporting me by providing your contacts, helping me resettle, and welcoming me into your homes. A special thank-you to Daniel's grandmother, Minna Mendel de Pincus, with whom I share a unique bond.

And finally, to my own family: Mama, Baba, and Fnona. *Shukran.* I am who I am because of you. When I close my eyes, you are with me. Until I can see you again in person, I will count these dreams as one of the biggest blessings in my life.

Shukr, or gratitude, plays an important role in Islam, as it does in Christianity and Judaism. By focusing on what we have instead of what we lack, we can be truly happy. I believe that is true, and in having so many people to thank, I realize how incredibly blessed I am and how much I want to live up to the example so many have set for me. Thank you all, and let us move toward peace.

INDEX